THE
DUTY MEN

THE DUTY MEN

THE INSIDE STORY OF THE CUSTOMS

PETER GILLMAN
WITH PAUL HAMANN

PHOTOGRAPHS BY ALAIN LE GARSMEUR

BBC BOOKS

To Charles Gillman
Officer of Customs and Excise 1919–1940

Additional research: Roger Courtiour

Published by BBC Books,
a division of BBC Enterprises Limited,
Woodlands, 80 Wood Lane, London W12 0TT

First published 1987   © The authors 1987

ISBN 0 563 20507 5

Typeset in 11/12½ pt Times and printed in England
by Butler and Tanner Limited, Frome and London

CONTENTS

Renaissance: The Red Sammy	7
Renaissance: The Couriers	40
The Red and the Green	71
Surveillance	123
Auntie's Bag	145
Poteen	167
The Chancers	185

ACKNOWLEDGEMENTS

It would be impossible to mention every one of the remarkable number of people who helped to produce both the television series, *The Duty Men*, and this book. But we would like to acknowledge, with special gratitude, the following:

From HM Customs and Excise – Leonard Harris, Dick Lawrence, Alan Huish, Bill Newall, Henry Snodden, Andy Lennon, Bill Hay, Hugh Donagher, Graham Dick, Graeme Hammond, Roy Devereux and Graham Smith. We recommend Graham Smith's books, *Something to Declare* (Harrap, 1980) and *King's Cutters* (Conway, 1983) as authoritative works on the history of the Customs.

From BBC TV – Patrick O'Shea (cameraman), Andrew Willsmore (film editor), Sally Benge (production assistant), Deborah Johnstone (transcriber), Roger Law and Will Wyatt.

Above all we thank Roger Courtiour, assistant producer, for his invariable steadfastness and support, and Alain Le Garsmeur, whose photographs are all the more remarkable for having been obtained in the teeth of perpetual difficulties and discomfort. All photographs in this book were taken by him, with the following exceptions:
Australian Customs Service pages 50 (top & centre right); BBC © pages 103, 107 (bottom), 111 (bottom), 134 (bottom right) & 165 (bottom); BBC Hulton Picture Library pages 77 (bottom), 79 (bottom), 119 (centre) & 127; The J. Allan Cash Photolibrary page 100 (top); Mary Evans Picture Library pages 77 (top) & 79 (top); Peter Gillman page 9 (top); Paul Hamann pages 50 (top & bottom left), 100 (bottom), 104 (top) & 105; Mansell Collection page 83 (top); The National Maritime Museum, Greenwich page 104 (bottom). Pictures on pages 9 (top right & bottom), 18, 34, 44, 51 (top right), 99 (top), 103 (centre), 104, 119 (top & bottom), 136 (top) & 169 reproduced by kind permission of the Commissioners of HM Customs and Excise.

CHAPTER ONE

RENAISSANCE: THE RED SAMMY

When Anthony John Favell arrived at London's Heathrow airport on 5 December 1985 he was, it is fair to say, a marked man.

A short, white-haired man in his fifties, wearing a brown suede coat, blue jeans and a pair of white shoes, Favell had already been watched by two officers of the Investigation Division of Her Majesty's Customs and Excise as he climbed into a minicab in Gipsy Hill, south London, at 3.12 that afternoon. When the minicab reached Heathrow a third officer saw Favell pay the driver and walk into Terminal Two. Two more officers were waiting inside, and they watched as Favell went to the Air France desk where he checked in for flight AF817, leaving at 5.30 p.m. for Paris and connecting there with a flight to Brazil.

Favell's progress through Terminal Two was observed just as closely. When he handed his passport to Home Office officials on the passport desk, two Customs officers were there too and they memorised his passport number. Yet another officer followed Favell into the departure lounge. He saw Favell pause outside the 'Caviar House' delicatessen to tuck his passport and airline ticket into the inside pocket of his coat and light a cigarette. Then he watched from a discreet distance as Favell disappeared into the duty-free shop, emerging a few minutes later with a yellow carrier-bag.

The officer sat a couple of tables away in the departure lounge snack-bar as Favell perused a newspaper, drank a cup of coffee and smoked another cigarette. Finally, when Favell's flight was called, the officer followed him to the departure gate to watch him hand over his flight coupon and go on board. The officer then retrieved the flight coupon from the Air France staff and noted down the details that showed where the ticket had been bought, how it had been paid for, and when Favell was due to return.

While all this was going on, still more Customs officers had been concentrating on Favell's baggage. He had checked in two items at the Air France desk, a large brown soft-sided suitcase and a grey zip-up holdall equipped with a pair of wheels, keeping a third, a dark briefcase, as hand baggage.

Two officers were waiting by the conveyor belt in the Air France baggage-sorting area as Favell's suitcase and holdall arrived from the check-in desk. They removed the cases from the belt, opened them and searched through his belongings. They also marked the cases with an ultra-violet pen before closing them and putting them back on the belt.

Shortly after 5.30 p.m., undoubtedly relieved that everything had gone smoothly, Favell was on his way to Paris and Brazil. The officers of the Customs' Investigation Division were relieved that everything had gone so smoothly too, as that afternoon's events were the latest stage in a major long-term investigation. For they suspected that Favell was a vital link in an international cocaine-smuggling operation whose profits, they believed, could be counted in millions of pounds. They reckoned that Favell was a courier who was travelling to Brazil to collect a consignment of cocaine that he would attempt to smuggle back into Britain in a week's time.

The third group who were relieved that everything had gone so smoothly that afternoon were the BBC. The account of Favell's movements comes partly from the Customs' own observations and partly from a remarkable film sequence obtained by a BBC crew. When Favell passed through the Terminal Two passport check and reached the departure lounge, a BBC cameraman, Pat O'Shea, was waiting for him too. O'Shea was equipped with a camera concealed in his shoulder bag, and he filmed Favell lighting his cigarette outside the delicatessen and drinking his coffee in the departure lounge snack-bar. That dramatic sequence opens the BBC series *The Duty Men*, first transmitted in October 1987.

The co-operation between the Customs and the BBC to make *The Duty Men* was as remarkable as the sequence itself. The Customs and Excise are one of Britain's longest-established institutions, with their activities recorded in Magna Carta. The story of their 750-year history is often one of a battle against public hostility, from the officers who fought the wreckers and smuggling gangs of the eighteenth century, to their successors who scrutinise passengers' baggage today. They are also one of the more closed bodies of British society, whose inner workings are only rarely exposed to the glare of publicity, if at all. That is especially true of the Customs' Investigation Division, whose habit of secrecy is compounded by an understandable desire not to reveal their operational methods to their adversaries.

Yet the Customs allowed the BBC unprecedented access to make a documentary series about their work. The lives of the officers in the Investigation Division are particularly subject to stress, as they spend

Operation Renaissance was led by Hugh Donagher, head of the Investigation Division's 'Romeo' team – and it was Donagher (*above left*) who co-ordinated the surveillance of cocaine courier Tony Favell when he passed through Heathrow en route to Brazil on 5 December 1985. Both Customs and BBC were secretly photographing and filming at Heathrow (see sequence *above right*) and were ready when Favell came into the frame (*left*). Favell had been watched since arriving in Britain the previous day – and went on his way entirely unaware that he was the object of so much attention.

working hours that would make most people shudder collecting evidence against some of today's most determined criminals. To have a BBC camera crew recording their more intimate thoughts and discussions, their anxieties and mistakes as well as their moments of triumph, added a burden that many could have done without.

The BBC team, headed by producer Paul Hamann, also went through moments it could probably have done without. It spent two days and nights with the crew of a Customs cutter during a force nine gale in the Irish Sea at the climax of an operation to intercept £4 million worth of cannabis. It was in the forefront of raids against professional criminals and it was present at more than a dozen arrests. It filmed inside the notorious stuffers' and swallowers' suite at Heathrow, where the most repellent aspect of modern drugs-smuggling is uncompromisingly revealed. Like the officers themselves, it spent endless hours watching and waiting as the Customs pieced together the evidence they needed against their targets.

This book records both the events depicted in that series, and the background to many of the cases and incidents that television was unable fully to show. It is intended to complement and enhance the programmes in depicting the lives and work of Britain's Customs officers, as well as conveying the skill and dedication behind one of the most remarkable television series ever made.

The day after Anthony Favell flew to Brazil, a group of senior officers met at the headquarters of the Investigation Division, invariably known inside the Customs as the 'ID', and housed in an undistinguished office block in New Fetter Lane near Holborn Circus, London. The meeting was chaired by Brian Clark, head of B3 branch which consists of the ID's four cocaine teams, and its aim was to review the progress of the operation, codenamed Renaissance, of which the Favell surveillance formed part.

Clark had just attended the weekly briefing given by the ID's intelligence division to the ID team heads, and he passed on the main points to the rest of the group. Then he asked for an account of the previous day's activity at Heathrow. It was given by Hugh Donagher, the head of the ID's Romeo team.

Donagher, a Scotsman from Ayrshire in his mid-forties, joined the Customs at the Clydeside port of Greenock in 1959. He joined the ID in 1972 and became a team head – in the Civil Service rank of senior executive officer – in 1985. A tall, bulky man, with distinguished silver hair and a Scottish accent that had been moderated by his years in the south, he was regarded as one of the ID's most determined and bullish investigators.

Unswervingly loyal to the Customs' traditions of secrecy, Donagher was at first not best pleased to have the BBC tracking his every move. At the same time he was well equipped with the diplomatic skills needed for negotiating the Customs' bureaucracy, as labyrinthine and prone to rivalries as any other government department. He was especially practised at the conduct of meetings, where he displayed a sense of confidence to reassure his superiors, whatever private doubts he may have felt.

Donagher and the Romeos had been pursuing their investigation for almost a year. They believed that the cocaine involved came from Bolivia, one of the two principal cocaine-producing countries of South America (the other is Colombia). Donagher suspected that there had been several previous runs, which had evaded the Customs' scrutiny, and which had been conducted by a method known as the 'suitcase switch'.

Two couriers would arrive at Heathrow on the same flight. The first would have brought a suitcase containing drugs, the second an identical suitcase packed with clothes. Once at Heathrow, the second courier would pick up the suitcase containing drugs and take it into the Green Channel, signifying that he had nothing to declare. If he was successful and passed through, the first courier would simply follow with the suitcase containing clothes. If the second courier was stopped and searched, he would claim that he must have picked up the wrong suitcase by mistake. He and the officer would go back to the baggage carousel and find the suitcase containing his clothes. It was, said Donagher, 'a fairly clever smuggle'.

Would Favell attempt the suitcase trick on this occasion? Here Donagher was less sure. The only firm knowledge the Romeos had was that Favell was due to return to London from Rio via Paris a week later. But the work of the ID is based to a daunting extent on deduction and guesswork – so perhaps the fact that Favell was travelling via Paris, even though there were plenty of direct flights to London from Rio, was significant. Donagher appeared at his most persuasive as he argued the case.

'It would seem logical to me, and it would certainly be a lot cheaper for them if they were going to work that system, to do it in Paris,' Donagher told Clark. 'Then all they have to do is to send somebody out on a day trip to Paris with an identical suitcase and board the same flight as the courier from South America.'

Donagher therefore proposed that he should go to Paris in a week's time to watch Favell as he passed through on his return from Rio. 'If I can see the suitcase being checked in, I can go and photograph it, mark it, and prove that it was boarded in Paris, so that when he comes down to his story of saying, "That's my suitcase which has travelled all the way from Rio de Janeiro," then we've seen it in Paris. That's the value of it.'

For the moment, Clark proposed postponing the decision whether Donagher should go to Paris. But there was a larger decision to be made, as Donagher also explained. If Favell did try to bring cocaine into Britain, should he be arrested? It was far from the straightforward question it appeared. If the Romeos were correct in supposing that Favell was a courier of the international cocaine trade, then it followed that other more important figures were involved too. If Favell were arrested on his return to Heathrow, then any colleagues could take fright and go to ground.

Having acknowledged this problem, Donagher advanced a solution. Favell *should* be arrested: but in such a way that the Romeos' previous interest would not be revealed. He would almost certainly try to pass through the Green Channel, where uniformed Customs officers should stop him. They were to make it appear that they had done so purely by chance, and Favell was to be questioned on the same basis, so that he remained unaware, Donagher said, 'that there have been any long in-depth investigations at this stage. This is so that we can go to the future and look forward to bigger consignments.' Brian Clark nodded his head in agreement.

In the event, Clark agreed that Donagher should watch Favell in Paris, and Donagher flew there on 11 December. His place as controller at the London end of the operation was taken by John Barker, the head of the ID's Quebec cocaine team. On the morning of 12 December Barker held a meeting for the Romeo team in New Fetter Lane. He explained that Favell was due to reach Paris from Rio at 1.30 that afternoon, connecting with an Air France flight to London at 2.30. Their aim was to arrest him, but in a way that preserved their overall goal, which Barker now outlined.

'The object of the exercise today is hopefully to trace the target as he arrives at Heathrow, to challenge and search him and potentially locate the drugs. And we want to do so in such a manner that he is totally unaware of our previous knowledge of his existence or suspicious of his movements. To that end we've got one or two plans afoot, and we'll try to see that they go as smoothly as possible.'

The plans that Barker explained covered every eventuality he and Donagher could think of. In Paris, Donagher would watch both Favell and his baggage. If Favell attempted a suitcase switch with a new courier, then Donagher should be able to identify the new figure who would be arrested in London with Favell. Donagher's presence in Paris would guard against another danger which sometimes blights international operations: that the French Customs or police might succumb to the temptation of arresting Favell themselves.

At Heathrow, even more officers would be waiting for Favell than had seen him depart a month before. There would be three in the Terminal Two immigration area – two to follow him through to the baggage hall, the third to receive any last-minute news from Donagher, who would arrive on the same flight. A rummage crew – the term originally referred to Customs officers who searched ships' holds, and now includes aircraft as well – would make sure that Favell had not hidden his consignment on the plane, to be retrieved later by a member of the airport or airline staff. A tarmac crew would watch Favell's luggage as it was taken to the baggage carousel, guarding against what is termed a 'rip off' – an attempt by an airport baggage handler to divert the luggage and smuggle it out of Heathrow.

Two more officers would be judiciously placed in the arrivals area to see if anyone was there to meet Favell. Finally, and most crucially, two uniformed officers were to be briefed on exactly how to deal with Favell when he attempted to pass through the Green Channel. 'If we can all make our way as expeditiously as possible to Terminal Two,' Barker asked in conclusion, 'and hope by then that we have got the okay from Hugh that all is well in Paris.'

During his briefing Barker had managed to convey a sense of confidence that overlaid the anxieties all investigative officers are prey to. It was another member of the Romeo team, Graham Dick, who revealed his doubts to the BBC as he drove to Heathrow along the M4. 'It's looking terrible,' he confided. 'It's going so smooth something's bound to go wrong. That's usually the case.'

The first thing that went wrong was that Favell missed his plane. As Donagher reported, his flight from Rio was forty-five minutes late and Favell missed the connecting flight to London. The second thing that went wrong was that although Favell missed the London plane his baggage did not. By some miracle of airport efficiency his cases were transferred to the London flight without mishap, so that not long after the Romeos arrived at Heathrow they learned that the baggage, minus Favell, was on its way.

However, the baggage was at least as important as Favell himself, and Donagher had further news to impart, which Graham Dick now relayed. 'He's told Air France out there that his baggage is one red Samsonite and one grey-blue holdall with wheels,' Dick reported, 'which is superb.'

To the Romeos that information was vital. A week before, they had seen Favell leaving Britain with a brown suitcase and a holdall on wheels. Favell had evidently disposed of the brown case and was returning with a Samsonite case instead. With their hard, curving sides, Samsonites (the Customs use the term to refer to all such cases, not just those manufactured by Samsonite themselves) were considered ideal for fitting with false compartments where layers of drugs could be concealed. But there was more to Dick's excitement than that. The Romeos were on the lookout for one particular Samsonite, and they hoped this might be the one – although they did not yet reveal that to the BBC.

Then came even more positive news from Paris. Hugh Donagher had managed to sneak a quick look at the bag before it departed and was firmly reporting that it was a 'DB' – a Customs acronym standing for 'dirty bag', and signifying that it almost certainly contained cocaine.

So what would happen now? The fact that Favell had missed his flight in Paris, while his suitcase had not, presented the Romeos with an almost limitless range of possibilities. They were added to by the latest news from Paris: Donagher had discovered that Favell had told Air France he had lost his ticket and had bought a new one.

Did this mean Favell had missed his flight deliberately? If so, would someone else try to collect his luggage in London? Would his accomplice be a passenger who had flown to Paris that morning and was now returning on Favell's flight? And why the apparent subterfuge over his ticket? Had he bought a new one so that it would appear he had flown to London from Paris instead of Rio? Or to get rid of the baggage tags that would identify him as the owner of the Samsonite?

As the Romeos wrestled with these alternatives, they found that they faced a new set of questions: now that the red Samsonite was heading for London by itself, what would happen to it when it arrived? According to airline procedures, the Samsonite should be retrieved by the Air France staff who would keep it at their baggage reclaim desk until the next flight arrived. It should also be checked by the airport security staff and the Customs would normally be asked to clear it too. All of that would take time and might go wrong as well. At worst, it could mean that when Favell arrived he would be unable to find his case. 'He might even walk straight through and not pick it up,' said Graham Dick gloomily. 'We haven't got a clue.'

That was the last thing the Customs wanted, and so Dick suggested an alternative. The Romeos should collect the Samsonite and take it to the Air France reclaim desk themselves. 'We'll leave it there and then hopefully when he comes through he'll take a wander up there and pick it up and then go to one of the channels,' Dick proposed. John Barker agreed.

So when Favell's original flight arrived, the Romeos retrieved his baggage themselves. Then John Barker made another suggestion. Since they still had two hours to spare before Favell arrived, why not open the Samsonite and see what was inside? Dick considered it an excellent idea. 'Okay,' he said, 'we'll have a peek.'

The Romeos had already enlisted the help of two of Heathrow's most experienced uniformed officers, Alasdair McDonald and Brian Waite, who had been asked to perform the task of stopping and questioning Favell when he tried to take the Samsonite through the Green Channel.

Both Scotsmen, McDonald and Waite had started work together at Heathrow on the same day in January 1978 and had since won reputations for being calm and imperturbable characters, which would suit them well for their role. Now Graham Dick asked them to search the Samsonite to see if they could find anything that would definitely link it to Favell, in case he tried to deny that it was his.

Favell's baggage was brought into an office behind the Green Channel. Waite lifted the Samsonite on to a table while McDonald produced an ample bunch of keys. It took him only seconds to select one to open the Samsonite, and he and Waite deftly sorted through Favell's freshly laundered clothing, laying it to one side so that it could be replaced in the same order. But although they looked through pockets in search of items – bills, hotel receipts, calling cards – that would identify the Samsonite as Favell's, they could find nothing of the kind.

They also examined the top and bottom of the Samsonite, and Waite tapped it knowingly. 'It's a very good concealment,' he said. 'Just looking at it you wouldn't be able to tell – you've got to feel it to actually know it's there.' How much cocaine did he think the suitcase contained? 'Three, four kilos perhaps – that's just a guess.'

Favell's flight from Paris was now due. His cases were spirited back to the arrivals hall, where John Barker instructed that they were to be left 'tantalisingly outside' the Air France desk in the hope that he would pick them up on his way through. Assuming that he then made for the Green Channel, McDonald and Waite were to stop and question him. Graham Dick told them that he or a colleague would point Favell out, and he reminded them to make it all seem as casual as possible – 'The whole idea is that this chap thinks that it's a chance pull.' He offered McDonald and Waite an intriguing phrase by way of explanation: Favell, he said, could be 'the key to bigger things'.

In acting out a 'chance pull', McDonald and Waite had several strong cards to play. As Graham Dick had told them, Favell was travelling on a new passport issued by the British Consul in Alicante. He had obtained it several months previously after claiming that his previous passport had been damaged by a hot iron. That would give McDonald and Waite the ideal excuse to take the passport away and check it.

Second, far more damagingly for Favell, the Customs' computer, known as CEDRIC, contained the information that he was wanted for questioning by the Customs on suspicion of having helped to import 12.5kg of Thai sticks, a form of cannabis consisting of dried plants coiled around a stick. That incident dated from 1983, when a friend of Favell's had been arrested. On checking the airline passenger list the Customs had found that he and Favell had travelled together and they had wanted to question him ever since.

When Favell stepped off the Paris flight, a virtual army of plain-clothes officers tracked his journey through immigration and into the baggage hall. So far so good, the Romeos thought. But Favell did not now behave according to plan. He appeared unaware that his baggage was standing at the Air France reclaim desk and stood dutifully waiting for it by the carousel.

The Romeos now decided to take a chance. An officer removed Favell's bags from the Air France desk and placed them on the conveyor belt beneath the baggage hall. As the cases came into sight, toppling gently on to the baggage carousel and beginning to revolve around it, the Romeos held their collective breath. Who would retrieve the Samsonite? Would it be Favell? Or would an accomplice now appear? All their worries, their endless permutations of possibilities, came to an end when Favell pushed his way into the crowd around the carousel and picked up first the grey holdall, then the Samsonite itself. He loaded them on to a trolley and headed for the Green Channel with his head down. Alasdair McDonald was waiting for him.

'Yes, sir,' said McDonald. 'Where are you travelling from?'

Favell looked up with a start and seemed to catch his breath. 'Er – I'm from Brazil, Paris....'

'And you live here normally?'

'No – I live in Spain.'

'You live in Spain – can I see your passport, please?'

Favell fumbled inside his jacket and produced his passport. McDonald looked at it ruminatively and said, 'That's a new one, is it?' He added, with an air of bonhomie, 'Can you bring your luggage round the corner? Is this all your luggage, is it? Did you pack all this luggage yourself?'

'Every bit, uh huh, yes,' replied Favell, almost inaudibly.

In that seemingly innocuous exchange, McDonald had already secured a crucial admission: Favell had identified the Samsonite as his. McDonald could see that Favell was immensely nervous: his stomach was pounding and his breathing had quickened. At the same time McDonald was struggling to contain the excitement most officers feel when they sense they are on the verge of a major find. With practised impassivity he took Favell through a well-tried routine.

McDonald first asked Favell whether he was aware that he was coming through the Green Channel, meaning that he had nothing to declare. When Favell said he was, McDonald asked to look inside his holdall. Meanwhile Brian Waite disappeared with Favell's passport. McDonald continued to question Favell about his trip while he perused Favell's belongings.

'How long have you been away?'

'I've been away – about ten days, ten days.'

'What was that – a business trip?'

'No, I've got a baby out there.'

'You've got a baby out there?'

'Yeah.'

'Have you lived out there as well?'

'No, I went out to see a football match two years ago, and stayed longer than we thought and I ended up becoming a father.'

'Good grief,' said McDonald. 'It's funny how things like that happen.'

McDonald secured further confirmation that the baggage was Favell's when Favell agreed that several items in the case – some tobacco and tape-cassettes – were his. Then Waite returned with Favell's passport.

'Did you do that check, Brian?' McDonald asked.

'Yes,' Waite replied. 'Actually there is a bit of an irregularity. We would like to have a chat with the gentleman. There's an awful lot on the computer, actually.'

Favell appeared not to have heard what Waite said. McDonald addressed him directly.

'Mr Favell, we'd just like a quick word with you. Apparently there's something come up . . .'

'. . . on the computer,' added Waite.

Favell took a step back and looked at McDonald. 'Well, what?'

'Well that', McDonald replied, 'is what we've got to find out.'

McDonald asked Favell to close his suitcases and load them back on to his trolley. With McDonald and Waite by his side, and a senior Customs officer hovering behind, Favell was led into the unprepossessing set of offices which comprise the Customs' inner sanctum at Terminal Two. Favell was shown into a confined interview room, followed by McDonald and Waite. They told him he was under arrest.

At first Favell appeared surprised at what had happened. But he was soon presented with the Samsonite suitcase, whose lid had been slit open to reveal a neatly packaged layer of cocaine. Favell offered little or no defence: in a crucial interchange, he admitted that he knew it was illegal to bring cocaine into Britain, and that he knew his suitcase contained cocaine. 'Beautiful,' said Graham Dick when Waite told him afterwards. 'Beautiful.'

Later, Dick joined Favell in the interview room. He gave Favell a formal caution, explaining that he was not obliged to say anything but if he did it would be taken down in writing and could be used in evidence.

Favell was evidently hoping for some less formal conversation. 'There's no off the record or anything like that?'

'No, we will take down what you say,' Dick replied.

'I've already answered his questions,' Favell said.

'Well, we want to cover it in depth, obviously – we'll have a chat—'

When Favell returned to Britain from Brazil on 12 December 1985, he was watched as carefully as before. There was alarm among the Romeo team when he missed his connecting flight in Paris, and his red Samsonite suitcase (*top*) arrived without him. The suitcase was retrieved – and when Favell attempted to take it through the Green Channel, he was arrested. The case contained 3 kg of neatly-packed cocaine, as shown in the Customs' photograph (*centre*), later produced as evidence in court. The Customs' photograph *below* shows how intelligence officers had secretly marked Favell's suitcase several months before.

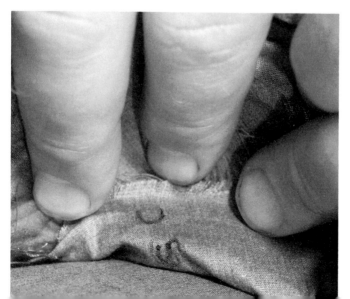

'I'd rather have a chat.'

'We will have a chat but we prefer to get it down in writing.'

'All right, you can do all that but I mean – look, I know that I'm up to here.'

Gradually – although Dick acted as if he did not realise it – Favell was making himself clear. 'I'm looking for a way out for me . . .'

'Okay,' said Dick, cautiously.

'Well, can you help me?'

'I don't know what you mean by that.'

'I don't expect to walk out the back door but I mean as it stands now I'm going to – I know what's been happening to people who have been done the same way.'

'Yes,' said Dick.

'And the thought of it isn't very fucking pleasing.'

Although he pretended not to, Dick knew very well what Favell was getting at: he was trying to suggest a deal. Perhaps in return for a full confession, providing the Customs with information about accomplices, Favell might receive a reduced sentence when he was convicted. Dick found it an embarrassing proposal, not because such arrangements are improper – they are sanctioned in guidelines laid down by the Lord Chief Justice – but because at that precise moment he did not want too much information from Favell.

If Favell *did* name names, then the Customs would be compelled to act upon his information, for to do otherwise would appear immensely suspicious. But the Romeos were not ready to make such a move. So Dick admitted that he knew what Favell was driving at – and then made a show of turning it down on the grounds that the Customs did not indulge in 'chats' of the kind Favell had in mind.

'We're not in a position to make deals,' Dick said. 'It's as simple as that. We're going to write down what you say, and if you have something to say, then tell us.'

Favell made himself clear. 'What do I get in return?'

'Well, that's not for us to say. Christ, we're not in the position of doing that.'

Favell persevered. 'I've never been in contact with you people before.' By 'you people', he meant the Customs. 'I've been in contact with the other people lots of times.' The 'other people' were the police.

'Yes, okay,' said Dick tolerantly.

'And I know – scratch my back and I'll scratch yours. Whatever way you say it, things are done amicable to both parties.'

Dick seemed unmoved. 'All we're concerned about is finding out exactly what has happened, exactly what was to happen. And we're going to stick it down in writing.'

As the evening progressed, Favell did tell the Customs a lot of what had happened – but almost nothing of what was supposed to happen next. He said he had been paid five thousand pounds for making the round trip to South America, plus all his expenses. He said that he was supposed to hand the suitcase over to someone in Britain, but declined to say who that was.

Outside the interview room, Dick – not yet betraying his true motives – went through the motions of discussing a deal for the benefit of the BBC cameras. Was there no chance of Favell getting what he wanted? 'He could do,' Dick replied, 'but we need names and addresses.'

Was Favell likely to provide them in return for a hint that his sentence could be reduced?

'I doubt it very much,' Dick replied.

So what sentence did he face?

Dick guessed that since Favell had tried to bring through around three kilos of cocaine he was facing a sentence of at least ten years. Then, in a moment of apparent sympathy, Dick added: 'He's the poor sod that's up front. That's why he's paid such a seemingly enormous amount of money.'

The trail which for Tony Favell ended at Heathrow began 5000 miles away in the South American country of Bolivia. Entirely land-locked, with half its population living on a 12,000-foot plateau between two chains of the Andes, Bolivia is the prime source of the coca plant, a low, sturdy bush with brilliant green leaves a little larger than those of a privet hedge. The plants occupy hundreds of thousands of acres of rough farmland, often deep in the jungle, and it is the coca plant from which cocaine is derived.

Bolivia is the poorest country in South America. Once its economy depended on tin, hewn from the rock of the Andes. Now tin has been replaced by cocaine, which employs almost half a million people and brings Bolivia two-thirds of its annual export earnings. While to the wealthy nations of the West cocaine is the cause of misery, exploitation, organised crime and death, to Bolivia cocaine means economic survival. It is this clash of interests and perceptions which makes it so much harder to eradicate the international cocaine trade.

The Indians of the South American Andes have chewed the leaves of the coca bush for 3000 years. Their priests used it to induce trances and it was chewed on ceremonial occasions at the royal courts of the Inca kings. When the fifteenth-century explorer Amerigo Vespucci first saw the inhabitants of the future Spanish colony of Peru he described how 'all had their cheeks bulging with a certain green herb which they chewed constantly'. At first the Spanish *conquistadores* believed that this mysterious green herb was a tool of the devil; but they changed their view when they discovered that it enabled their Indian slaves to toil in their silver and tin mines, helping them to draw breath and dull the pain of working at high altitude. It is still chewed by the miners of Bolivia today, and is served as coca-maté tea in the Sheraton hotel of La Paz, giving strength to the tourists who gasp for air in the highest capital city in the world.

The powers of the coca leaf are still celebrated in the name of the world's most popular soft drink, invented by an American pharmacist, Dr John Styth Pemberton, from Atlanta, Georgia. He had learned of a tonic wine made from coca leaves in Paris, whose devotees included Jules Verne, Alexandre Dumas and Pope Leo XIII, who gave the manufacturer a gold medal for his services as 'a benefactor to humanity'. Pemberton concocted a syrup which included coca leaves, mixed it with carbonated water and put it on sale at five cents a glass. When it proved successful he advertised it as 'the new and popular soda fountain drink', and he named it Coca-Cola.

Cocaine itself was first produced in the search for a replacement for morphine. Derived from the opium poppy – also the source of heroin – morphine had proved an effective painkiller for the half-million casualties of the American Civil War. But it also proved highly addictive and created almost 50,000 addicts among the survivors of both sides. After German chemists had isolated cocaine from coca leaves, doctors found that it was effective both as painkiller and stimulant, bringing enhanced feelings of energy, self-confidence and excitement.

Its properties were soon discovered by writers and intellectuals, like Robert Louis Stevenson who took it as a remedy for a breathing complaint and was certainly under its influence when he wrote the story of Dr Jekyll and Mr Hyde – with its obvious parallels – in a week. Arthur Conan Doyle prescribed cocaine for his character Sherlock Holmes, who injected it as an antidote to boredom in the intervals between solving his cases.

The most enthusiastic advocate of all was Sigmund Freud, the father of psychoanalysis, who gave cocaine to his patients as a treatment for depression and used it himself as a tonic when he was tired. He called it a 'magical substance' and his article, *Über Coca*, remained a standard text until well into the twentieth century. Following Freud's work, cocaine was discovered to be an ideal local anaesthetic for eye surgery and is still used for that purpose today.

Ironically, it was Freud's work which began to turn the legislators against cocaine. One of his patients died of an overdose and another became hopelessly addicted. In Britain there were several well-publicised cocaine deaths and the sale of cocaine to British troops was banned during the First World War.

That law was replaced by the Dangerous Drugs Act of 1920 on which Britain's subsequent anti-drugs legislation has been based. Most US states made cocaine illegal too, while the US government led a series of international moves to ban cocaine along with other drugs such as opium and heroin. And the manufacturers of Coca-Cola had long since changed its formula, so that it contained an innocuous flavouring derived from purified coca leaves. (The official history of Coca-Cola makes no mention of the coca plant at all.)

One of the dilemmas of the fight against drugs is that when a commodity is made illegal it attracts the attention of organised crime. It was the ban on alcohol during the Prohibition era which more than anything else enabled the US Mafia to organise and prosper. The same process has proved sadly true in the case of heroin. Cocaine is now providing the latest example – only this time entire countries are being corrupted.

For forty years after it was banned, cocaine was hardly perceived as a problem. In Britain its use was confined to high-society circles, surfacing occasionally in the press in scandalous tales of overdoses and the occasional death. In the US it remained part of a confined subculture, peopled by jazz musicians and the beat writers. But in the early 1970s it became the suddenly fashionable drug of the American music and entertainment industry, and its use soared. Cocaine was offered to guests at movie receptions or post-concert parties, to be sniffed from tiny spoons, or 'snorted' through straws from 'lines' laid out on mirrors. While rock stars claimed, improbably, that cocaine boosted their creative abilities, it certainly enhanced the image of a glittering life-style and became known as the 'champagne drug'. Its illegality gave it a certain cachet but its greatest boost came from the belief that it was 'safe' – i.e. it did not bring painful withdrawal symptoms like heroin and was believed to be non-addictive. In the US today some six million people are believed to use cocaine regularly and a further twenty-five million to take it from time to time.

Virtually all the cocaine used in the US is supplied from Bolivia and Colombia. While there is considerable dispute (of the chicken-and-egg variety) over which came first, the explosive growth of the cocaine habit in the US has brought profound changes to the economies of these two South American countries. Twenty years ago Bolivia and Colombia had well-established coca industries which provided coca leaves for the home market and the raw materials for the international pharmaceutical trade. As US demand rose vast tracts of land were cleared to grow coca plants, and what had been a traditional peasant industry became the preserve of major crime syndicates of staggering wealth and power.

In Colombia, the coca industry was taken over by three Mafia-style families who have come to dominate at least seventy-five per cent of the country's cocaine trade. They control it at all levels, from the farms where the plants are grown to the processing plants where the leaves are converted into cocaine paste. Their power is so brazen that in 1984 they offered to pay off Colombia's national debt, then valued at $13 billion, in return for an amnesty and a repeal of Colombia's extradition treaty with the US. When Colombia's President Betancur turned down their offer they retaliated with a succession of brutal assassinations.

Their victims include a journalist who wrote articles revealing their methods and judges who sent their henchmen to prison. The head of the US Drug Enforcement Administration was killed by a bomb planted inside the US Embassy in Bogotá. Colombia's justice minister was murdered for ordering a raid on a cocaine-processing plant. For his own safety, his successor was made Colombia's ambassador to Hungary and posted to Budapest. The cocaine gunmen tracked him down even there and he was seriously wounded when he was struck down in yet another assassination attempt.

Although the Colombian government makes some attempt to stem the cocaine trade, it is now doubtful whether it could manage without it. Cocaine brings Colombia $8 billion a year in exports, most of which feeds the economy by financing the importation of consumer goods. The cocaine barons act like benevolent despots, building houses for their farmers and process-workers, buying banks, zoos, cattle farms, hotels and soccer teams almost at whim.

Cocaine's hold on Bolivia is even more powerful. Its spectacular growth in the 1970s was encouraged by Bolivia's president, Hugo Banzer, with the assistance of the former Gestapo chief Klaus Barbie, who found sanctuary in Bolivia for twenty years before being hauled back to France to stand trial for war crimes. Barbie recruited a squad of 'enforcers' to protect the trade and ensure that supplies reached the processing plants of Colombia. When Banzer was toppled and replaced by General Garcia Meza, the coup was funded by cocaine money and assisted by Barbie's private army. When Meza gave way to an elected government in 1982, the new regime found that the cocaine trade was virtually beyond the law, as it had become by far Bolivia's largest source of overseas earnings.

In the province of Cochabamba, 150 miles from La Paz, thousands of families cultivate their coca plants on smallholdings which may bring them $2000 a year. That is ten times what they could earn from the backbreaking task of growing coffee, Bolivia's traditional crop. They are organised into growers' cooperatives and at harvest time are helped by up to 250,000 migrant workers. Since cocaine prices can fluctuate enormously – a kilo of cocaine paste has swung between $300 and $5000 in the past five years – farmers and traders have organised a commodity market to bring stability to their incomes. Deals are struck between suppliers and traders in the street cafés of Cochabamba in the spirit of the coffee houses of London in the seventeenth century.

But there is no shortage of modern technological aids: airstrips dot the coca fields of Cochabamba, and the Bolivians and Colombians have joined forces to ensure that their cocaine is transported safely to staging posts in the Caribbean. From there it is shipped to the US by sea and air, most of it through Miami and the rest of Florida. The size of some loads beggars belief: in 1986 the US Customs and Drug Enforcement Administration seized over *three tons* of cocaine from a vessel attempting to land it on the Florida coast and seizures of a ton or more have continued since.

The flood of cocaine has brought massive medical and social problems. While some users still insist that cocaine is comparatively safe when inhaled in small quantities, many have been tempted into such risky practices as 'freebasing' (burning cocaine and inhaling the fumes), or 'speedballing' (injecting it directly into the bloodstream, sometimes mixed with heroin). Once touted as non-addictive, cocaine has also been found to cause both physiological and psychological dependence. With them come depression, hallucinations and paranoia. Overdoses can cause convulsions and fainting, and doses as low as one gram have proved fatal.

In the mid-1980s a new form of cocaine, a highly-purified version known as 'crack', arrived in the US. Smoked through a glass pipe or on the tip of a cigarette, it reaches the brain within seconds. While it brings an almost instant 'high', it also creates addiction far more rapidly. It is sold for as little as $5, threatening to expand the use of cocaine into an even wider market than before.

Crack is also blamed for a vast increase in crime. Out of 169 murders in one area of New York in six months of 1986, the police blamed crack for almost half. Both it and cocaine have brought new groups into organised crime, the most awesome being the Colombian distributors who enforce their territory with reprisals more horrifying than those of any of their predecessors. Whereas the New York Mafia would execute transgressors and dump their bodies in the Hudson River, the Colombians slaughter their families or even entire bars where they drink.

Over the past ten years the US government has made desperate efforts to stem the cocaine trade at source. Headed by the Drug Enforcement Administration, with the backing of US military forces, its campaign has included spraying herbicides to defoliate the coca fields and carrying out gunship raids on processing plants. It has also enacted extradition treaties to try to bring South American traders into US courts. But such is the hold of the cocaine industry that supplies have continued to reach the US unabated, leading Bolivia and Colombia to protest that the US government should concentrate on stemming the demand for cocaine at home. In 1986 the *Financial Times* bleakly concluded that, no matter what efforts the US made, the power of the cocaine barons had become 'unassailable'.

The report in the *Financial Times* formed part of a spate of media interest in the American cocaine trade which inevitably raised the question of whether anything similar was likely to occur in Britain. Certainly there was a worrying trend. Rock musicians who visited the US in the early 1970s brought back news of cocaine when they came home, and by 1980 the British Customs were seizing increasing amounts. In 1975, for example, seizures stood at 6kg. In 1980 the figure had risen to 36kg and in 1985 it was 78kg. In 1987 the Customs made their record single seizure when they raided a flat in London's Harley Street and found 57kg of cocaine.

Interpreting seizure statistics is always a controversial matter. Do they mean that the Customs are becoming more efficient? Or simply that more cocaine is being imported? The answer is probably a combination of both. Either way, the British Customs came to the view that they were facing a marked increase in attempts to smuggle cocaine into Britain – and guessed that they were intercepting between one-tenth and one-fifth of the total amount.

By the same yardsticks, however, the British figures did not remotely approach the size of importations into the US. The record seizure made by the US Customs and Drug Enforcement Administration in Florida in 1986 was ten times the entire amount of cocaine ever seized by British Customs. Nonetheless, some British authorities concluded that Britain was facing a parallel threat.

A party of MPs who visited the US in 1985 warned that Britain faced 'a cocaine crisis on an American scale'. In 1986 David Mellor, then the Home Office minister responsible for fighting drugs, toured the cocaine-producing countries of South America. He distributed £1.5 million to the anti-drugs forces of Bolivia, Ecuador and Peru and said on his return that Britain would do all it could to resist 'ruthless traffickers' who threatened them. Two days later, in the most dramatic warning of all, John Dellow, Assistant Commissioner of the Metropolitan Police, declared that 'violent and evil criminals' from South America were about to organise a distribution network in Britain, and could even use the proceeds to finance international terrorism.

Claims such as these leave the Customs with mixed feelings. They fear that to overstate the case can do harm by glamorising drugs and stimulating demand. They are wary of panic measures which can overwhelm a more considered response. Individual Customs officers might even say that Mr Mellor's £1.5 million could be better spent on the

British Customs, since they represent the front line of Britain's defences. And despite warnings they too had been receiving from the US, the Customs considered it unlikely that the Colombia drugs-mafia were about to invade Britain, whether in alliance with international terrorists or otherwise.

It was true that in 1986 at least twenty Colombian couriers were arrested trying to smuggle cocaine into Britain. But many of these attempted to do so by the repellent methods known as stuffing and swallowing (described more fully later in this book), which limit the amount that can be carried to an average of 200–250g. And the Customs estimated that it would be far harder for the Colombians to set up a distribution chain in Britain than the US, which was so much closer to the point of supply.

The Customs had nonetheless been quietly reorganising their own resources to deal with cocaine. In 1984, only one of the Investigation Division's seventeen teams, code-named the Hotels, worked on cocaine. That year the ID formed a second cocaine team, the Romeos, followed in 1985 by two more, the Sierras and the Quebecs. The Romeos and the Sierras were also given a new brief. Previously where cocaine was concerned the ID had mostly carried out 'referral' work, which entailed following up seizures made by the uniformed officers at the main points of entry such as Dover and Heathrow. Now the Romeos and the Sierras were to concentrate on 'target' work, which meant identifying suspects and piecing together the evidence that could lead to an arrest.

The Customs believed that they faced the greatest threat from British smugglers who travelled as couriers to South America with well-rehearsed cover stories and returned with amounts of up to 3kg skilfully concealed in their baggage: smugglers like Tony Favell, whose cocaine, they believed, came from Bolivia, and who was a most suitable adversary for target teams like the Romeos.

But the Romeos had a further aim. Commonsense alone told them that Favell was hardly likely to be operating on his own – and Favell had admitted as much himself, when he told them that he was supposed to hand the Samsonite to an accomplice in Britain, although naturally declining to say who that was. In the Romeos' estimation, Favell was a typical small-time professional criminal, with a long record for offences ranging from possessing cannabis to dealing in stolen travellers' cheques, and several spells spent in Her Majesty's prisons. He was also, at least so the Romeos suspected, typical of the cocaine trade in that as a courier he would almost certainly be regarded as expendable.

That was what Graham Dick meant when he said, in a sudden moment of apparent sympathy, that Favell was the 'poor sod up front' who ran the risk of a heavy prison sentence in return for his fee of £5000. Another of Dick's phrases now assumed significance too: his explanation to the two uniformed officers, Alasdair McDonald and Brian Waite, when asking them to make it appear that Favell's arrest was a matter of chance, as he could hold the key to 'bigger things'. From the very start of their investigation, in fact, 'bigger things' were what the Romeos had in mind.

The arrest of Tony Favell has already shown the amount of inference, deduction, instinct and sheer guesswork involved in Operation Renaissance. It was in fact a comparatively simple transaction, that entailed watching Favell in Paris, tracking him and his suitcase, and arresting him in London. Yet there had been so many possibilities at hand that the Romeos were driven almost to distraction trying to calculate the various permutations before Favell ended the discussion by delivering himself into their arms.

That episode was typical of the Romeos' work. To be an investigative officer, particularly on a target team, is to spend a large part of life in a haze of speculation and doubt. One officer says that working on an operation like Renaissance is like trying to complete a jigsaw puzzle with only a few of the pieces available at the start – and, he adds, 'you've no idea what the final picture is supposed to look like'. Much of the investigation is devoted to searching for further pieces and trying to decide what that final picture might be.

To these difficulties are added others that result from the changing role of the Customs over the past twenty years. For 750 years the Customs were principally a revenue-collecting body, dedicated to filling the coffers of the Treasury with taxes and other dues, and imbued with the same traditions of caution and circumspection as the rest of the Civil Service. Now, as a law-enforcement agency dedicated above all to the fight against drugs, they have had to learn how to respond to the fast-moving, fast-changing world of professional criminals.

The Customs have a proud record in this field, often winning praise for the thoroughness of their fieldwork and its presentation in court. It is also a demanding and competitive life. One ID team calculated that in 1986 it had worked 223 hours a month, or an average of almost $7\frac{1}{2}$ hours a day, 365 days a year, including Christmas and all other holidays – and on the Christmas Day in question they had been called to Heathrow at 8.55 a.m., returning home at 10 o'clock that night. The competition is both internal, where it is usually good-natured, and with other law-enforcement agencies, where there is a certain territorial rivalry. In this climate the view is sometimes expressed that you are only as good as your last case; mistakes are deeply felt and may take time to live down.

Operation Renaissance had the further and unique complication of the presence of the BBC. When the BBC team began work on its series in 1985, it was first told by the head of the ID, Dick Lawrence, that it would not be able to record the progress of a cocaine investigation as the work was difficult enough as it was. Eventually the Customs relented, and the BBC became privy to the Romeos' innermost thoughts and discussions, as they attempted to interpret the information they were painstakingly acquiring. In those sessions, the Romeos were to argue their theories and beliefs with considerable force and conviction.

Eventually those beliefs were also advanced at a six-week criminal trial at Isleworth Crown Court in 1987. For the Romeos the trial represented the culmination of a two-year investigation that had started long before the arrest of Tony Favell. Their case was based on a series of detailed observations of the five accused men, including Favell, and on documentary and other evidence they had gathered.

In the course of the trial, very little of that factual evidence was challenged. But the interpretation placed upon that evidence by the prosecution, in line with the beliefs the Customs had formulated during their investigation, most emphatically *was* challenged. In some instances the defence put forward an alternative explanation to account for the evidence the Customs presented; in others, they argued that the evidence simply did not substantiate the charges that the defendants faced.

Whether the Customs' case ultimately proved convincing was, of course, for the judge and jury at Isleworth to decide.

Operation Renaissance was born, in effect, at Heathrow airport on 13 February 1985. Early that evening two Customs officers, Frank Munoz and Steve Clark, were on duty in Terminal Two, watching passengers checking in for an Air France flight to Paris.

While it is well known that the Customs scrutinise passengers and their baggage as they enter Britain, it is less widely known that they also keep a discreet watch on those who are leaving. They may be looking for a particular 'face' – someone known to them already for involvement, or suspicion of involvement, in nefarious practices such as the drugs trade. Or they may merely be on their guard for anything unusual or out of place – anything, in short, that would arouse the sensibilities of the 'revenue nose', the centuries-old term for the awareness Customs officers are supposed to develop for the unlikely or the untoward.

On 13 February Munoz and Clark, two laconic Liverpudlians who have operated as a partnership at Heathrow for four years, were on the lookout for a very particular 'face': someone they suspected of smuggling cocaine and who they believed was due to fly via Paris to La Paz, the capital of Bolivia. They had not in fact seen him when a tall, slim passenger with fair hair and a trim moustache came into view. Quite simply, to their innately suspicious minds, he appeared to merit clo-

attention. Munoz was especially interested in the man's baggage, which included a red Samsonite suitcase.

That is another facet of the Customs' work at Heathrow that has largely escaped the public's awareness. Passengers who deposit their baggage at the airline check-in desk may fondly suppose that it proceeds on an uninterrupted journey to the hold of their aircraft. As the travels of Tony Favell have already shown, this is not necessarily so – and on this occasion Munoz walked briskly through the Customs area to the rear of Terminal Two, where a line of baggage containers was waiting to be towed to the Paris flight.

Munoz found the red Samsonite suitcase inside the transit container intended for baggage for destinations beyond Paris. It carried a label – number AF466930 – which showed that its ultimate destination was Peru. It bore the name 'M Mescal' and the address 2 Merlin Gardens, Romford. Although the suitcase had a combination lock, to Munoz's practised eye discovering the number was a simple matter.

Munoz tipped the suitcase forward so that he could peer past the combination numbers and look at the spindle on which they revolved. He then moved each of the numbers in turn until he saw a groove appear in the spindle, signifying the figure to which each had been set. It took Munoz less than a minute to discover that the combination of Mescal's Samsonite was 185.

Munoz jotted the number in his notebook and returned to the departure hall where he conferred with Clark. They decided to speak to Mescal and waited for him by the passport desk. When Mescal proffered his passport, Munoz asked him where he was going. Mescal replied that he was bound for South America in his business as a gemstone dealer and that he might also buy some land. Munoz memorised Mescal's passport number – 923934E – and he and Clark recorded the encounter in their notebooks.

The information also reached the Investigation Division at New Fetter Lane. Munoz and Clark had filled in what is termed an 'SMR', or Suspicious Movement Report. The report was referred to the Romeo team, headed by Hugh Donagher. The Romeos consulted the computer, CEDRIC, but it had nothing to offer on Mescal. A new file was opened, headed Michael Mescal, and the SMR was fed in.

A month later the Romeos received further news. Among the Customs and law-enforcement bodies of other countries, the ID maintains the closest links with the Drug Enforcement Administration, the American anti-drugs body with its headquarters in Washington and around 300 agents abroad. Since Bolivia is one of the two prime sources of cocaine reaching the US, the DEA naturally has a number of officers there. Now Mescal – who after reaching Peru had flown to Bolivia's capital, La Paz, before moving on to Rio de Janeiro on 19 February – came to the DEA's attention.

While in South America, the DEA reported, Mescal had met three expatriate Americans whose activities had already aroused their interest, and it now reported its suspicions to the British Customs. The point when that information reached the Romeos, thus seeming to give them two pieces for their jigsaw puzzle (the first was the report from Heathrow), was the point when Operation Renaissance was truly launched. It was also the point at which it received its name.

During subsequent investigation the Romeos naturally learned more about Michael Mescal. Aged thirty-two, from Romford – 2 Merlin Gardens was his grandmother's home – he was a gem-dealer operating between Britain, South America and the Far East. He had a girlfriend in Thailand named Toy, the daughter of a prosperous farmer in a village 600 kilometres from Bangkok. In 1978 Mescal had been convicted of attempting to smuggle heroin into Germany and had spent three years in prison there.

Not all of this was yet known to the Romeos, but they did know that Mescal had recently become a Muslim and had adopted the name Omar – Michael Omar Mescal. The Customs have a liking for private jokes or puns and Hugh Donagher first thought of calling it Operation Reborn as a reference to Mescal's religious conversion. Donagher eventually plumped for Operation Renaissance as he felt it had that extra touch of class.

With Operation Renaissance in being, it was the tireless activities of Frank Munoz and Steve Clark at Heathrow that now brought them the next piece in the jigsaw. It came from another of the Customs' less publicised methods, namely their examination of airline passenger lists. Some members of the Customs consider this a delicate matter, for it could be considered an abuse of privacy. And while the airlines co-operate both fully and officially, they are hardly open about doing so. When British Airways decided that its passenger manifests should be made available to the Customs, its board showed its sensitivity on the subject by deleting the item from its minutes. The co-operation of other airlines was secured by an agreement between the European Customs Co-operation Council and the international airlines association, IATA. That provided a 'frame-work' within which airlines would work, although its precise nature was left suitably vague.

So it was that by perusing a passenger manifest supplied by the Brazilian Airline, Varig, on 10 April, Frank Munoz learned that a passenger named Mescal had booked to fly to Rio. At around 8 p.m. Munoz saw a tall, square-jawed man in his twenties arrive at the Varig desk for the flight. His first name was David and he was the younger brother of

Michael Mescal. He had two items of baggage: a black travelling ward-robe, which he checked in, and a tan-coloured Samsonite briefcase which he carried as hand-baggage.

Munoz went, as usual, to the rear of the terminal and retrieved the travelling wardrobe. He opened it and found that it contained clothing. He also borrowed Mescal's flight coupon from Varig and discovered that he was intending to fly on to Santa Cruz in Bolivia, returning to London on 24 April. Munoz duly reported his findings to the Romeos.

When David Mescal arrived at Heathrow on 24 April, there was a small reception party waiting. Munoz was accompanied by the Romeos' Graham Dick, who had been appointed the Renaissance case-officer by Hugh Donagher. When Mescal reached the baggage-reclaim area, Munoz pointed him out. Both officers were quick to notice that he no longer had the Samsonite briefcase.

Back at New Fetter Lane, the Romeos considered where the new piece in their jigsaw might fit. For one member of the Mescal family to leave Britain with a Samsonite case could hardly be considered significant; but for another to do so, and then return without it, so it seemed to the Romeos, most certainly was. In addition, one of the brothers had been drawn to their attention by the DEA, and both had gone to Bolivia, a prime source of cocaine. To the Romeos – and this was to form part of the case they eventually presented in court – it all suggested that one or more Samsonites were being used to smuggle cocaine into Britain. But as Graham Dick later starkly summarised the position at that time, 'we had no idea where or when'.

Two months passed. In that time the Romeos learned what little they could about Michael Mescal and his younger brother David, who was a carpenter by trade and lived with his wife in Rainham, Essex – also the home of the Mescals' parents. But where was Michael himself? The Romeos did not know. They did not even know if he had remained out of Britain since leaving in February, or whether they had missed his return. The next piece in the jigsaw arrived on 26 June. That evening Frank Munoz was on hand to see David Mescal embark on another Varig flight to Rio and Santa Cruz. He was carrying another Samsonite case – this one was coloured maroon – which Munoz removed from the Varig baggage conveyor at the rear of Terminal Three.

By now Munoz was finding the Mescals' Samsonites easy to open, as they were all set to the same combination, 185 (the Romeos later dis-covered that Michael's birthday was the key – he was born on 18 May 1954). The only item Munoz considered of possible significance was a Budget car-rental receipt. He noted down the details before closing the case and putting it back where it belonged.

This time the Romeos tried to learn more about David Mescal, and employed a somewhat brazen subterfuge to do so. In Terminal Three a Romeo officer asked an airport security guard to stop Mescal and search him under the pretence of carrying out a random security check. When the guard frisked Mescal he found a sizeable wad of currency in one of his pockets. He riffled through it and noted that it appeared to be made up of $100 bills – to a total value, the Romeos later estimated, of £10,000.

As jigsaw puzzles went, the fact that someone was carrying a sizeable amount of US cash rated as a fairly small piece. But David Mescal was due to return to Britain on 3 July – and when he did the Romeos would see how much more of the puzzle they might be able to fill in. They particularly hoped that David Mescal might lead them to his brother Michael, as they still had no idea where he was.

When David Mescal arrived at Heathrow on 3 July he was first observed by Frank Munoz, who noted that he was wearing a purple tracksuit. Munoz asked a uniformed officer in the Green Channel to examine Mescal's baggage. The officer searched Mescal's holdall and found several hotel bills and business cards which he handed to Munoz, who discreetly photocopied them before handing them back. Once again, the maroon Samsonite Mescal had taken out of Britain was missing.

After leaving the Customs area Mescal walked through the tunnel leading from Terminal Three to Heathrow underground station. Following a short distance behind was a Romeo officer, Martin Wilson. Inside the station Wilson handed over to a second officer, Chhotubhai Patel. Known to most of his colleagues as 'Chats', Patel was the operation's deputy case-officer. He joined Mescal in the booking-office queue and heard him ask for a ticket to Earls Court. He radioed that information to Customs control and then followed Mescal on to an eastbound train.

By the time the train reached Earls Court several of the Romeos were waiting, including Martin Wilson who had headed there at some speed along the M4. It was Wilson who followed David Mescal as he left the station and walked down Earls Court Road. Mescal turned into Old Brompton Road, eventually reaching Harrington Road and turning from there into Queensberry Place. He stopped at No. 4, climbed the steps and rang the bell. There was no answer. Mescal came down the steps and read a note which had been left on the windscreen of a blue Ford Granada parked outside.

Mescal went back up the steps to No. 4 and let himself in. Two minutes later he left again and walked towards Harrington Road. He had just reached the corner when he met a tall man with fair hair and a trim moustache who was carrying several video cassettes. It was Michael Mescal.

For the Romeos, the mundane fact that the brothers had met outside a flat in Earls Court ranked as a major breakthrough. First, they had found Michael; second, the meeting indicated to them that the brothers were acting together in some way. The sighting also suggested to them that the flat served as some kind of rendezvous – and it presented them with the opportunity to mount a surveillance operation to see who else called there.

Surveillance operations are among the most uncomfortable aspects of investigative work. Tucked away in a Southwark back-street is a garage containing a collection of nondescript and often dilapidated vehicles whose identities the Customs understandably do not want revealed. The vehicles are usually parked as casually as possible outside the premises under observation, leaving the officers to spend up to twelve hours at a stretch inside. They have to peer through a tiny peep-hole, camera at the ready, in the hope of seeing and/or photographing something of interest. In the winter it can be bitterly cold, in the summer unbearably hot, and there is no escape until the colleague who has parked the car arrives to take it away. For sustenance, officers take sandwiches and thermos flasks; for other bodily needs, a portable camping lavatory which provides up to forty flushes.

The Romeos began to watch 4 Queensberry Place that night. They also called in Dick Palmer and his box of tricks. Palmer, whose formal title is Principal Photographer, HM Customs and Excise, inhabits a room on the first floor of New Fetter Lane that is cluttered with photographic equipment of every kind. The Romeos told him they wanted pictures of anyone entering or leaving 4 Queensberry Place, day or night, for the foreseeable future.

The next problem was to find premises which offered a view of 4 Queensberry Place and whose owner was prepared to help. After Chats Patel had done so, Dick Palmer installed a video camera with a special 'low-light' lens that operates both day and night. Palmer set it to run at one frame per second, so that one three-hour cassette would last for three days. Every third day an officer called at the premises to remove the cassette which – as a rule of thumb – took three hours to replay, using the fast-forward button when nothing was happening and freezing the frame when something of interest came into view.

The initial results were disappointing. Ironically, the low-light lens worked perfectly at night but gave only murky pictures by day. On the earliest videos, the Romeos could see that *someone* was visiting Queensberry Place but they could not tell who. Other frames clearly showed Michael Mescal carrying something in his hand, but it was hard to see what it was. Palmer returned to install *two* cameras, one for day and one for night, which meant that a member of the Romeos had to call in twice a day to switch over the video lead.

For three months in the summer of 1985, the Romeos kept watch on a flat in Queensberry Place, Earls Court, photographing occupants and visitors and recording their comings and goings with a secret video camera installed nearby. There seemed to be frequent activities to record, particularly as suitcases were brought in and out, as shown in the Customs' surveillance photos and video stills. *Top to bottom*: Michael Mescal leaves the flat empty-handed; so does his brother, David Mescal; Michael enters carrying suitcase; Michael leaves with two suitcases.

Although the pictures were vastly improved, the Romeos suffered a further disappointment when they learned that Michael Mescal was due to fly into Heathrow from Rio on 4 August. They watched him pass through the Customs carrying a black canvas holdall and a large brief-case, to be met by David Mescal who drove him back to Queensberry Place in a Ford Granada. Their disappointment stemmed from the fact that they had missed Michael when he left Britain, leaving them with a sense of frustration that they were hardly on top of events.

Quite soon, however, the Romeos' spirits were lifted by a flurry of activity. Four days after returning to Britain Michael Mescal took a suitcase into Queensberry Place, leaving with it again that evening. The following day, 9 August, he arrived with a Samsonite case. Another figure who appeared was an Asian woman who, they deduced, was Mescal's Thai girlfriend, Toy.

A new visitor also entered the picture. His name, the Romeos later discovered, was Maxwell Treacy, an antique dealer who lived in Gipsy Hill in south London and who had a shop in Brighton. Treacy brought a suitcase into Queensberry Place on 8 August and took it away the following day. On 14 August Treacy arrived with a package and left without it. The pattern of entrances and exits, sometimes with cases and sometimes without, continued for the rest of the month.

The Romeos felt that *something* was afoot: but they were still hard-pressed to say what. In September, however, events seemed to move apace. On 10 September David Mescal arrived with a red suitcase; on 11 September Michael left carrying a holdall and a red Samsonite. The following morning he and David brought the Samsonite back. At 11.44 a.m. Treacy called. At 3.36 p.m. Michael Mescal left, Samsonite in hand, and walked to South Kensington underground station. There he caught a train to Heathrow.

By the time he reached Heathrow, the Romeos were there in force. At 5.10 p.m. they saw Mescal check in for an Air France flight to Paris, connecting with a flight to Rio. The indefatigable Frank Munoz, with his partner Steve Clark, retrieved Mescal's Samsonite from the Air France conveyor belt. When they opened it – using the usual combination number, 185 – it seemed they had struck gold. The Samsonite contained a false bottom that appeared ideal for carrying concealed goods. The Customs were later to say that it was one of the most skilfully constructed they had ever seen.

Before closing the case, Clark pulled out the inner lining of one of its elasticated pockets and marked it with his initials, 'SC'. Munoz inscribed his initials, 'FM', inside the housing of one of the locks. Chats Patel photographed their handiwork and the case was locked and returned to the Air France transit baggage container.

In the developing jigsaw puzzle, this counted as by far the biggest piece of all. Following the puzzling comings and goings at Queensberry Place, here was Michael Mescal heading for South America once more – taking with him a Samsonite equipped with a secret compartment. His journey also yielded another admittedly smaller piece. When the Romeos checked the reservation list for the flight, they discovered that Mescal had not travelled to South America alone, as they had initially supposed.

He had a companion who, for the purposes of this account, has been given the fictional name 'Tom Ashton', and who came from Rainham, Essex – and the Romeos felt the fact they had not spotted him at Heathrow to be significant in itself. They believed that Mescal had taken care to avoid being seen in the company of Ashton, which in their eyes constituted 'sussy' behaviour – a term they apply to people who seem surveillance-conscious.

Ashton returned to London on 19 September. By now the Romeos had identified him from their videos as a visitor to Queensberry Place, and this time they were ready. The Romeos asked a uniformed officer to give his baggage a thorough search. The officer handed some of Ashton's documents to Steve Clark, including his ticket and passport, and Clark photocopied them before handing them back. Outside in the arrivals hall Ashton made a telephone call, and a Romeo officer overheard him saying: 'I've been given the whole works.'

To the Romeos, Ashton's remark appeared to pose a new danger: that of 'showing out'. During surveillance operations there is a fine line between gathering evidence and alerting your targets, with one false move destroying months of patient work. The judgement on how far to go is another that contributes to the investigation officer's state of permanent anxiety, since it too has to be based on guesswork and intuition. Ashton's comment served to increase that anxiety.

For that reason Michael Mescal was not given the 'whole works' when he returned to Britain on 3 October. From a safe distance, Chats Patel saw him arrive in the baggage area. The most crucial question was whether Mescal had brought back the red Samsonite with the false compartment the Romeos had examined three weeks before. As the baggage arrived on the carousel, Patel saw Mescal collect a black suitcase but no Samsonite. He was allowed to go through the Green Channel unmolested.

The next two months were immensely frustrating for the Romeos. They felt that they had a considerable amount of suggestive evidence about Mescal's activities: the jigsaw puzzle, it could be said, was beginning to make sense. But as they pondered their next move, Mescal disappeared. The flat at Queensberry Place was vacated, and they later learned that just two days after returning to Britain on 3 October, Mescal

The Romeos pored over the surveillance video and photographs, trying to interpret their significance and decide on their targets' respective roles. *Above*: Hugh Donagher points out an item of interest, although Graham Dick's attention appears to be drawn elsewhere. The photographs of the targets were displayed to all members of the Romeo team (*left*), to be memorised for future reference.

had flown to Bangkok. It became pointless maintaining surveillance at Queensberry Place, and so Dick Palmer removed his equipment.

The Romeos continued to make such observations as they could: on 23 October, Graham Dick saw David Mescal and Tom Ashton at Mescal's house in Rainham; later that day David was spotted at a local bank where Michael had opened an account. On 25 November David flew to Rio, and after that, an officer says, 'it all went a bit quiet'. The Romeos once again felt that something was afoot: once again they could not tell what, and their main feeling was fear that whatever it proved to be they might miss it.

Early in December the Romeos had the break they were waiting for. How it came is something they refuse to disclose, in keeping with their determination to preserve the secrecy of some of their most important operational methods. In this, the Customs are no different from the other law-enforcement agencies of the modern state. Yet the public does secure occasional glimpses of the Customs' inner workings. In March 1987, for example, Lord Justice Lloyd delivered a report on telephone tapping to Parliament. He described how Customs officers engaged on drug investigations can obtain warrants to listen to or record from both private lines and public telephone boxes, and he praised them for the 'notable successes' they had achieved.

Like the police too the Customs use informants, and here they are prepared to go to extraordinary lengths to protect their sources. They once abandoned a heroin trial at Reading rather than concede a defence demand that the name of an informant should be revealed, a decision taken by the ID's head, Dick Lawrence. Since Lawrence is a cricket enthusiast, his decision could be said to accord with a sense of fair play that other law enforcement agencies might consider outdated, particularly in the amoral world inhabited by professional criminals – and by some police too.

There is no telling whether it was by one of these methods, or another, that the Romeos acquired a sizeable new piece for their jigsaw. It consisted of the information that a new character had come into the reckoning: his name was Anthony John Favell, and he was due to fly to London from Alicante the next day. His ample criminal record, together with the information supplied by CEDRIC that he was suspected of helping to smuggle cannabis into Britain, made him of immediate interest. The Romeos learned that he was linked in some way with Maxwell Treacy.

There was thus a full Romeo reception committee to watch Favell when he arrived at Heathrow on the afternoon of 4 December. Graham Dick saw him wait by the carousel in Terminal Two to collect his baggage, comprising his brown soft-sided suitcase, zip-up holdall, and briefcase. When Favell reached the arrivals hall he was met by Treacy.

Favell and Treacy were photographed as they walked to the Terminal Two car-park. Another officer watched as they loaded Favell's baggage into the boot of a blue Ford Cortina and drove off. Shortly after four o'clock two more officers saw them arrive at Treacy's flat in Gipsy Hill.

By the following morning, even more officers were in position to track Favell's return to Heathrow for the first leg of his journey to Brazil. Seven days later the Romeos saw him return. This time he was carrying a red Samsonite case. When Frank Munoz and Steve Clark examined the Samsonite after Favell's arrest, they had the satisfaction of confirming that it was the same case they had marked with their initials on 12 September, and which had been taken to Rio by Michael Mescal.

CHAPTER TWO

RENAISSANCE: THE COURIERS

The fact that the Mescal suitcase had been used in an attempt to smuggle cocaine into Britain came close, for the Romeos, to being the 'smoking gun' they were looking for: a smoking gun, in the lore of detective literature, is the conclusive evidence from which an accused can find no escape. Certainly the discovery marked a watershed in the case. The Romeos now considered that the most important question was no longer who was at the heart of the cocaine operation they were investigating, but how much more evidence they needed to acquire and when they should make their arrests.

Their terminology began to reflect that conviction too. Mescal was now a 'main man' of the operation, a status embodied in the charges the Customs eventually brought against him in court. They also referred to him as Tango One: Tango stands for T which stands for Target. There were target names for the other suspects they were watching: thus David Mescal became Tango Two and Maxwell Treacy was Tango Eight.

The Romeos also came to feel that, rather than constructing a jigsaw, they were now engaged in a game of poker with opponents who, they suspected, were becoming very worried indeed. Although they did not yet know precisely what role Treacy played, they were certain he was a puzzled man since he had come to Heathrow to meet Favell on 12 December and had waited there, as the Romeos knew with their customary precision, from 2.35 to 5.12 p.m. before giving up and going home.

But what conclusions would Mescal, Treacy and Co. reach about the arrest of Favell? Would they consider it, as the Romeos intended, a 'chance pull' – the kind of unlucky break that could happen to any courier, who was after all being paid to run precisely that risk? Or would they suppose that the Customs knew a great deal about their operation and realise that they too were at risk?

The Romeos felt there was one important factor on their side. It was true that their opponents appeared to be innately cautious and might well be tempted to suspend their operation there and then. But against that were the financial considerations involved. The Romeos calculated that, including the price of the cocaine in Bolivia, Favell's run would have cost around £15,000. They believed that when sold in one-kilo amounts on the wholesale market in Britain it would fetch £100,000. (On 'the street', where it would be sold in tiny 'deals' of a few grams each, it would eventually net £750,000.) They did not know if the organisers could afford to forgo profits on such a scale – and they hoped that there was a powerful psychological factor on their side. Would their opponents really be able to admit to themselves, after months if not years of preparation, that their scheme had been laid to waste?

It was therefore with their customary mix of expectation and anxiety that the Romeos continued their observations. David Mescal returned to Britain on 19 December and Treacy visited at his home in Rainham the following day. On 15 January 1986 David met Treacy at a Wimpy Bar in Brixton and handed him a plastic carrier bag. The following week, Treacy visited David again in Rainham.

Michael Mescal returned to Britain from Bangkok on 3 February. David met him at Heathrow and there was a spate of activity over the next two days, with Treacy meeting Michael twice at a restaurant in Earls Court Road. On 5 February Michael Mescal left for Rio. Treacy saw him off at Heathrow, and he was carrying yet another red Samsonite case. A Romeo officer, Keith Bowen, opened it in the usual manner and marked it with the date '9.12.48' – Bowen's birthday.

The Romeos were certain that matters were now coming to a head, and on 14 February Hugh Donagher met Brian Clark at New Fetter Lane to review events. Donagher gave one of his most confident performances, leaving no doubt that he saw Michael Mescal as principal target and that he felt that the Romeos were now fully in control. 'Last week,' announced Donagher, 'the main man flew in from Bangkok. He arrived at Heathrow and had a series of meetings with our target suspects in the UK. We believe that they've recovered from the first one and they're looking forward to doing another quick one to recover some of their financial loss.'

In what proved to be a precise summary of the case as it was eventually presented in court, Donagher pointed out that the Romeos had now secured 'good association' between Mescal and Treacy, who was in turn linked to the arrested courier, Favell. And he speculated – with customary bravura – that their meetings had been designed to devise another cocaine run. 'Everything is ready to send out another courier,' Donagher said. 'We've been working on that, and we'll continue to work on it.' As for Mescal's departure for Rio, Donagher guessed that he was intending to arrange 'the purchase of the cocaine. He will get the concealment done, and then we will see some movement here.'

Clark asked Donagher if he thought Mescal was likely to be suspicious over Favell's arrest, but Donagher revealed no doubts. 'I'm quite convinced the team regard the last pull as unlucky. There was something in his past that caused him to be pulled. I'm quite sure they don't realise we are with them.' Clark also asked Donagher whether the 'team' was likely to remain quite so calm if another courier were arrested. 'My own view is that I don't think they'll stand another suitcase bust on a courier, and that the next time we should go and scoop the lot,' Donagher replied. He guessed that the next cocaine run could take place in two or three weeks' time. 'We run the risk that if we don't take them out on this run, we could lose them. I don't think we should take that risk. I think we should go for it.'

'All right,' said Clark.

So far as the Romeos could judge, the next three weeks were spent in attempts to recruit couriers to replace Favell. Their main point of attack was Treacy, who appeared to be assuming a more and more important role. He was followed on several occasions from his home in Gipsy Hill to a Streatham pub, the John Company, which he appeared to favour as a meeting-place. The Romeos had to remain on their guard, for Treacy seemed particularly 'sussy', driving around his home several times as if to see whether anyone was following him before setting off.

On 20 February – with the BBC in attendance – the Romeos staked out the John Company in the belief that Treacy was attempting to recruit a courier whom they had dubbed 'Andy'. The pub had a lot of new customers that day, as successive Romeo members strolled in for a drink, while others played pool. One officer spent an hour apparently deep in conversation with the BBC's production assistant Sally Benge, who had been borrowed for the occasion, although he was really straining to hear what 'Andy' might have to say. While Sally ended the session somewhat sozzled, it proved a frustrating day for the Romeos as they remained unsure whether 'Andy' had anything to do with the case.

On 26 February the Romeos tried again. 'Operation Renaissance again, chaps,' Donagher said breezily in a briefing that morning. 'It's all hotting up and we've got an important operation involving fifteen or sixteen officers tonight. We believe there's a meeting taking place tonight between the London organiser and one of the next couriers. This is a meeting prior to the departure of the courier out of the country, so I don't need to tell you how important it is. And I don't need to tell you how important it is to make sure there's no silly moves, no stupid manoeuvres on surveillance that might show out. If you show out at this stage it's a tragedy. So very, very cool.'

In keeping with Donagher's description of him as the 'London organiser', the Romeos' main target that night was, once again, Treacy. They had by now identified 'Andy': he proved to be a painter and decorator in his late forties, Michael Bond. Once again the John Company's trade was swollen by Romeos, this time to more conclusive effect. An officer came into the pub soon after 7.30 to find Treacy already there. He saw Bond arrive just before eight o'clock and spend twenty-five minutes talking to Treacy and taking notes. Treacy then departed, leaving Bond to finish his drink before he too left. It was, Hugh Donagher observed later that night, 'a good meet'.

The Romeos reassembled at New Fetter Lane the following morning. This time Donagher told them that he believed Treacy would be attempting to buy tickets for his courier or couriers. 'I don't want to follow him everywhere he goes today because that's dangerous, so I'm going to look at selected travel agents that I suspect might be used,' Donagher said. 'We expect a development next week for his couriers to go out of the country to get the cocaine, and they've got to get their tickets, so that's what we're setting up to do today.'

The Romeos believed that there were two travel agents where Treacy was likely to call: STA Travel in Old Brompton Road and Top Deck Travel in Kenway Road, Earls Court. The Romeos were expecting Treacy to be partnered by Bond but another newcomer appeared: James Flanagan, a stocky man of about fifty with a greying beard.

At least a dozen pairs of Customs' eyes tracked Treacy and Flanagan in their journey around west London. An officer followed them into STA Travel on the pretence of asking about the cost of flying to New Zealand and overheard Treacy book a flight to Rio for the following Tuesday, 4 March. Treacy said he would be paying cash – a telling detail, investigation officers consider, since (unlike cheques or credit cards) it leaves no traces. Treacy in fact visited *three* travel agents – the third was Travelscene in Baker Street – and booked three tickets in all, for himself, Bond and Flanagan. What was more, they were not for return flights to Rio, as the Romeos had first assumed, but were round-the-world tickets, continuing across the Pacific, via Easter Island and Tahiti, to Sydney, before returning to London via Bangkok.

The news that the three men were heading for Australia prompted an urgent meeting at New Fetter Lane. Donagher and Clark were there, together with the head of the Sierra cocaine team, Bill Newall, who was assisting the ID's liaison with the BBC. As Donagher explained, it seemed that the main result of Favell's arrest was to switch the smuggling operation as far from Britain as possible. That presented the Romeos with a new set of problems, which the meeting now considered.

The growth of international drugs trafficking has prompted laws which

When he left London for Brazil in December, Tony Favell was photographed from all angles (*left*). After his arrest, a new courier entered the frame – a London painter and decorator, Michael Bond. Bond was photographed (*centre*) coming out of a travel agent's in Fulham after buying round-the-world tickets, and he later attempted to smuggle cocaine into Australia. The Romeos were still watching Michael Mescal too, and had photographed him (*below*) during one of his departures from Heathrow.

transcend national boundaries. Thus under Britain's Misuse of Drugs Act it is an offence to conspire in Britain to import drugs into another country – in this case, Australia. There are also formal extradition treaties between a large number of countries, which cover serious offences such as drug smuggling. Donagher was confident that they would be able to use their alliances and contacts to ensure that the couriers were arrested wherever they ended up. There were nonetheless pitfalls to overcome of the kind that occur when a law-enforcement agency of one country seeks to operate in the territory of another.

Bluntly stated, the problem was this. If the British Customs told the Australians that three cocaine smugglers were heading their way, would the Australians be content to arrest them and hand them over to the British? Or would they put them on trial in Australia themselves? Brian Clark had a contact in the Australian Customs he felt he could rely on. But already he and Donagher started to rehearse the arguments they might need to deploy. 'What I see is our conspiracy evidence is here, in this country,' said Donagher.

'Except the couriers,' warned Clark.

There was also the question of Michael Mescal. Supposing he returned to Bangkok at the time of the cocaine run? That would require further diplomatic moves, as Donagher explained. 'We're going to have to approach the Bangkok police at the time it's going down and ask them to search his premises and take him in for questioning and advise them of the strength of our case. We want him back here and have our case here because this is where the meat of the conspiracy is, where all the evidence is.'

The Romeos hoped that if any of the couriers were offered the choice over where they wished to stand trial, they would opt for Britain anyway. Bill Newell considered that particularly true of anyone arrested in Bangkok: 'They shoot them there,' Newell said.

The first approaches to the Thai and Australian authorities were made that weekend. The following Monday, 3 March, the Romeos watched Treacy collect his air tickets, in company with Bond. (They were also filmed in a dramatic sequence by the BBC.) Treacy visited the three agencies in turn and paid out over £5000 in cash. 'So much for their plan to book them all separately,' Donagher remarked to Graham Dick. 'They've all been well and truly pulled together by that surveillance today. I think we should just leave them to potter around now – I don't see any purpose in following them any more at this stage. Tomorrow's our big day at the airport. Well done. That was a super day's work.'

'Not bad,' said Graham Dick, cautious as ever.

When the 'big day' came, Donagher first met Brian Clark. Clark reported that a deal had been struck with the Australians: they could keep the couriers and the cocaine, while any principals would be returned to Britain. By that, Clark understood that Bond and Flanagan would stand trial in Australia and Treacy would be extradited. Donagher would fly to Australia to ensure that all went smoothly, and Graham Dick would go with him. They would stop in Thailand en route to seek the help of the Bangkok police, if necessary. 'We're in business,' Clark told Donagher.

There were more Romeos than ever, together with reinforcements from the ID teams, at Heathrow that evening to see Treacy, Bond and Flanagan on their way. Dick Palmer scored a notable first by setting up a video camera in the British Airways office overlooking the check-in area at Terminal Three. (Although many of their overseas counterparts have permanent video facilities at airports, the British Customs' had never done this before.)

All worked perfectly. The three men arrived at Terminal Three in the same car. Then – faithfully recorded by Dick Palmer's video camera – they studiously ignored each other while queueing for the check-in. Once all three had passed into the departure lounge, an officer radioed to Donagher to tell him that the pictures were 'very nice to say the least'.

'Super duper,' said Donagher. 'That's it. Came together in a car and went through controls separately. Didn't associate, didn't speak. So far, very good. They're on their way now. In about thirty-five minutes they'll be in the air and it's obviously all systems go.'

From those welcome certainties, the Romeos passed once again into their more familiar state of doubt. They supposed that the couriers' first move in Rio would be to collect the cocaine awaiting them there, together with the suitcases they needed to smuggle it into Australia. They learned that Michael Mescal was in Rio himself, but were surprised to learn that he held a ticket to return to London. Was he really going to walk so easily into the Romeos' arms?

Hugh Donagher and Graham Dick, meanwhile, set off on their travels. They spent four days in Bangkok, where they secured promises of the assistance they might need. Once in Sydney they embarked on a round of meetings which were complicated by the differences between their own jurisdictional boundaries and those of their Australian colleagues. In Britain the Customs have the power to investigate international drugs smuggling no matter where the goods end up; in Australia the Customs' powers are restricted to ports and airports, and beyond those limits the Australian Federal Police take over.

Hugh Donagher hinted at the problems they were encountering in a telephone call to the Romeos on 14 March. 'We're getting very good co-operation from the Australian Customs,' he said. 'I'm quite sure that everything will go very well next week.' But Donagher offered one caveat. Referring to the Australian police, he said: 'It's possible that they might try a few tricks like letting one of the couriers run, but nothing definite has been decided.'

Donagher knew more than he was letting on. He and Graham Dick were dealing with Chief Inspector Ken Curnow, then acting as head of the Sydney drugs squad of the Australian Federal Police. Although a former British police constable, Curnow appeared to have mixed feelings at the arrival of two British Customs officers on his patch, mirrored in the tendency of members of his squad to refer to Donagher and Dick as 'Pommie bastards'. Curnow was preparing a plan of his own to allow at least one of the couriers to pass through the Customs in the hope that he would lead the police to his Australian connection. Donagher could appreciate why Curnow would want to do so; but it conflicted with his own understandable desire to ensure that all three couriers were arrested with as little fuss or risk as possible.

In London the Romeos had two false alarms. They twice discovered that Michael Mescal had made a booking to return to London, and twice turned out in force at Heathrow to meet him. On both occasions they learned from the passenger manifest that he was not on board. The Romeos assembled again on the evening of Thursday 27 March, together with reinforcements from other ID teams. They were briefed by John Barker, who this time promised that the operation was for real – and 'hopefully the finale' of a case which by now had occupied the Romeos for a year.

Barker reported that after spending a week in Tahiti, Treacy, Bond and Flanagan had taken off for Sydney, where they were due to arrive in two hours' time. Once they had been detected, and either arrested or allowed to 'run', the London end of the operation would begin.

Early the following morning, 28 March, which happened to be Good Friday, the Romeos would raid four addresses in London: the homes of David Mescal, Maxwell Treacy, 'Tom Ashton' – the man who had flown to Rio with Michael Mescal the previous September – and a friend of Treacy's to be named, for this account, 'Terry Robinson', who had accompanied Treacy, Bond and Flanagan to Heathrow when they flew to Australia earlier that month.

Mescal, Ashton and Robinson were to be arrested on suspicion of drug trafficking and their homes searched; and although Treacy would be in Australia, his wife, who had driven the car taking him to Heathrow, was to be arrested and their home searched too. The teams would have search warrants issued by a magistrate, as well as Writs of Assistance, the all-purpose warrants, dating back to Charles II, which give the Customs wide powers to enter premises and seize property.

As for timing, Barker briefly referred to Donagher's tribulations in Australia by saying: 'There is some pressure from Australia to delay but this is being resisted'. The Australian police, in fact, wanted the British arrests to be delayed as long as possible, for fear of alerting the couriers they decided to let 'run'.

Barker predicted that the London raids would take place around 1 a.m. on Good Friday morning, adding: 'I would prefer entry, with Easter weekend looming, to be by a knock on the door and a pleasant answer. I do not expect to be consulted should that not be the case. Each of you has an experienced officer in attendance and it must be an on-the-ground decision as to whether force is used to enter.'

Finally, Barker revealed that if all went well there could be a 'tremendous bonus' later that day. Michael Mescal had made a confirmed booking to return to London from Rio, and should be touching down at Heathrow towards midday on Good Friday. For some reason which the Romeos found difficult to fathom, it appeared that Mescal had boxed himself in.

Since Mescal's flight was due to leave Rio before Treacy, Bond and Flanagan reached Australia, Mescal would be in mid-air when the arrests in Sydney and London were being carried out. The first knowledge he would have that anything was amiss would come when he was stopped and questioned at Heathrow. 'Tango One', said Barker, 'is a little bit elusive, and if he comes in tomorrow that really will be super.'

After the Thursday evening briefing the four teams made their final preparations. Some officers strapped on body-harnesses that look like gun holsters but in fact carry their personal radio sets. No Customs officers are ever armed: they would regard that as a violation of long-held beliefs about the way they should conduct themselves, no matter how provocative their opponents. The most powerful weapons they carried that evening were what they term the 'keys' – picks and sledge-hammers to be used if any doors had to be broken down. Even so there was something incongruous about the sight of Civil Servants, which all Customs officers are, going about their business in such a way.

The four teams left New Fetter Lane at 9.30 p.m. on Thursday evening. They first drove to the nearest police station to their target addresses, where they were to ask for a uniformed police officer to accompany them. (The Customs are obliged to take a police officer with them when carrying out searches by night: the police role is defined as 'providing reassurance to the occupier and preventing a breach of the peace'.) The teams then settled down to wait for the news from Australia. The team bound for Robinson's home in Lewisham sat in the cheerless canteen of Ladywell police station, drinking instant coffee served in beer mugs. The team heading for Treacy's flat in Gipsy Hill was more fortunate: their police station was equipped with a pool table, which at least helped them pass the time.

At precisely the moment that a Romeo officer was lining up a shot with his cue in south London, Hugh Donagher was watching Treacy, Bond and Flanagan as they walked towards the immigration control at Sydney airport. Donagher could see them on the Australian Customs' video system: Treacy, casually dressed in a white tracksuit and carrying a slim attaché case, was in the lead; Bond, looking smart in a collar and tie, was next; Flanagan, carrying his jacket, came last.

The three men kept apart from each other, and when Treacy joined the queue at the immigration desks he turned in the direction of Bond, standing two places behind him, but did not acknowledge him at all. Donagher could not conceal his glee. 'That's a good shot,' he told the officer with him. 'Two of them in the queue with one between them, not talking to each other. Let's get that one.'

Graham Dick was ensconced in the baggage-handling area below the arrivals hall with an Australian Customs officer, looking for the three men's baggage. He was gratified to discover that it included three Samsonite-type cases, of which the largest belonged to Bond. That case had a travel sticker over one corner, and the Australian officer pulled it aside and drilled a hole in the surface beneath. When he removed the drill, white powder was clinging to the bit; the officer tested it and found that it was cocaine. The other two Samsonites were found to contain a similar powder too. Dick loaded the three Samsonites on to the carousel and they were carried up into the arrival hall.

By now Treacy had collected his case, a soft-sided holdall, and had been allowed to pass through Customs. When Flanagan's cases arrived, including one of the Samsonites, he collected them from the carousel and tested the locks with a key. 'Very cool,' said Donagher, who was watching him on the airport video. Flanagan headed for the Customs barrier and, like Treacy, was allowed through.

Then Bond's two cases, both Samsonites, were sent up. Bond loaded them on to a trolley and walked towards the barrier, while Donagher supplied a commentary: 'Bond's going towards the control now, he's at the control now, and he shouldn't be going anywhere.' On the radio an Australian voice said: 'He's all yours.'

Bond was directed towards a Customs officer named Joe Homer. In the same practised manner as his British colleagues, Homer asked Bond a standard set of questions.

'Is this all your baggage?'
'Yes.'
'Did you pack all the bags yourself?'
'Yes.'
'Are you fully aware of the contents of your baggage?'
'Yes.'

The climax to Operation Renaissance was played out in two continents 13,000 miles apart. In Sydney, Hugh Donagher (*left*) waited for Michael Bond and colleagues to arrive from South America. Bond was recorded on video as he approached the Australian Customs and as Australian officer Joe Homer examined his bags (stills from video sequence *above*). Bond was arrested, and his two Samsonite suitcases – one is shown *below* – were found to contain 3 kg of cocaine. Bond pleaded guilty and was sentenced to sixteen years.

As Homer removed Bond's clothing and tapped the suitcase lids, Bond looked distinctly grim. 'He is not a happy man,' said Donagher. Then Homer seemed to indicate that Bond was free to go, and Bond broke into a wide grin. 'He's happy now, isn't he?' said Donagher. Bond's hopes were dashed when other officers appeared by his shoulder and he was led away to a Customs' ante-room, behind a bare brick wall.

Despite all that had occurred, Donagher and Dick were feeling rather disappointed as they had hoped that one of the three targets would be carrying a Samsonite they had previously seen leaving Britain at Heathrow, but that proved not to be. 'Unfortunate,' said Donagher, 'but there we go.' An Australian officer told Donagher that, having avoided each other until then, Treacy and Flanagan had met up outside the airport and headed into Sydney with the police on their tail. 'The main thing is the conspiracy's still strong,' Donagher said. 'We've got the importation and we've got the gear.'

Donagher asked if he could make a phone call to New Fetter Lane. 'It's Hugh,' he announced to the waiting Romeos in London. 'It's a bingo.'

The news of Donagher's success in Sydney reached the four London teams at 11.30 p.m. on Thursday night. John Barker told the teams to prepare to move and at midnight they received the further instruction: 'Away we go.'

The tactics of the team assigned to 'Terry Robinson' were typical. At 12.15 a.m. on Friday morning the officers arrived at the Lewisham council estate where Robinson occupied a second-floor flat. They drove past, taking care not to look up too ostentatiously, and parked two streets away. After making a reconnaissance on foot, officer Ken Newhouse told two of his colleagues to watch the rear windows in case anyone tried to throw anything out or even to make an escape – although since there was a fifty-foot drop that was considered unlikely.

At 1 a.m. the measured tones of John Barker crackled on the radio again: 'Could you all enter your premises now, please?' The officers drove to the estate and walked briskly up the stairs to Robinson's flat, officer Paul Smith carrying a sledgehammer as unobtrusively as it is possible to carry a sledgehammer. Without further ado Smith banged hard on the opaque glass of the front door. 'Police and Customs,' he yelled. 'Open the door, we've got a warrant.' When nothing happened, Smith shouted: 'You've got five seconds to open the door.'

After exactly five seconds Smith started swinging at the door with his sledgehammer. Then a figure appeared at the glass and Smith shouted: 'Open it NOW.' The figure called: 'Hold on,' and finally the door swung open. Immediately Smith told him: 'Mr Robinson, you're under arrest on suspicion of importing drugs. You don't have to say anything unless

As soon as Hugh Donagher passed on news of the arrests in Sydney, the Romeos went into action in London, raiding a series of homes at 1 a.m. on Good Friday 1986. *Above left*: An officer pulls on his jacket over his radio harness. *Above*: ID equipment includes handcuffs and radio – but never arms. If suspects are likely to be carrying guns, armed police always go in first. The police must also accompany the Customs when they carry out raids at night, as in the picture *centre*. *Below*: Officer Jim Newhouse searches the kitchen drawer at a flat in south London.

The Operation Renaissance raids continued past daybreak. *Above left*: An officer carries one of the 'keys' – Customs slang for a sledgehammer or other tool, also shown *above right* – used for forcing entry where necessary. *Below*: Searches are always immensely thorough, and not even bedrooms are sacrosanct.

you wish to do so but what you say may be given in evidence. Do you understand?'

Robinson, a man in his sixties who was wearing grey trousers with braces and a vest, did understand. 'I ain't got no drugs, mate,' he assured Smith.

Similar scenes were enacted at the three other premises. In David Mescal's home in Rainham, where the raid was led by Chats Patel, the door was opened by Mescal's wife Simone, hastily pulling on a dressing-gown. Where was David? Mrs Mescal said he had gone out to see a friend – 'and that is all I know'. Chats Patel told her that they intended to search the house, adding: 'Before we make a start, can I just ask you one question? Are we likely to find any drugs on the premises?'

'God, I should hope not. No.'

The team in Gipsy Hill spent some time hammering on the door of Treacy's flat before realising it was empty. They broke open the lock with a pick and had just started their search when Mrs Treacy, who had been taking her dog for a walk, arrived. 'What's all this about?' she asked indignantly. An officer showed her the search warrant and told her she was under arrest.

'What for?' she asked.

'I'm arresting you on suspicion of being involved in drug trafficking.'

'Oh don't be so ridiculous,' Mrs Treacy said.

Between 3 a.m. and 4 a.m. that morning Robinson, Mrs Treacy and Ashton were brought into New Fetter Lane, which in accordance with the Police and Criminal Evidence Act, in force since January 1986, had been equipped with a Custody Suite. A Custody Officer carefully read the three suspects their rights and they were placed in separate interview rooms. David Mescal was still missing, but John Barker professed himself 'more than happy' with the night's events – 'a just reward for all the efforts that have gone in so far'. It soon appeared that a further prize awaited them: the return of Michael Mescal.

The confirmation that Mescal had left Rio came from the Varig passenger manifest at 9.15 that Good Friday morning. For the umpteenth time, and despite their evident weariness, the Romeos went into their tried and tested routine. One officer was stationed at the 'finger', the movable corridor where the passengers disembark from their plane. Another group lounged in the immigration area. Two uniformed officers – Brian Waite and Alasdair McDonald, who had arrested Favell three months before – were deputed to stop and question Mescal. Whatever he said, he was to be arrested.

At 11.40 a.m. Michael Mescal walked into the immigration area, a tall lean figure, wearing a brown leather jacket and light trousers. He waited calmly in the passport queue and then – watched closely in case he stopped to make a telephone call – went down the stairs into the baggage hall. At least a dozen Customs officers did their best to appear unconcerned as Mescal waited for his suitcases, among them a red Samsonite which he loaded onto a trolley before walking towards the Green Channel. Brian Waite stepped forward and asked to see his passport and then steered him to a baggage desk.

'You've come into the Green Channel for Customs – that's "nothing to declare". Do you understand that?' Waite asked.

'Yes,' said Mescal.

Mescal looked on impassively as Waite opened his Samsonite and began to sort through his clothes. Waite asked Mescal why he had been to Rio and Mescal replied that he had been there to buy clothes for a beachwear business and to look at apartments as possible investments. Then Waite asked Mescal to go with him and McDonald to be searched.

As soon as Mescal had disappeared, Keith Bowen sprang forward and examined his Samsonite. Bowen found the date he had marked six weeks earlier and announced: 'It's the same one he took out.' Waite reappeared and probed at the lid of Mescal's case with a penknife, finding that it was 'clean'. When Mescal returned Waite asked if they could have 'a few words'.

'What's all this about, please?' Mescal asked.

'I'll explain it to you,' Waite told him. 'You've been arrested on suspicion of being involved in the importation of drugs.'

Neither then, nor at any time later that day, did Mescal offer any indication that he accepted Waite's charge. Still pushing his baggage trolley, he was led into an interview room where McDonald told him that a Custody Officer would shortly come and explain his rights.

'What's the reason?' Mescal asked.

'You've been told that you're under arrest on suspicion of being involved in an importation of drugs.'

Mescal sat back and opened his hands. 'Yeah – but why?'

McDonald said that would be fully explained once Mescal had been advised of his rights, unless Mescal wanted to say anything more now.

'I don't see any reason – that's the only thing, there's no reason for it.'

As Mescal watched with a quizzical air, Waite and McDonald began a methodical examination of his belongings. Then the Custody Officer came in and asked Mescal his name and address. When the Custody Officer asked Waite for the time of arrest, Mescal interjected: 'What have I been arrested for?'

'We'll get to that in a moment,' the officer told him. He explained to Mescal that he had the right to have someone informed of his arrest, the right to consult a solicitor, and the right to consult the Code of Practice relating to the Police and Criminal Evidence Act.

Shortly before midday on Good Friday, Michael Mescal, whom the Customs suspected to be a central figure in the smuggling operation, returned to Britain from Brazil. He was stopped when he entered the Green Channel (*above*) and filmed by the BBC too. Although no drugs were found in his baggage, he was arrested by officer Brian Waite (right in picture *left*) accompanied by Alasdair McDonald.

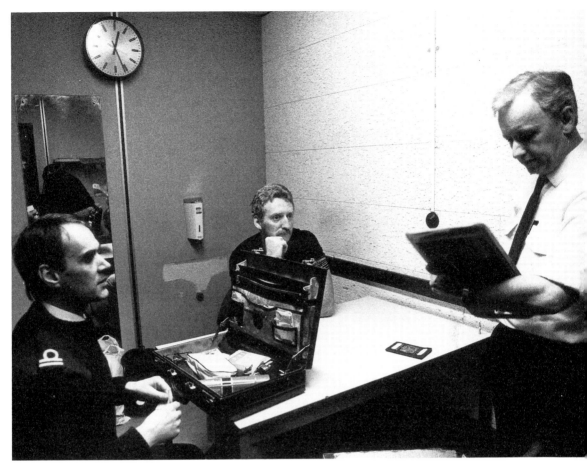

Mescal was taken to a Customs interview room (*above*) by Waite and McDonald. Later ID officer Keith Bowen took over questioning, which lasted until that evening. Although Mescal later admitted that he had smuggled jewellery into Britain – and some gems were found in his briefcase – he consistently denied having any connection with drugs. That evening he was taken to Heathrow police station in handcuffs (*left*). He spent a year in custody before standing trial at Isleworth Crown Court, where he was acquitted on all charges.

'Yeah, but I don't understand everything yet,' Mescal replied.

'Well, this is the process that we have to go through as to what the law dictates that we do.'

'Yeah – but you've got to have reasons – right?'

'The reason is that you've been arrested on suspicion of being concerned with the importation of drugs.'

'And why?'

Brian Waite intervened: 'That will all be explained to you later.'

The Custody Officer added: 'I'm just here to explain all your rights.'

Mescal was still asking why he had been arrested when two Romeo officers, Keith Bowen and Len Watson, came to interview him half an hour later. Mescal and Bowen sat facing each other, their elbows on the table, looking for all the world as if they were settling down for a game of chess. Bowen first asked Mescal why he had been to Rio.

Mescal replied that he had spent seven weeks there, both as a tourist and on business, 'to check up and see how much apartments were, to try to get people to buy them'. He explained that apartments in Brazil were 'very cheap' beause of the fall of Brazilian currency and the difference between official and unofficial rates of exchange. 'But it's all legal', he added.

Bowen asked Mescal where he lived. 'I'm resident in Thailand, at Loi, a place about 600 kilometres from Bangkok,' Mescal told him. 'My girlfriend, her father owns land up there, rice fields.'

Before long Bowen came to the point. 'It's been mentioned to you that you've been arrested today in connection with suspicion of being involved in the importation of drugs, right? Are you aware that it is illegal to import drugs into the United Kingdom?'

'Of course, yes,' Mescal said quietly.

'Okay. If I specify cocaine, are you aware it's illegal to import cocaine into the United Kingdom?'

'Yeah, for sure I am.'

'Likewise with cannabis?'

'Everything.'

'Heroin?'

'Everything I know is illegal.'

'And likewise perhaps into most countries of the world – the United States, Canada, Australia?'

Mescal nodded. 'I understand that, yeah.'

'Okay, fine. Have you ever imported drugs into any of those countries?'

'Never,' said Mescal.

'Have you ever organised the importation of any drugs into those countries?'

'Never.'

Bowen asked Mescal how much he earned each year. Mescal replied, a little vaguely, that he was a gem-trader and that his potential profits were both large and variable. Bowen asked where he kept his bank accounts, but Mescal responded with a question of his own.

'First of all I want to know why you're asking all these questions? Is it tax? You're a tax man?'

'No, I'm investigating international drug smuggling.'

'But there's got to be a reason to ask me all these questions, right?'

'Well, to be involved in international drug smuggling, one has to look into the aspects of finances, and that sort of thing.'

'I see,' said Mescal.

When Bowen asked him if his bank accounts had ever been used in connection with drug smuggling, Mescal protested again. 'You haven't told me nothing about why you're asking me all these questions, all that you've said is that it's drugs, and drugs is illegal. Right?'

'Yes,' said Bowen.

'But I've nothing to do with any drugs.'

'You've not – okay.'

'So I don't want to answer any more questions.'

Bowen pursued the point. 'Can we just go to your recent trip in Rio? Have you met anybody over there who's been involved in drug smuggling?'

Mescal seemed exasperated. 'I've met nobody over there who's involved in drug smuggling that I know of.'

'Have you organised any trips for anybody to go over there?'

Mescal paused. 'What does that mean – tourist trips?'

'No, I'd say drug smuggling trips.'

'I've never organised any drug smuggling trips – never.'

The questioning lasted, with several breaks between sessions, for four hours. Mescal's answers gradually became shorter and he finally refused to answer some of Bowen's questions altogether. He admitted knowing Max Treacy – 'as a friend, just as a person I know' – but declined to say any more about him. 'I don't know where you're leading to,' he told Bowen. 'All I know is I've got nothing to do with drugs.'

Bowen asked if he knew anything about 'false-sided suitcases'.

'No,' said Mescal.

'Have you ever been to Bolivia?'

'I was there briefly about two years ago.'

'What was the purpose of the visit?'

'Emeralds.'

'Are you aware that in fact Bolivia is a source country for cocaine?'

'I know that South America's a place for drugs, yeah.'

'Just going back to Treacy. Did you meet him in Rio this time?'

'I don't want to answer any more questions. I don't understand what everything is leading to.'

'Do you understand the question?'

'I don't want to answer any more.'

Later Bowen asked Mescal about his Samsonite suitcase. Mescal agreed that he owned one but denied ever having lent it, or any other red Samsonite, to anyone. Bowen showed Mescal photographs of the red Samsonite he had taken out of Britain in September and asked if it was his, but Mescal refused to reply. After several more inconclusive exchanges, the interview was at an end. At 8.30 p.m. Mescal was taken in handcuffs to Heathrow police station, where he was to spend the night.

Elsewhere other dramas had unfolded. That lunchtime David Mescal had been tracked down at a pub in Chadwell Heath. When officers approached him he seized a snooker cue while other customers blocked the officers' paths. Mescal ran out of the pub and was eventually arrested in a nearby garden. When he was brought into New Fetter Lane he explained that he had not realised that the men who had come into the pub were from the Customs. 'You don't look like Customs officers,' he said. 'I don't know what a Customs officer looks like. The only ones I see is when I get off a plane – they've got blue suits on.' He scoffed at any notion that he was a 'drugs baron' or a 'multi-millionaire'. He and his brother Michael were remanded in custody, as was Ashton. Robinson received bail while Mrs Treacy, who was never charged, was released.

The fracas in Chadwell Heath was far surpassed by events in Australia, where the decision to let Treacy and Flanagan 'run' became all too literally true. Bond's suitcases contained just over 3kg of cocaine, and he was safely under lock and key. Treacy and Flanagan, who was carrying a case estimated to hold $1\frac{1}{2}$ kg of cocaine, had been followed to their separate hotels. Treacy made several phone calls and then arranged to meet Flanagan at the Intercontinental Hotel. The two men missed each other and Treacy returned to the Wentworth Hotel. At the Intercontinental, police officers were installed in the room next to Flanagan's. At 3 a.m. Flanagan was overheard making a telephone call. A woman told him to hang up and Flanagan called out: 'Got to get rid of the gear.' The police burst into his room and he was arrested and taken away.

That left Treacy. At 6.30 a.m. police officers saw him appear in the foyer of the Wentworth Hotel wearing his tracksuit. Treacy then stripped off to reveal a pair of running shorts and dashed out of the hotel. A plain-clothes officer managed to follow him on to a train heading for the Sydney suburbs and sat next to him. Treacy turned and asked the officer if he knew where he could buy some clothes, and the officer suggested Bondi Junction. Treacy took the officer at his word. When the train reach Bondi Junction he got off and disappeared.

While the Australian police issued lookout notices to airports, harbours, bus stations and taxi ranks throughout Sydney, the feelings of Hugh Donagher and Graham Dick on learning that their target had escaped can probably be better imagined than described. They spent the morning waiting for news at the Federal Police Headquarters and finally learned at lunchtime that Treacy had been found at Sydney Airport. He had got as far as the departure lounge for a flight to Bangkok before a Customs computer, which was monitoring passenger lists, flashed a warning and Treacy was arrested just before he boarded the plane.

'Thank Christ for that,' said an officer who was with Donagher when he heard the news.

'Thank Christ for that,' echoed Donagher.

'Bit of a relief,' said the officer.

'I suppose I might buy you a beer now,' said Donagher.

'About bloody time.'

'Don't say that,' said Donagher.

The trial of Michael and David Mescal opened at Isleworth Crown Court on 30 March 1987. They faced two charges: conspiring to import drugs into Britain, culminating in the attempt by Tony Favell to smuggle cocaine to Heathrow in December 1985; and conspiring to do so into Australia, leading up to the cocaine 'run' by Treacy, Bond and Flanagan in March 1986.

There were three other men alongside them in the dock. The first was Favell himself, who was also accused on both charges. The second was 'Tom Ashton', who had accompanied Michael Mescal on his journey to Rio in September 1985, and was accused of the conspiracy charge relating to Britain. The third was 'Terry Robinson', who had accompanied Treacy, Bond and Flanagan to Heathrow in March 1986, and was accused of conspiracy over the Australian run.

Someone conspicuously *not* in the dock was Maxwell Treacy. Originally, of course, the Romeos had hoped that Treacy would be extradited from Australia to stand trial alongside the Mescals. In the event, the Australian authorities had wanted to put him on trial themselves; and in London, officials of the Director of Public Prosecutions had decided not to press the point, advising the Customs that they had a good enough case without him. Even in his absence he featured prominently in the case, being referred to frequently by both the prosecution and the defence.

Also missing were three Americans who were named in the indictment as co-conspirators – they remained beyond the Customs' reach in South America. With one exception, the five men in court pleaded not guilty to all the charges: the exception was Favell who, while denying the

Australian charge, admitted conspiring to smuggle the cocaine into Britain in December 1985, the offence for which he had been caught 'hands on' – Customs jargon for red-handed. (Favell's guilty plea gave rise to an interesting conundrum: since he admitted taking part in a conspiracy, who had he actually conspired with? Favell certainly denied conspiring with the Mescals; but the indictment was also against 'persons unknown' and it was they, Favell said, who were his fellow conspirators.)

The prosecution case took four weeks to present. In the year before the case came to court the Romeos had gathered a considerable body of information to complement their original investigation. Witnesses came from as far afield as South America and Australia, and their testimony was backed with evidence from airline bookings, hotel reservations, bank statements and telephone accounts. Taken with the Romeos' original observations, it added up to a picture that, in the prosecution's eyes, appeared satisfyingly complete.

The prosecution first described the defendants' alleged roles in the conspiracies. Michael Mescal, of course, was a principal; his brother David was his 'trusted lieutenant'. Favell was the man who 'took the risk' of actually carrying the cocaine; Ashton and Robinson were 'workers' or 'general assistants'. As for the missing Treacy, he, the prosecution argued, had played a crucial role as Michael Mescal's 'right-hand man'.

Then the prosecution developed its case. Conspiracy charges often depend heavily on patterns of events and links between the alleged conspirators, and that was how the prosecution case unfolded. Michael Mescal, the prosecution showed, had travelled extensively around the world – and certainly more extensively than the Romeos had originally supposed. The Romeos had first seen Mescal leave Britain for South America in February 1985. In fact, he had been to Rio twice in 1984. Apart from the trips which the Romeos had observed in 1985, he had also been to Canada and Australia. His brother David had been with him on several trips, to both South America and Canada.

Favell and Treacy had travelled widely too. The only trip by Favell the Romeos had previously known about was his journey to South America to collect his consignment of cocaine in December 1985. They had since discovered that he had made earlier visits to South America, and others to Australia, in 1984 and 1985. As for Treacy, he too had visited South America and Australia before coming to the Romeos' notice in the summer of 1985.

It was when the prosecution demonstrated how the defendants' paths had crossed on their travels that the picture became more compelling. In May 1984, for example, Michael Mescal had travelled to Rio with Favell. In March 1985, Mescal and Treacy had travelled to Australia together, to be joined soon afterwards by Favell. In August 1985 Mescal and Treacy had been in Rio at the same time, together with another man who did not appear in court. Mescal then returned to London, followed by Treacy and his companion. In October 1985 the same pattern recurred: Mescal and Treacy were back in Rio, where they were joined by Favell, together with one of the Americans named in the indictment. Mescal returned to London, while Treacy and Favell went on to Australia. According to the prosecution, this pattern precisely matched the defendants' roles. Mescal and Treacy would go to South America to organise a cocaine shipment; Mescal would withdraw, leaving Treacy and a colleague to make the shipment themselves – Treacy as overseer or 'minder', the colleague as the actual courier.

That pattern was repeated, once again, before the two final cocaine runs. In November David Mescal, acting on Michael's behalf, had gone to Brazil. He was joined there by Favell, and they stayed in the same hotel – in adjoining rooms – in São Paulo, before Favell returned to Britain with his consignment of cocaine. Before the Australian run in 1986, Michael Mescal had once again travelled to Rio. He was joined there by Treacy, Bond and Flanagan, together with one of the Americans. Mescal had remained there after Treacy, Bond and Flanagan went on to Australia, returning to London on the very day that they were arrested.

The prosecution added to this picture with the photographs and video-recordings made at 4 Queensberry Place in the summer of 1985. There had, of course, been a flurry of activity in August, with numerous visits by Treacy, usually with suitcases or packages, and the prosecution argued that he and Mescal had been distributing cocaine from the flat and preparing their next run. The prosecution also produced bank statements showing that large amounts of cash had passed through Michael Mescal's accounts. They included £60,000 in one three-week period in the autumn of 1984; £65,000 in September 1985; and £15,000 in cash withdrawn in January 1986, on the very day that David Mescal had been seen to hand a package to Treacy in Brixton.

Finally there were the Samsonites: the fact that the Mescals had been seen to take Samsonites out of Britain and return without them, the prosecution said, suggested that they were being used to transport cocaine. The clinching argument, it seemed, came with the Samsonite suitcase which Michael Mescal had taken to Rio in September and which Favell had used in his attempt to smuggle three kilos of cocaine into Britain three months later. Although the suitcase was now in pieces, the prosecution naturally missed no opportunity to display it to the jury. The jury also saw a video-recording of Treacy, Bond and Flanagan arriving in Australia, together with film showing the three Samsonites being dismantled to reveal the packages of cocaine.

As the prosecution evidence unfolded, what became noticeable was how little of it the defence actually challenged. There was a minor dispute over whether all of the Mescals' cases had been set to the number 185, derived from Michael's birthday; Michael said that he had later reset David's case to 612 (David's birthday was 6 December). But little else of the factual evidence was in dispute. Michael Mescal's counsel, Ronald Thwaites QC, nonetheless made some intriguing interventions.

Thwaites took a close interest in Mescal's Samsonite, and was anxious to demonstrate just how its false compartment had been constructed, especially in comparison with those in the Samsonites that had been used to carry cocaine into Australia. They consisted of layers of hardboard secured with glue, so that the only way to remove the cocaine was to hack them apart. Although Mescal's Samsonite had been dismantled by the Customs too, in fact its false compartment had been secured by rivets with screw-tops so that the compartment could be replaced and the case used again.

Thwaites also questioned the Customs about what they had found when they searched Mescal's briefcase after his arrest. An officer said that concealed in the lining of the case he had found a number of gemstones: seven sapphires, a ruby and an emerald ring. Was it not obvious, Thwaites asked, that Mescal had attempted to smuggle the gems into Britain? The officer agreed that it seemed that way.

As yet, the points that Thwaites was making remained to be explained, and the Customs believed that their jigsaw remained largely intact. At the end of the prosecution case, however, they lost some of their pieces as a result of rulings made by Judge Bathurst Norman. The barristers acting for Ashton and Robinson had argued that there was insufficient evidence against them to place before the jury. The judge agreed, and Ashton and Robinson were discharged.

More significant, perhaps, were two similar rulings over the Australian conspiracy charges faced by Favell and David Mescal. In Favell's case, the judge said that although the pattern of events appeared 'highly suspicious', it would require 'a great leap' to convict him. However, Favell was not discharged from court as he had pleaded guilty on the first count. After these rulings only the two Mescals were left in the dock, Michael facing both conspiracy charges, David the first.

Michael Mescal entered the witness box on 5 May. Although his counsel had challenged very little of the Customs' factual evidence, what he did dispute, of course, was the prosecution's interpretation that Mescal was a 'main man' of a cocaine-smuggling operation. Over the next four days Mescal presented his own account.

Mescal said – as he had indeed said when he was first questioned by Frank Munoz in February 1985 – that he was a gem-dealer. He had become involved in the gem trade at an early age, having left school at sixteen and then gone for a holiday in Europe which had turned into a nomadic four-year trip to the Middle East, including Iran and Afghanistan. He eventually settled in Thailand, where he had a colourful life which included taking part as an extra in the film *The Deer Hunter*, starring Robert de Niro. He also acquired a Thai girlfriend whose father, Mescal said, was a farmer who produced 'cattle, shrimp, sugar-cane, rice, and peanuts', and who was the 'head man' at a village named Loi. Her full name was Phenchan Mansiri, but Mescal called her Toy.

Mescal explained that his business required him to travel a great deal. At first he had imported stones from Sri Lanka, selling them to tourists. He also took parties of tourists to jewellers who paid him a commission on their sales. 'I was earning a living,' Mescal said. As his activities expanded, assisted by finance from Toy's father, he imported gems from Cambodia and Burma. Burmese rubies proved especially profitable, yielding up to 200 per cent profit, so that a stone bought for $6000 could be sold for $18,000.

Then Mescal looked further afield, to South America, and he began to export emeralds and amethysts from there to the Far East and Europe. His business became more complex as it expanded, and he joined a world of financiers, stake-holders and middle-men, where deals are made by telephone and payments made in cash, delivered in person or by trusted couriers. It was also a trade, Mescal related, which did not always observe the rules of the orthodox business world – or rather which framed rules of its own. In fact, Mescal admitted, he was not just a gem-dealer but a gem-smuggler.

Thus from the very start his activities had meant breaking the law. The stones he purchased in Sri Lanka were known as 'carborunda'. These were 'worthless stones' which could be burned and polished so that they looked like blue sapphires. They had to be smuggled into Thailand and this Mescal did, 'some on my person and some in a bag'.

Mescal's dealings with Cambodia and Burma had entailed travelling to their borders and circumventing the official gem markets. 'You were supposed to buy at government shops but they were three or four times higher than the cost of buying from locals,' he said. He took part in an 'underground currency market', exporting dollars from Thailand by using promissory notes which could be cashed in Singapore.

Many of Mescal's dealings in South America and Europe were conducted in the same way. In March 1984, for example, he had smuggled an assortment of sapphires, rubies and emeralds into Britain. 'I didn't declare them,' said Mescal. 'I had them tied around my waist in a money belt. I had no trouble getting them in.' He smuggled emeralds and amethysts into Britain in his money belt again three months later. In fact, he added, 'I have never declared stones I've brought back to the

UK.' Later he pointed out that the only time he was caught was when he was arrested on the cocaine-smuggling charges on 29 March 1986 and the Customs found gems worth £450 hidden in the lining of his briefcase.

It was against this background that Mescal described his dealings with other characters named in the case. He had first met Maxwell Treacy in Bangkok near the end of 1983. Treacy, he learned, was an antique dealer with a shop in Brighton, who also sold jewellery, and he told Mescal that he would be interested in any gems Mescal brought into Britain. 'He felt he could make a little bit of money,' Mescal said.

Mescal became close to Treacy – whom he knew as Mac – both as a business colleague and friend. In Bangkok Mescal introduced Treacy to a supplier of imitation Rolex watches. Later Treacy said he wanted to sell gems in Australia (his father was Australian) and Mescal helped supply those too. He also got to know Treacy's family: his daughter was a singer who came to Bangkok to work in a night-club, and Treacy would call Mescal from time to time to ask how she was.

It was through Treacy that Mescal met Favell in 1984. Mescal understood that Favell sold holiday apartments in Spain, 'and he was asking if he could get involved in the gem business,' Mescal said. They also discovered that they shared a common interest in soccer. As for the Americans named in the indictment, Mescal knew them as gem-dealers. He had met the first American in 1983, and it was through him that he started to trade in South America. The American purchased emeralds from Brazil and Bolivia and supplied them to Mescal for sale on credit in both Thailand and Britain. Mescal met the second American in Brazil in November 1984, after he had been supplying Mescal with gems through a middle-man. Before long they cut out the middle-man and from then on, said Mescal, 'we dealt direct'.

Finally, there was his younger brother David. Mescal appeared to have adopted a protective role towards him – he had paid for his wedding in 1984 – and he also employed him as a courier in his gem business on a number of occasions. When Michael first asked David to go to South America he was, Michael said, 'thrilled to go'.

Michael Mescal now turned to the journeys the Customs had so assiduously logged. Beginning with his visit to Britain in March 1984, almost all, Mescal said, were in connection with gem-dealing – or gem-smuggling. He had sold the gems he had smuggled on that occasion in Hatton Garden, the centre of London's jewellery trade. In May 1984 his brother David had travelled to Rio to deliver a payment to one of the Americans, and Michael had gone to Rio later that month for more stones.

But why had Favell gone to Rio with him? Mescal explained that Favell liked soccer and 'nightlife': they had gone to see England play Brazil in Rio together (England won 2–0) and there Favell met a Brazilian woman who later gave birth to their child. On returning to London, Mescal had smuggled gemstones through the Customs as usual. He had gone back to Brazil in August to obtain some more. In February 1985 – as he had told Frank Munoz at the time – Mescal had travelled to Brazil and Bolivia to obtain more gems. He acquired some emeralds from the second American in Bolivia and then travelled with him to Rio. He also bought emeralds on Treacy's behalf; Treacy was planning to sell them in Australia, and Mescal arranged for them to be collected in South America by Favell.

So why had Mescal gone to Australia with Treacy in March? That, Mescal explained, had come about almost by chance. Treacy was already planning his trip to Australia, while Mescal was intending to return to Bangkok. Then Mescal discovered that it only cost £100 or so to fly on to Australia, so he decided to join Treacy for a holiday. The two men travelled together and were later joined by Favell, who had collected Treacy's diamonds in Paraguay en route. 'I travelled widely in Australia with Treacy and Favell,' Mescal said. 'We went to Queensland, to Surfers Paradise.'

The pattern of business deals resumed soon afterwards. In April 1985 David Mescal visited Bolivia – the first occasion he had been spotted at Heathrow – to deliver $24,000 that Michael owed to one of the Americans. David returned to Bolivia and Brazil in June for similar reasons. It was true that David had returned without the two Samsonite cases he had taken with him. The first was a Samsonite briefcase which he took out for one of the Americans, who had been unable to buy one in South America. The second, a maroon suitcase, had been lost or stolen.

In July 1985, Michael and David had travelled to Canada together. Michael explained that he was delivering some gems, while David was considering moving to Canada with his wife, Simone. 'My brother's a professional carpenter,' Michael said. 'He was playing with the idea of emigrating there and working in construction.' The trip, Mescal added, was 'not a success', save in one respect. While in Montreal, Mescal said, he had met some gem-dealers who showed him a Samsonite suitcase containing a false compartment which they used to carry jewels and currency between Canada and the US. Mescal considered the case ideal for his own business and he bought one for $250. 'I have a lot of stones in my possession and I have a hard time finding a good place to hide them,' he said. 'I thought it would cover that problem because a lot of the apartments I stay in don't have safe deposit facilities.' At $250, he added, 'it was cheap anyway.'

On his return from Canada, Mescal rented the flat at 4 Queensberry Place. He needed somewhere to stay because his girlfriend, Toy, had come over from Bangkok for the summer. So why, Mescal was asked, had he and Treacy gone to Rio in August? Why did Treacy visit him so many times at Queensberry Place afterwards – and what was in the suitcases and packages that they kept taking in and out? Mescal explained that his aunt had set up a wholesale business selling baby-clothes. He had gone to Rio for gems but had also looked at baby-clothes for her. Treacy was thinking of joining the business and he had brought back a number of samples from Rio – and they were in the suitcases which the Romeos had seen. Treacy also helped to compensate for a certain lack in Mescal's diet. Toy preferred Thai food, which she could buy in Earls Court, but Mescal had a hankering for traditional English fare. Treacy's wife had come to the rescue: she was an enthusiastic cook and among the packages the Customs had seen was one containing several of her steak-and-kidney pies.

In September Mescal left Queensberry Place. Toy returned to Bangkok, while he planned another trip to Brazil. His brother David helped him clear out the flat and on 12 September he flew to Rio. He took with him the Samsonite he had bought in Montreal, using it to carry $25,000 which he owed to one of the Americans. Mescal now explained what happened to the Samsonite in Brazil. In Rio Mescal met Treacy, who was on his way to Australia. 'I was telling Mac about the bag and said that I was going to Bangkok in October. Mac said, "Will you need the bag in Bangkok?" and I said no. He asked to borrow it as it would be useful for moving stones.' Mescal said that he had heard nothing more of the suitcase until the following March.

In November 1985 Mescal sent his brother David to Rio to meet one of the American gem-dealers. So how had David finished up staying in the next room to Favell in a hotel in São Paulo, shortly before Favell returned to London with a consignment of cocaine? Michael explained that he had provided David with enough expenses to last for ten days, but David had spent more money than expected and went to São Paulo to borrow some from Favell. David did not go into the witness box to give evidence, but Michael was emphatic that neither he nor David knew anything about Favell's plans. 'I had nothing to do with cocaine,' Michael said.

Nor, for some time, did either of the Mescals know that Favell had even been arrested. They and Treacy continued to do business together in January, when David handed over £15,000 in cash as a loan from Michael for Treacy to buy gems. When Michael visited London briefly in early February, Treacy met him at Earls Court and repaid £10,000 of the loan. 'Treacy said he was doing good business in diamonds and would pay the balance when he was paid,' Mescal said.

Later that month, Mescal went to Rio to buy more gems. Why were

Treacy, Bond and Flanagan there? 'I had not met Bond or Flanagan before that time,' Mescal said. 'I was told they were investing in the diamond business.' Mescal helped them find somewhere to stay, and soon afterwards met Treacy alone. Now, at last, he learned what had happened to his Samsonite case. 'He told me that Tony had got himself into trouble in England. I asked what sort of trouble and he told me trouble with drugs. I couldn't believe it. . . . He told me that he had given Favell my bag that he had borrowed from me. I was shocked and very angry. I told him that we could not go on being friends if he did that sort of thing. I only saw him by accident after that.'

In court Mescal would not be drawn on precisely what he believed Treacy's role in the smuggling attempt had been. His barrister was less reticent. 'You may conclude,' he told the jury, 'that Maxwell Treacy is the Mr Big who uses other people and is prepared to sacrifice them for his own ends. Using other people is the staple diet of drugs smugglers.'

On 28 March Mescal left Rio for Britain, bringing with him the gems he intended to smuggle once more. Instead, to his surprise, he was arrested for allegedly helping to smuggle drugs. He agreed that in his long interview with the Customs he might have seemed anxious or evasive at times – but that, as his counsel said, was partly because he was tired after his long flight, and partly because 'he was smuggling jewels, on which duty should have been paid'.

Mescal also agreed that he had lied when asked about his Samsonite, that was because he had learned by then that it had been used to smuggle drugs. 'I did not tell the truth when I was asked about the bag,' he admitted. 'I might have been evasive about Max Treacy but I did not want any part of what he was involved in. I thought they would not believe me, but I thought as I had nothing to do with that, they would let me go.'

When Mescal was asked about the money that had flowed through his bank accounts, he replied that it was all connected with his business as gem-dealer, and he called a number of witnesses to help confirm his account. They included his aunt, who had set up the wholesale clothing business; David's father-in-law, who had bought some gems; and Max Treacy's daughter, who had known him when she was singing in Bangkok.

Most striking of all was a witness from Thailand who arrived to give evidence on the final day of the defence case. He too was a gem-dealer and he told how he had paid Mescal up to $16,000 a kilo for diamonds. When the prosecution challenged him to produce the documentary evidence, he laughed. 'He would give me the gems, I would give him the money – what need for writing things down?'

The virtue of Mescal's account was that it provided a twofold explanation for the events the Customs had observed. His travelling and transactions were all part of his trade as a gem-dealer; and if there were evasions and subterfuges, that was because he was a gem smuggler too. The jury retired shortly before lunchtime on 14 May 1987, and spent just over an hour considering their verdict. They found Michael Mescal not guilty on both charges. The judge had already ruled that if Michael was acquitted, David must be too. Both were awarded their costs. For conspiring to smuggle cocaine into Britain, which he had admitted, Favell was sentenced to twelve years.

In Australia, Bond pleaded guilty to smuggling cocaine and received sixteen years. Treacy and Flanagan at first denied the charges against them and stood trial in August. But halfway through the trial they changed their pleas; Treacy – who had been described in court as general manager and recruitment officer for a shadowy 'Mr Big' – received eighteen years, Flanagan fifteen. To the Romeos' gratification, *The Times* headlined the verdicts: 'Undercover team breaks international cocaine ring'.

Outside the court at Isleworth, Michael Mescal shook hands with Graham Dick and said: 'No hard feelings.'

'Michael,' said Dick, 'you're the luckiest man alive – you were looking at twenty-eight years.'

'You're wrong,' said Mescal. 'I had nothing to do with it.'

'Bollocks,' said Dick.

Mescal grinned. 'I was innocent,' he said.

CHAPTER THREE

THE RED
AND THE GREEN

In the heart of Heathrow's Terminal Three, beyond the Red and Green Channels which are all that most airline passengers see of the Customs, beyond even the Customs' own offices equipped with their grey government-issue desks and filing cabinets, is a bare cell. The floors, walls and ceiling are polished stone; the light is hidden behind a pane of protective glass; and the only item of furniture is a rubber mattress resting on a ledge. The door, which locks from the outside, is fitted with a narrow pane of one-way glass, so that anyone inside cannot see out. This cell is where the suspected stuffers and swallowers are brought.

The stuffers and swallowers represent all that is most foul and degrading about the work of the Customs today. The 'stuffers' are passengers who, not to put too fine a point on it, have concealed illicit goods in their bodily orifices; in the case of the 'swallowers', the goods are in their stomachs. The contraband is usually packed in plastic capsules or contraceptive condoms, and these days it usually consists of drugs.

There are in fact two such cells alongside each other in Terminal Three; and once the Customs have detained a suspected swallower there is little they can do except wait, on the assumption that what has gone in one end will have to come out the other. In most cases this happens within forty-eight hours, but in 1986 a Dutch passenger set a remarkable record by holding out for *nineteen days*. Sooner or later, however, the suspect will have to visit the third room in the holding suite. A notice on the door gives due warning of what lies inside. 'Unpleasant though it is to work in here, this is what we are reduced to. Please therefore try and keep it as clean and tidy as possible.'

The third room is known as the throne room, and the 'throne' consists of a portable lavatory on a plinth at the top of two metal steps. The officers accompany their suspects in here, equipped with a face mask and rubber gloves. The lavatory bowl is lined with a continuous plastic tube; when the suspect has performed, the officer presses a foot pedal which draws the tube down into the plinth where it is automatically cut and sealed. The officer carries the sealed bag to a washbasin, tips the contents into a plastic colander, and sluices them away with a hose. If he or she finds any smuggled goods they are placed in a sample jar which is then sealed inside a polythene bag and labelled as evidence.

In the nature of things the stuffers will have to visit the throne room too. Young Customs officers are warned that this is not a place where they should follow their natural instincts and avert their eyes, in case the stuffers try to jettison whatever it is they have stuffed.

The stuffers' and swallowers' suite was installed at Terminal Three five years ago. Before then suspects were sent behind a screen to squat over a cardboard potty which the Customs had obtained from a nearby hospital, and the contents were examined in a washbasin. The new suite was equipped with an impressive medical isolator for sifting faeces but officers found it too cumbersome and replaced it with the more basic plastic colander, purchased at Marks and Spencer.

In keeping with the spirit of the place, someone pinned up a series of sardonic warnings, like the one on the throne room door. Another reads, 'Always use protective clothing as far as it is available. . . . Always dispose of your pax gunge in the loo – do *not* leave it for others.' 'Pax' means passengers; 'gunge' is best left to the imagination.

Officers are divided over which is the most repellent part of this task. Some say it is the smell, which penetrates even the stoutest face mask; others that it is the sifting process that follows. Some find it hard to talk about it at all. It certainly does not feature in their small-talk at social occasions and one officer admitted that he had never told his wife about that part of his work. 'I think she'd throw me out if she knew,' he says.

Princess Diana was not spared the gruesome details when she visited the Customs at Heathrow in December 1985. An officer, Mike Sandy, held up a sample jar which had just been filled with plastic capsules that looked like pickled onions, and told her, 'This is the bottom end of the market.' She was not amused.

This repellent method of smuggling has a long and almost respectable history, for the eighteenth-century French writer Voltaire, in his satirical novel *Candide,* portrayed one of his female characters using the stuffing method to smuggle diamonds. However, the first swallowing incident that anyone at Heathrow remembers occurred in 1974.

The Customs had become suspicious of three young Americans who were making frequent return trips to India and Pakistan. The officers guessed that they were smuggling cannabis into Britain but could never find any evidence. Finally an officer made a covert search of their baggage on one of their outward trips, and found a supply of condoms that exceeded any normal sexual capacities. Even now the full implications did not dawn on the Customs. 'We had heard about it but could not

The stuffers' and swallowers' suite at Heathrow's Terminal Three represents one of the most degrading aspects of the illicit drugs trade. Passengers suspected of having concealed drugs by either swallowing or 'stuffing' are held in a spartan cell (*top*). It contains a minimum of furniture, denying them hiding-places for their contraband. Sooner or later they will have to visit the 'throne room' (*centre*) where drugs that have been swallowed will eventually reappear. Sifting through faeces in search of drugs is not the most popular task among Customs officers, although Mike Sandy (*below*) puts on a brave face as he presents a sample find – condoms packed with heroin. Some astonishing records have been set. The most packages swallowed by one person was 739 capsules of cannabis; the greatest weight was 1.5 kg. One flight in 1986 contained fourteen suspects, seven of whom proved positive. The longest wait before a passenger visited the throne room was nineteen days. In the end, says Sandy, 'nature will have its way – but that's the length some people will go to'.

really believe it would happen,' the officer says. When the three Americans returned to Heathrow they were stopped and questioned once again, and two finally admitted what they had done. The third proved more resistant. He was put in a room and handed a rubbish basket lined with a plastic bag, while an officer sat outside. 'In the morning,' says an officer, 'there was the most awful smell.' There was also a pile of condoms filled with cannabis oil.

The numbers of stuffers and swallowers rose gradually at first. Then came a dramatic acceleration, reaching twenty-six in a single month, August 1986. The numbers of packages have risen too: a dozen stuffed or a hundred swallowed are now far from uncommon. The highest number of items swallowed was 739 capsules of cannabis resin, weighing half a kilo. That was by a man. The greatest weight swallowed, again by a man, was $1\frac{1}{2}$ kg of cannabis. The largest item ever stuffed was a 260-gram package of heroin the size of a ripe avocado. That was by a woman.

From interviews with stuffers or swallowers, the Customs have now learned a considerable amount about their methods. Swallowers first practise by swallowing entire grapes intact. Before swallowing the actual capsules they take a dose of a binding agent, like Lomotil or kaolin-and-morphine, which should give them two days' grace. They also coat the capsules with syrup so that they slip down more easily.

The first problem for uniformed officers in the Green Channel is that neither stuffing nor swallowing leaves any outward signs. In their search for suspects, the officers concentrate on nationalities known for stuffing and swallowing – the 1986 league table was headed by Nigerians, with Ghanaians second and Colombians third. Most officers follow their usual routine of probing passengers' reasons for travelling. If they cannot give satisfactory answers they are regarded as suspects and their baggage is likely to be searched. If an officer finds nothing incriminating but remains convinced of his or her hunch then the next step, in one officer's indelicate phrase, is to 'put them on the crapper'.

Once suspects have been consigned to the strip cell they are usually held until they have made two bowel movements. If these are clear they are allowed to go. As a rule of thumb the Customs reckon that anyone who does not visit the throne room in the first twenty-four hours is likely to be guilty – 'either that or they're loony,' an officer says.

Then the manoeuvring begins. For obvious reasons, swallowers usually refuse to eat. If they do ask for a meal, officers usually serve them with baked beans on toast – a tried-and-tested laxative. Officers may also offer to take them for a walk, which may induce their bowel muscles to relax. But the couriers are learning too. For a time the Customs gave suspects a urine test which frequently showed traces of drugs from the covering of the packages. The couriers are now careful to clean the packages and results from the test have declined sharply.

Suspects must also be watched continually in case they try to dispose of their goods. The first holding rooms were far more civilised than the present strip cells; they contained a bed, clothes stand, even a carpet. These provided an astonishing array of hiding-places – and once packages have been disposed of, suspects can deny that they were theirs, claiming that they must have been hidden by a previous occupant of the cell. Even in the new strip cells suspects still search for hiding-places and in some extreme cases have tried to re-swallow packages that have emerged from their body. Sometimes this causes them to vomit the package back up – and officers witnessing this spectacle have come close to vomiting too.

Personal feelings apart, the greatest problem caused by the stuffers and swallowers is the large number of Customs staff they occupy. It takes two officers to watch each suspect and if three or four have been detained there may be no officers left to check passengers on subsequent flights. Officers at Terminal Three still talk about the day in September 1986 when a single flight from Lagos, Nigeria, produced *fourteen* suspects of whom seven proved to have stuffed or swallowed drugs. Reinforcements were summoned from other terminals and their holding cells were pressed into use. 'But we were overwhelmed,' an officer says. 'Anyone could have walked through with ten kilos of heroin for all we knew.'

The Dutchman who went for nineteen days before visiting the throne room thus single-handedly tied up almost eleven weeks of continuous Customs time – and the irony is that at the end of that time no drugs were found. There is still controversy at Terminal Three about this case: was the Dutchman another 'loony', or did he manage to conceal his packages when the two watching officers relaxed their guard? The longest productive wait was thirteen days, when the suspect in question finally excreted thirty-seven packages.

The introduction of the Police and Criminal Evidence Act in 1986 has relieved the Customs of some of this work load, as, like the police, they can now hold suspects for only ninety-six hours. After this time suspects must be released or charged; and, once charged, they must be remanded in custody or on bail. Suspected stuffers or swallowers are remanded to Brixton prison, where the task of watching them – to the Customs' unconcealed relief – passes to the prison staff.

There is considerable disagreement among individual officers over how stuffers and swallowers should be handled in future. Some officers complain that their treatment amounts to 'pussy-footing', and suggest that compulsory medical examinations or forcible enemas would not go amiss. So far the only change in the Customs' procedure has been to take away suspects' clothes and give them a set of white paper overalls, with elastic cuffs and ankles and a zip-up front, so that any attempt to pass the drugs and reconceal them will be obvious.

Other officers take a softer line. They point out that forcible medical treatment raises serious issues of individual rights and that most passengers suspected of stuffing or swallowing are innocent. In 1985 44 out of 180 suspects were found to have drugs. In 1986 the figures for suspects soared, but out of 1093 only 198 proved positive – a lower proportion, 18 per cent against 24 per cent, than the previous year, and leaving 895 passengers with every right to feel aggrieved at their treatment.

Some officers also point out that even the guilty passengers may only be pawns in a multi-million-pound game. In a recent issue of the Customs' staff newspaper *Portcullis,* officer Janet Leonard, who has worked at Heathrow for thirteen years, told the story of a peasant woman from South America who swallowed a dozen packages of cocaine. She passed through the Green Channel unchallenged but when she met the organisers of the run in a London hotel she found herself unable to produce the packages on demand. The organisers threatened to cut her stomach open and she was so frightened that she ran away and gave herself up to the police. Thinking that she was safe, she squatted on the floor and produced the cocaine.

The woman was arrested and brought back to Heathrow. After confessing, she told Janet Leonard how she had been recruited. She had a crippled child who needed medical treatment she could not afford. One day a stall-holder in the local market said that he knew how she could earn the money her son required. He introduced her to a gang of cocaine-smugglers who told her that they would finance her son's medical treatment if she made the run.

After her interview the woman complained of feeling ill. Janet Leonard guessed that some of the packages she had swallowed had leaked and she was rushed to hospital. She recovered, and eventually received a prison sentence of six years.

In general, it is the woman officers at Heathrow who feel more sympathy for their suspects. 'They must be really desperate,' one acknowledges. Nonetheless, she adds, 'I wouldn't do it for a million pounds.'

Nothing epitomises more potently than stuffing and swallowing the changes that the British Customs have undergone in the past twenty years. They are changes as profound as any in their 750-year history, dating back to Magna Carta which refers to the 'ancient and rightful Customs' – an adaptation of the phrase, 'the customary duties', which were payable to the King on goods landed at England's ports. The duties were levied on items such as wine, cheese and wool and were collected under a free-enterprise system known as 'the Farms' by officials with

Some distinguished figures of British literature have been Customs officials. Geoffrey Chaucer (*left*), author of *The Canterbury Tales*, was 'Controller of the Custom and Subsidy of Wool, Woolfells and Hides' at the Port of London from 1374 to 1386. (It was a family tradition, for Chaucer's father and grandfather were Customs officials too.) Controllers were appointed by the king, and their task was to check on the assessment and collection of duties. Chaucer's annual salary of £16 13s 4d was boosted by seizure awards – in 1374 he received £71 4s 6d as his share of a penalty imposed on John of Kent, who had tried to export wool without paying duty. The characters Chaucer met in his work almost certainly helped to inspire the pilgrims of *The Canterbury Tales*, like the Seaman – 'hot summers had made his hue all brown', and he liked to 'draw off a draught of Bordeaux wine' when his colleagues' backs were turned.

The poet and playwright John Dryden (*left*) was Collector of wool duties at the Port of London from 1683 to 1692. His salary was a tiny £5 a year but, like Chaucer, he received considerable bonuses in the form of 'fees and profits thereof' which were paid by merchants on all Customs transactions. Dryden's pension as poet laureate was also paid for out of Excise duties. By Dryden's time the Customs and Excise had been formally established under a Board of Commissioners set up by Charles II – previously they had been run under a free-enterprise system known as the farms. The Customs and Excise are still headed by a Board of Commissioners today.

titles which are still in use today. Thus the Collector gathered the taxes, the Controller watched over the Collector, and the Surveyor made a further check on both. Some distinguished figures have held those posts: Dick Whittington was Collector of the Wool Subsidy; Geoffrey Chaucer was Controller of the Customs and Subsidy of Wool, Woolfells and Hides at the Port of London.

The Customs were brought into full government control in the mid-seventeenth century when Parliament placed them under a Board of Commissioners during the Civil War. The Board introduced a new tax to help pay for Cromwell's army: named the Excise, it was the first tax to be levied on home-produced goods like beer, cider and soap, and provoked widespread riots.

When the monarchy was restored, Charles II kept the Board of Commissioners and used the Customs to draw up the first 'balance of payments' account. (Britain had a trade surplus of £1,080,487 11s 9d in the first year.) King Charles also used the Customs as a slush fund to finance both the English secret service and his exploits with Nell Gwyn – an Excise officer paid her £500 a month in cash, contrasting with his own pay of £50 a year, from which he had to provide his own horse. Some of the Customs' considerable powers date from this period, including the Writ of Assistance, which permits the Customs to search premises and seize goods without a magistrate's warrant (it is still used around 600 times a year today).

For much of the seventeenth and eighteenth centuries the Customs and Excise were engaged in a virtual civil war, as they fought the notorious smuggling gangs which operated with impunity around the British coast. The gangs unloaded contraband tea, tobacco and wine almost under the officers' noses. When challenged they fought back ruthlessly, murdering officers and their witnesses and storming Custom houses to repossess confiscated goods. In the nineteenth century the smugglers went so far as to help Napoleon during the war with France, selling him details of Britain's coastal defences. After Napoleon had been defeated the British government declared war on the smugglers and their power was finally broken.

Throughout this time the Customs' principal function had been to collect revenue, and that remained true in the twentieth century. By now they had come to occupy a more stable and peaceable role: at ports and airports smuggling was little more than a game between officers and passengers who might try to smuggle in the occasional contraband item, such as cameras or watches. Certainly that was true at Heathrow in the 1960s. Although it was already one of the world's busiest airports, it was known among Customs officers as one of Britain's less eventful – or desirable – posts. Quite simply, one Heathrow veteran says, 'there was nothing happening'.

Tom Paine (*left*), writer and radical, was an Excise officer between 1762 and 1774. The author of *The Rights of Man* and *The Age of Reason*, which helped fuel revolutions in France and America, he also took up the cudgels on his colleagues' behalf. Paine joined the Excise service in Norfolk in 1762 but was sacked three years later for not carrying out his duties. He was reinstated in Sussex in 1768, and in 1772 published a pamphlet, *The Case of the Officers of Excise*, calling for an increase in pay. He pointed out that officers took home a miserly £46 a year, from which they had to provide their own horse, and that they had not had a pay-rise for 70 years. He sent the pamphlet to the Board of Commissioners and MPs, but the Treasury rejected his case. To the government's relief Paine was sacked again two years later, this time for being absent without official permission.

In contrast to Paine, Robert Burns (*left*), Scots poet and balladeer, was content with his pay as an Exciseman. 'I find £50 per annum an exceedingly good thing', he wrote. Previously a farmer, Burns was an Excise officer in Dumfries from 1789 until his death in 1796. He evidently led a demanding life, riding 30 or 40 miles a day, 'besides four different kinds of book-keeping to post every day'. He used his travels to collect Scottish songs, as well as writing and publishing his own. Yet he did not neglect his Excise work, as a contemporary staff report testifies: 'The Poet does pretty well.' Burns was promoted to supervisor shortly before his death, and his widow received an official pension of £8.

Then came drugs.

Geoff Yerbury is a Senior Customs Officer who has worked at Heathrow for almost twenty years. Now at Terminal Three, he recalls the quiet days at Heathrow, but then 'in 1971 or 1972 we began to find cannabis, cannabis oil, opium – that kind of thing'. Yerbury was determined to go on the offensive against the drugs smugglers, and he did so in a manner that some colleagues regarded as unconventional or even unsporting. His method was to take a surreptitious look at passengers' cases before they were delivered to the baggage hall. He found it surprisingly easy to pick out suitcases with false sides or bottoms.

'You could squeeze the sides together and see what you could smell,' he says. It was usually the glue from suitcase concealments that gave the game away, rather than the drugs themselves. 'Or you could see what happened when you lifted them up' – suitcases with false compartments had often been packed unevenly, so that they tilted to one side. Yerbury also made a number of finds with what he calls his 'portable X-ray machine' – a penknife with which he probed the contents of suitcases without bothering to open them first.

Yerbury eventually received the MBE for his success in detecting drugs. But in the early 1970s his superiors were less enthusiastic, as he discovered one afternoon when he was summoned before a senior Customs official at Heathrow. Yerbury assumed he was about to be praised for his efforts; instead he received a stern reprimand. 'We're not here for drugs,' the official told him. 'We're here for revenue.'

For a time cannabis remained the principal illegal drug imported into Britain. Although there was an increasing number of seizures of Class A drugs, the so-called 'hard drugs' like heroin and cocaine, these were still measured in grams. Then came an incident which brought home the new threat the Customs faced.

One day in 1974 Mike Waddington, an officer who had worked at Heathrow since 1968, was watching passengers collect their baggage off a flight from Amsterdam. Waddington – who appears in the BBC film *The Red and the Green* – was with an officer from the Investigation Division, and remarked that although increasing amounts of heroin were supposedly entering Britain, none of the smugglers ever seemed to be caught. On a whim which he still finds impossible to explain, Waddington pointed out an Asian passenger and said: 'There's your man.'

The ID officer left at that point. But as Waddington watched the passenger he became increasingly intrigued. In the first place he had no hand baggage, which was most unusual as Amsterdam was renowned for the value of its duty-free goods. Second, he was chain smoking. When the man collected his suitcase and headed for the Green Channel, Waddington decided to stop him.

The passenger's initial answers seemed innocuous enough. He explained that he was a bank clerk from Kuala Lumpur in Malaysia and had come to Britain to visit relatives. But when Waddington looked at his suitcase and compared its internal and external depths he suspected that it could have a false bottom. Half-jokingly, Waddington says, 'I decided to go for a quick confession.'

'What's in the bag?' he asked.

Without hesitating, the man replied: 'Heroin.'

To Waddington's astonishment the passenger admitted that he was carrying 2kg of heroin. He explained that he had incurred huge gambling debts in Malaysia and had taken the heroin to Amsterdam in the hope of selling it there. But he had failed to find a buyer and had come to London merely to catch the next flight home. Instead he was sent to prison for eight years.

For Waddington and his colleagues the find marked the moment when the myths and the rumours about heroin became fact. 'All of a sudden it was for real, not just something you heard about,' Waddington says. 'It was not just small-user quantities either, but proper commercial smuggling.'

Even now it took some time for the Customs to adjust to their new role. Throughout most of their history, Customs officers have been paid seizure awards for detecting contraband. In the 1970s the size of the awards still reflected the Customs' traditional function as collectors of revenue: officers were awarded £25 for a smuggled camera, compared with £4 for a seizure of cannabis. This was the subject of some grievance among officers until the anomaly was finally resolved in 1979, when all seizure awards were simply abolished.

The year of Waddington's heroin find was nonetheless a watershed. It marked the first time that the Customs' annual report provided statistics for drug seizures under the three principal headings of cannabis, heroin and morphine, and cocaine. 'Before then it was just another bit of smuggling as far as we were concerned,' an official says.

The statistics provide a graphic picture of how Customs' seizures of the Class A drugs – the so-called 'hard drugs' – have soared since. Cocaine has risen from 6kg seized in 1975 to 94kg in 1986, heroin from 4kg to 175kg in the same period. Seizures of cannabis, a class 'B' drug, already stood at 4.4 tonnes in 1975; in 1986 the figure was 22.4 tonnes. The number of seizures has increased from 871 to 4182.

It should be said that precisely what these statistics show is a controversial matter. At face value, the dramatic rise in seizures could mean that the Customs have simply become more efficient. But other evidence suggests that it equally reflects an increase in importations. When drugs are in short supply it is usual for their price to rise and their average purity to fall. But in Britain both these indicators rose between 1980 and 1985. The street price of heroin rose from £70 to £75 per gram, and purity from thirty-five to forty per cent. In the same five years the price of cocaine rose from £65 to £70 per gram, while purity remained steady at thirty per cent. (Heroin and other hard drugs are always diluted or 'cut' before they are sold in the street: a figure of forty per cent means that the consignment consists of forty per cent heroin, sixty per cent other substances such as sugar. But heroin sold in Britain is invariably of far higher purity than in the US, where it is sometimes sold at as little as one per cent.)

The implication that importations have risen in step with seizures accords somewhat disconcertingly with officers' own instincts. In public some officers say that they believe they are intercepting no more than ten per cent of the drugs aimed at Britain. In private they may be even more gloomy: 'Five per cent – if we're lucky,' was one officer's view. Some researchers believe that these estimates may be unduly pessimistic: the Institute for the Study of Drug Dependency puts the figure between thirteen and twenty per cent. There could be no doubt, however, that by the 1980s drugs had become the main preoccupation of Customs officers at ports and airports, especially Heathrow.

As the seizures soared, the audacity and ingenuity of the smugglers mounted in proportion. Cocaine was found stuffed inside toy elephants, concealed under a consignment of grape nuts, strapped to the leg of a former PoW, hidden in women's corsets, soaked into designer shirts, impregnated into a cardboard suitcase, and packed into champagne bottles which were carried in duty-free bags. In April 1985 a courier was arrested at Heathrow carrying 13.2kg of cocaine from Bolivia in his baggage; three months later, even that amount was exceeded by a passenger carrying 20kg of heroin. The largest consignment of drugs ever seized in the Green Channel at Heathrow was 222kg of cannabis found in the baggage of a group of women arriving from Nigeria: when questioned, they said they had no idea it was there.

Most of the large-scale seizures, at Heathrow and elsewhere, are made as a result of enquiries or information supplied by the Investigation Division. The uniformed staff at Heathrow sometimes look askance at their ID colleagues, however, slightly resenting their knack of attracting the best publicity. They like to point out that when the *number* of seizures is considered, it is the officers staffing the desks in the Green Channels who make the most: around two-thirds of all heroin seizures and half those of cocaine. What is more, they add, ninety per cent of those seizures result not from tip-offs from the ID but from the officers' own instincts.

So how do they do it? What is the alchemy of intuition, experience and luck that enables them to pick out one passenger from another,

In the seventeenth and eighteenth centuries the Customs and Excise fought violent battles with the notorious smuggling gangs of southern England. The smugglers unloaded contraband tea, tobacco and wine from sailing ships and brought it ashore in small boats: out of four million tons of tea consumed in Britain in 1750, it is reckoned, three million had been smuggled in. When the Customs tried to halt their trade, the smugglers – as in the print *above* – resisted fiercely. Many officers were killed or injured, and smugglers sometimes stormed Custom houses to recover their goods. The gangs flourished until the nineteenth century and even sold Napoleon details of Britain's coastal defences. Once France was defeated at Trafalgar, the British government declared war on the smugglers instead. The Customs were reinforced with 7000 soldiers and the power of the gangs was finally broken. Nonetheless, similar methods of smuggling persist to this day. In 1986, the Customs seized $1\frac{1}{2}$ tons of cannabis packed in bales (*left*) that smugglers had attempted to land at a remote beach in South Wales.

especially when during the busiest times, like the morning rush-hour when one Transatlantic 747 after another is touching down, they may stop only one person in 400 or 500? Officers say, in short, that it all depends on the 'revenue nose', a centuries-old term which implies that officers can smell smugglers as they pass by. Since nervous smugglers tend to sweat the term is an appropriate one – even more so now that the most likely contraband is drugs, which often give off distinctive odours of their own.

Like Mike Waddington, Mike Sandy is a 'two-ring' officer at Heathrow, the two rings indicating that he is an executive officer of the Civil Service and corresponding to the prized status of officer in the days when the Customs had their own career grades. A confident, expansive man in his late thirties with a trim beard, he joined the Customs in 1974 and came to Heathrow after a spell in a London postal sorting office, where he stood by a conveyor belt and scrutinised parcels arriving from abroad to decide which should be opened and examined. Known as 'externalling', it was a frustrating job as the parcels sped by at a rate of one every two seconds. Sandy finds a more rewarding challenge at Heathrow.

'You stand for long periods and look at people and that's how you do the job,' he says. 'You look, you watch their reactions, you watch what they do after they've picked up their baggage. It's not just standing in the Green Channel, it's wandering round the terminal, watching people get off planes, whether they appear to be with somebody, whether they appear to be distancing themselves from somebody, whether they appear to be unnatural in any way. You can look at a hundred people walking by and nothing, and then all of a sudden somebody will walk by and something inside you says, I want to stop him. ...'

Some passengers, Sandy says, are known as the 'gimmes' or 'Mr Magics' of this world: 'They're the sweet ones – you can see them a mile off.' Once Sandy was about to take a break when he almost collided with a passenger carrying a suitcase. 'He just presented himself in front of me and without looking any further he was a person that I had to stop and have a word with. You ask for the passport, you look at the passport – two weeks in Bogotá – and then you look at the ticket, cash-paid ticket, all the good things, and then it was a matter of finding it. ...'

'Bogotá' is currently one of the cocaine-smuggling capitals of the world; 'cash-paid ticket', as Operation Renaissance showed, is viewed as another major clue, as smugglers dislike using cheques or credit cards. Sandy's instinct was spot-on: the man's suitcase had a false compartment containing 1.2kg of cocaine.

Sadly for Sandy, the Mr Magics have become far less frequent as smugglers become more knowing and experienced. Sandy now relies on one basic line of questioning: 'Why is this person travelling?' If a passenger's answers are vague, he probes. 'You've come here on business – what sort of business? To buy computers – what sort of computers?'

Questioning may produce clues by itself. 'Stop them and all of a sudden they're jumpy. Some go all quiet. Some won't look you in the eye.' Sandy persists and sooner or later a spurious story will collapse. 'The more you go into it the more they say and then suddenly the whole house of cards comes tumbling down.'

One passenger gave himself away by saying he had come to find a school for his son, listing as examples Eton and Gordonstoun – and the prominent girls' school Roedean. The hardest suspects to crack, says Sandy, are students, since they have a perfectly valid reason for travelling. 'They're bomb proof. All you can do is look and wonder: have they got the gear?'

Sandy's colleague Mike Waddington chooses a different rule of thumb to follow: he likes to size up passengers coming off a flight and homes in on those who somehow do not seem to 'fit'. 'When you've dealt with a lot of people for a long time, you're not looking for a particular type of person but someone who doesn't fit that type of person,' he says. 'Every passenger has his own reason for travelling and when someone stands in front of you, you soon get to realise whether someone is genuine or not. I suppose it's a sort of sixth sense, but people give off vibrations if they're nervous about something or if they're excited about a particular situation, and after a while you can latch on to this and you realise that something is not right somewhere.'

One of Waddington's best seizures came by following this instinct. Like Sandy, Waddington wanders the terminal building and had gone to watch passengers disembarking from a Varig flight from Brazil. One young woman seemed out of place. 'They're normally fairly upmarket South Americans, well dressed, fairly affluent, and she just didn't fit that category,' Waddington says. When the woman entered the Green Channel, Waddington stopped her. The first signs were promising. Although she said she was a photographic model who had gone to Rio for a holiday, she was only nineteen and had a cash-paid return ticket that had cost over £2000. With clues like that, says Waddington, 'you're on to a winner'. He felt the uncanny frisson of excitement officers experience when a discovery is near. 'It's almost impossible to describe – but you know there is something there and it's a question of where it is.'

The woman was carrying a holdall and a handbag. Inside the holdall, Waddington found a set of chess pieces. When the woman said it was a present, Waddington asked her if she had the board. When she replied that she had brought it to London on a previous trip Waddington knew the story was crumbling.

'Do you play chess?'

'Yes.'

'What's a pawn?'

'I don't know.'

'I knew then I was really warm,' says Waddington. 'The chess set was saying, "Look at me".' The pieces felt strange to the touch and they had a pungent, earthy smell. 'It's not something I would normally have associated with cocaine,' Waddington says. 'It was more like opium.' In fact, the chess set proved to have been moulded from cocaine paste.

The best smugglers are therefore those who merge most unobtrusively with their fellow passengers – and Mike Sandy admits that it is then pot-luck whether they are stopped. As with stuffing and swallowing, the Customs try to improve the odds in their favour by drafting in large numbers of officers for particular flights. One that normally proves fruitful is British Airways' flight 262, which arrives from Jamaica at around midday four days a week.

Since rum is the traditional Jamaican drink, and since it costs three times in Britain what it costs in Jamaica, passengers often attempt to bring in more bottles than they are permitted under the duty-free rules. The officers in the Green Channel who unwrap the bottles and line them up affect a stern air that may belie the amused resignation they really feel. The passengers usually appear astonished that so many bottles have been found and claim that a relative must have packed them as a present. Since the officers will already have asked whether they packed their own suitcases, the excuse invariably fails. Passengers who have tried to smuggle only one or two bottles, and readily confess on being found out, are usually only asked to pay the duty and are allowed to go. Where larger amounts are concerned the Customs pursue a deliberate policy of holding the offending passengers for questioning, reckoning that the delay and inconvenience will make them think twice next time.

Flight 262 often brings another of Jamaica's national products: cannabis. Sometimes that too is simply wrapped in newspaper; or it may be concealed more ingeniously, like the cannabis shown in the BBC film found in a bunch of coconuts which had been sliced open and resealed. Rastafarians, for whom using cannabis is part of their religion, find they are stopped and searched more than other passengers.

Customs officers are naturally aware of the argument that cannabis should be decriminalised on the grounds that there is little evidence that it causes users any harm. At present the government is doing its best to avoid any debate on the subject in case it is suspected of being 'soft' on drugs. Officers themselves are most likely to say that they are there to enforce the law and if cannabis is illegal there is no point in even discussing the issue. Brian Clark, the head of the ID cocaine teams, was

To some passengers, going through the Green Channel may feel like running the gauntlet, as the officers watch and wait (*top*). For the officers, the key decision is which passengers to stop out of the thousands who pour through. *Centre:* Passengers arriving from Karachi have brought in some fresh oranges. This contravenes the Plant Health Act and the oranges are confiscated. *Below:* Flights from Jamaica usually produce finds of rum above the duty-free allowance. This passenger declined to pay the duty she owed, and simply left the rum behind.

more explicit still when he told the BBC: 'If dandelions are prohibited and people smuggle dandelions, I'll knock them off too.'

Nonetheless, the sheer volume of cannabis now entering Britain has compelled the Customs to make certain pragmatic decisions over how to deal with it. Among their considerable powers is that of being able to 'compound' offences – which means, in effect, exacting a private fine rather than taking offenders before the courts with all the waste of officers' time that entails. In 1982, with almost no publicity, the Customs decided that attempts to import small amounts of cannabis for personal use should be compounded. They set the limit at 10 grams and the charge at £50 – and two years later an official report concluded that the scheme had proved both sensible and successful. However, there are still anom‑ alies. Anyone paying the charge escapes a criminal record (although their name is still recorded on the Customs' computer, CEDRIC). But since that is only available for passengers who can pay at the time, or find someone else who will pay for them, it discriminates in favour of the wealthy. Furthermore, the charge was recently raised to £75 – and whereas previously anyone with cheque book and cheque card could pay, they can no longer do so if their limit is £50.

Flight 262 from Jamaica on 17 February 1986 brought one cannabis find. It was rather more substantial than 10 grams; and it came about because, in keeping with the category used by Mike Waddington, some‑ thing about the passengers did not seem to 'fit'. An officer stationed at the finger had his curiosity aroused by one of the few white couples on the flight. The man was wearing a light-coloured suit with a white tie, the woman a short fur jacket – clothes that might be considered 'flash'. The officer alerted the uniformed staff and the couple attracted further attention by entering the Green Channel with two large duty-free boxes on their luggage trolleys.

A Scottish officer, George Shields, stopped the couple and asked them what the boxes contained. The woman passenger, Christina Hart, said that they contained four bottles of rum each – which exceeded the duty-free allowance, as she immediately acknowledged.

'You've chosen to come through the Green Channel,' Shields told her. 'The Red Channel is where you pay on excess goods.'

Hart appeared contrite. 'Sorry – I just walked through. I thought it was more sort of, er, if you get loads of perfume. Sorry.'

'Yeah, but you can't bring in as much booze as you want, you've already said you expected to pay on it.'

'Yes, sorry.'

The couple seemed uneasy; and although that could merely have been because Shields had found the excess rum, he continued his search. He took their suitcases away and examined them in an X-ray machine, but saw nothing to confirm his suspicions. Finally the duty-free boxes were cut open in front of the couple, and, to their apparent surprise, they contained not rum but a substantial amount of cannabis.

'What do you think that is?' Shields asked Hart.

'Well, you can only think it's drugs or something,' she replied.

'You think it could be drugs or something?'

Hart shrugged. 'Well, yeah – the way you reacted.'

Hart and her partner claimed that there must have been a terrible mistake, as they had been given the boxes at Kingston airport after ordering cigarettes and rum. Shields was sceptical.

'All over the world, I've bought a lot of stuff from duty-free shops and I've never been given anything like that.'

'Well neither have I,' Hart told him. 'It's the first time I've been to the West Indies. ....'

'Let's stop playing silly wee games,' said Shields.

Hart and her partner were led away to the interview rooms in the Customs suite. On further analysis, each box proved to contain 7kg of high-quality herbal cannabis. 'Very fresh,' Shields explained as he sniffed the dried cannabis plants. 'Normally it varies. Herbal cannabis from Nigeria is mostly seeds and is of very poor quality. But this is good quality stuff, very good quality. Not many seeds. A nice smell.'

Hart and her partner stuck to their stories throughout interviews that afternoon. 'They accept the fact that it was in their duty-free goods,' Shields explained. 'But they are claiming they didn't know it was there, and that basically the woman in the duty-free shop has stitched them up. According to them, they were buying rum, and were more than surprised to see it contained cannabis.' Shields considered it 'a very implausible story – that sort of thing doesn't happen in the real world.'

'Do you believe them?' Shields was asked.

'No – not at all, not at all, not at all.'

'So are the couple in your opinion guilty?'

'That', said Shields dutifully, 'is for the jury to decide.'

Seven months later, the couple stood trial at Isleworth Crown Court. Hart changed her story and pleaded guilty. She accepted sole responsibility for smuggling the cannabis, saying that she had done so without her partner's knowledge and in the hope of using it to pay for medical treatment required by an elderly relative. She was sentenced to eighteen months. Her partner denied any knowledge of the cannabis and was found not guilty.

Christina Hart's misfortune was to encounter an officer as persistent as Shields, who was prepared to back to the hilt his hunch that something was 'not right'. Not all officers, it should be said, are quite so determined. A recent internal Customs report revealed that a surprising number of officers appeared too timid, lacking in tenacity or simply unable to select the most likely targets. The Customs have since been reviewing their training procedures – until then officers received just three weeks in the classroom and three weeks' practice on the job – and improvements are on the way.

Assistance is also at hand from a growing number of technological aids. Foremost among these is CEDRIC – the acronym for one of those titles which, you suspect, has been made up simply to provide an interesting name. The 'Customs and Excise Department Reference and Information Computer' contains almost 200,000 names and has the capacity to store half a million more. Anyone who arouses the Customs' suspicions in any way is likely to become the subject of an 'SMR' or 'Suspicious Movement Report', even if they have not committed any crime. Members of the Investigation Department say it is surprising how often these suspicions pay off and, to drive the point home, uniformed officers were recently exhorted to make a greater effort to provide CEDRIC with information, especially when they are 'unable to locate an offence yet are still unhappy about the subject'.

The Customs at Heathrow now make an average of 400 CEDRIC enquiries a day. If an officer asks to borrow a passenger's passport and returns with it five minutes later, it is a safe bet that he or she had been checking what information CEDRIC has to offer. CEDRIC should also show if a passenger has a criminal record. For the details, the officer checks with the National Drugs Intelligence Unit, the joint police and Customs post at Scotland Yard which collects information about drugs offences and also provides access to the Police National Computer.

As Operation Renaissance revealed, the Heathrow Customs can scrutinise aircraft passenger lists. The boarding manifests from transatlantic flights are available moments after they close in the US, and officers can also inspect the reservation lists for details of where the tickets were issued, how they were paid for, whether passengers are travelling with companions, and their precise routing to Heathrow.

Not all airlines are quite so efficient – some from third-world countries merely bring a passenger list which is available to the Customs when they reach Heathrow – but it follows that anyone with previous convictions who attempts to import drugs into Britain is putting himself or herself at risk.

That is precisely what occurred when the BBC were filming on 17 February 1986 – the day Judy Carne, the British-born actress who starred in the 1960s' television series the *Rowan and Martin Laugh-In*, flew to Heathrow from New York on a British Airways Concorde. The Customs will not say precisely how they knew she was coming, other than to say they had received a 'tip-off', but they were waiting for her as she

In the perpetual contest with smugglers, high technology is coming to the Customs' aid. X-ray machines have been installed at Heathrow (*top*) to help search baggage or suspect items. Suitcases found with drugs or contraband are likely to be taken, together with their owners, into the Customs' offices (*centre*) for a closer search. The evidence from recent seizures is kept here too, like the coconuts (*bottom*) found by officer Louise Beard in the baggage of a passenger arriving from Jamaica, which were used in a bid to smuggle cannabis. The smuggler had sliced the coconuts in two and replaced the contents with herbal cannabis. He had glued them together again and covered the join with coconut dust. There were ten coconuts in all, says Louise Beard. 'But some weren't very good, because you could actually see the glue.' A more expert smuggler would have packed a small bottle of water with the cannabis, so that when shaken it sounded like coconut milk.

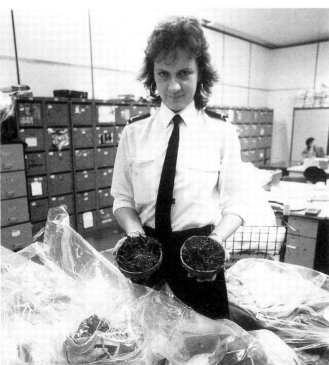

approached the Green Channel at Terminal Three.

Wearing a pale-pink tracksuit with a long matching pink and blue scarf, Judy Carne looked neat and elegant as she approached. She was stopped by officer Hazel Shopland. With elaborate courtesy Shopland asked: 'Where are you coming from, madam?'

'New York,' Carne replied.

'Where are you resident?'

'England.'

'Can I look at your passport, please?'

Shopland led Carne to a baggage desk and steered her through the standard line of questions. 'You've just been on holiday, have you?'

'No, I work in New York a lot.'

'Oh, you're an actress – that must be fun.'

'You get to travel, sometimes.'

'You travel quite a lot – you're fully aware of your allowances in the Green Channel, are you?'

'Yes, yes.'

'Good – have you any items that you purchased on this trip?'

'No – I have a carton of cigarettes and a bottle of booze and that's it.'

'I'd just like to look through your things.'

'Sure.'

Then came the question that closed the trap: 'Did you pack them yourself?'

'Yes.'

Rummaging through Carne's handbag, Shopland found a packet of pills. 'These are all prescribed for you, are they?'

'Yes.'

'What are the white ones for?'

'It's a drug for arthritis. I broke my neck in an accident and I have to take them.'

Shopland found another container and asked: 'What's this for?'

'Hmm?' said Carne.

'What's this for?'

Carne peered at it closely. 'It's a cosmetic thing,' she said. 'Dunno – somebody gave it to me for cosmetics.'

'Sorry,' said Shopland. 'I don't believe that.'

Carne put her coat on the desk and looked around distractedly.

'Do you want to take a seat?' Shopland asked.

Carne declined. Shopland turned to another officer and asked: 'Would you please go and test that for me? The lady says it's cosmetics. It isn't. It's a razor blade and a straw.'

'Somebody gave it to me in New York, really,' said Carne, who now sat down.

Shopland continued her search until the other officer returned and announced the result of the test: 'Positive.'

'Positive,' repeated Shopland.

Carne got up. 'What did you say?'

'We just tested the contents of that little box, the straw and the razor, and it's reacted positively to one of our local drug-testing kits,' Shopland told her. 'The blue is an indication that cocaine is being used. So we're going to have to search things very, very thoroughly. It might take a little time, do you want to take a little seat?'

'All right,' said Carne, and sat down again.

Shopland and another officer now painstakingly searched every item of Carne's belongings. 'There really isn't anything in my luggage, honestly,' Carne told them. 'I know you have to do this. . . .'

Then Shopland asked her if she had any objections to a body search.

'What happens?' Carne asked.

'Well, we make sure you've got nothing on your person, basically.'

'What happens if you object?'

'Well if you object to the search then obviously we don't do the search but somebody else will.'

Carne did not object. Shopland led her to a side room with another woman officer acting as a witness – 'to make sure that the search of the person is all above board'.

'Now what we do,' said Shopland, 'is with ladies we take the top part of your clothing off first and I'll go through it, and I'll give it back to you and you can dress, then we do the bottom half – that way you're not too embarrassed and you don't get too cold. All right, if you give them to me then I can go through them. Do you have anything on your person that you want to tell us about?'

'No.'

Soon after starting the search, Shopland noticed some marks on Carne's arm and asked what had caused them.

'From years ago,' Carne told her.

'What were you using?'

'Heroin.'

'Heroin?'

'Years ago.'

'You don't use it any more?'

'No.'

'Do you use any form of drug at the moment?'

'Not very often.'

'What do you use when you do?'

'Sometimes some coke, sometimes.'

'Have you any on you at the moment?'

'Yeah.'

'You do – what have you got?'

'I've got a bit of coke.'

'Where have you got it?'

'Here.'

Carne took two small bottles out of her pocket and showed them to Shopland, followed by a small sachet that was pinned to her clothing. They contained cocaine. In evident distress, Carne said they had been given to her as a present shortly before she left New York.

Shopland asked Carne if she was feeling unwell. 'When you've dressed we'll take you to another room, it will be a little more comfortable, and get you some refreshments.'

'What will happen to me?' Carne asked.

What happened to Carne was that in April 1986 she was given a nine-month prison sentence, with six months suspended. Apart from having used heroin earlier in her life – as she admitted both to Hazel Shopland and later to the *Sunday Mirror* – she was already on probation for possessing cannabis and cocaine when she came to London carrying both cocaine and the paraphernalia for using it. Yet although she had taken an absurd risk, the officers at Heathrow felt some sympathy for her plight. A senior officer said she was 'not a well girl'; Hazel Shopland thought she was 'very, very nice'.

The Judy Carne case raises another issue connected with the fight against drugs – and one which sees the Customs caught on the horns of a painful dilemma. It concerns the searching of suspects at ports and airports. By asking Carne to remove her clothes, the Customs at least found what they were looking for. But – just as with suspected stuffers and swallowers – the vast majority of searches prove fruitless. Although the Customs have been searching passengers for most of their history, the issue came into prominence in 1987 when a succession of cases were publicised by the news media.

The first case, reported in the *Observer* in February, concerned a pregnant woman who was returning to Britain with her husband and two of their children after a week's holiday in Tenerife. On arriving at Gatwick airport she was searched by Customs officers who suspected her of carrying drugs and asked her to remove her clothes. She told the *Observer* afterwards that she realised the officers suspected she was not really pregnant, but she had expected them to call off their search when they discovered she was. 'They did not,' she said. 'I felt totally humiliated. They acted like the KGB.'

A second case was reported by the *Sunday Telegraph* in March. It arose when an officer at Heathrow found a packet of condoms in the baggage of a woman returning from a holiday in India and suspected her of being a stuffer or swallower. The woman, a thirty-year-old solicitor from North London, was strip-searched and asked for a urine sample. She was arrested and cautioned, and released when the urine test proved negative. Afterwards she complained that it was 'absurd' that she should carry condoms as a precaution against AIDS, as the government advised, and find that she was treated as a drugs smuggler as a result.

Most striking of all were three cases presented by the BBC itself. On 1 March, the *That's Life* programme told the story of a family of four who returned to Cardiff airport after a holiday in Spain. Both the father and his seventeen-year-old son received a full body search: their hair, ears, armpits and mouths were all searched and finally they were asked to remove their clothes and bend over. The father, a practising Catholic, said afterwards that he felt 'physically sick' and complained that when the family were finally released after two and a half hours they received neither explanation nor apology.

That's Life received hundreds of letters, including two dozen describing similar experiences, and it returned to the subject in April. This time it reported the experiences of a couple who were held for seven and a half hours at Hull docks and received an internal search from a doctor using an instrument known as a sigmoidoscope. Their own doctor said that the man had been passing blood since and that his companion was taking tranquillisers as she had become 'trembly and distraught'. The programme also described the case of a seventeen-year-old girl in a school party returning to Dover from Amsterdam. An officer who searched her baggage found a beer-mat from an Amsterdam café where cannabis was known to be sold. She too was strip-searched and asked to bend over. The girl told *That's Life* it was a 'terrifying' experience.

The succession of cases caused tremors within the higher echelons of the Customs, particularly as they had been engaged in a campaign to win public sympathies over staffing and resources, as well as in a dispute with police over their territorial limits. The issue received a further airing in the House of Commons in April when a Scottish MP raised the case of a young woman constituent who had been strip-searched at Glasgow airport when she was having her period. But in dealing with the criticism, the Customs faced several difficulties.

The Customs were certainly aware of the problem as they receive up to 100 complaints a year from aggrieved passengers which they answer in as much detail as they can. And when the Board of Commissioners enquired about the cases raised by the media, they learned, for example, that some stuffers and swallowers are indeed careless enough to carry their surplus condoms in their baggage. The couple held at Hull docks were considered legitimate suspects because of an entry on CEDRIC. The seventeen-year-old schoolgirl was at risk because preventive staff are instructed to regard *any* evidence of association with drugs abroad, however indirect, as justification for a full search.

However, the Customs have made it a firm rule not to present the reasons for their searches in public, partly for reasons of personal confidentiality, but also to preserve their operational secrets. So when they responded in public they did so only in general terms. Their case was argued by Peter Brooke, the Treasury Minister who was then responsible for the Customs, in an answer in the House of Commons and in letters to MPs. Brooke said that 'the difficulties facing Customs officers as they seek to intercept smuggled drugs or apprehend those responsible can be readily appreciated'. He pointed out that 'drugs smugglers have been found among almost every category of passenger', and added: 'As far as possible the Customs endeavour to target their operations on likely carriers and it is not surprising that drugs smugglers present themselves as innocent passengers. At times they feign distress or become aggressive in order to persuade an officer not to conduct a search. Unfortunately babies and children have on occasion been used as couriers – the drugs being taped to their bodies.'

Brooke's statements served to remind the critics of the difficulties the Customs face in attempting to control drugs – and he went on to assert that they were instructed to do so 'with tact and courtesy'. But there was a further issue which related to the Customs' powers and how they are defined. Most Customs searches are carried out under the Customs and Excise Management Act of 1979. This allows officers to search passengers where they have 'reasonable grounds'. If passengers object, the Act gives them the right to go before a magistrate or senior Customs officer, who decides whether the grounds are indeed reasonable and whether the search should go ahead. Until the controversy broke, officers simply reported their suspicions to a senior officer, who almost invariably directed that the search should proceed. Now officers have been instructed to tell passengers they can appear before a magistrate if they wish.

Further confusion still exists, however, over what precisely constitutes a search. Under the 1979 Act, it can be anything from asking passengers to take off a jacket, to asking them to remove all their clothes and bend over so that they can be inspected from behind. But since January 1986 searches have also been regulated by the Police and Criminal Evidence Act, which applies to the police and Customs alike.

The Police and Criminal Evidence Act refers to 'intimate searches' and lays down safeguards over how they are to be conducted. They must be performed by a doctor or nurse, and suspects must sign a form giving their consent. Remarkably, however, the Customs and police define the word 'intimate' in different ways.

Home Office guidelines to the police stipulate that *any* examination of

OPERATION RENAISSANCE

A two-year investigation into international cocaine-smuggling brought
the Customs convictions in Britain
and Australia. Conducted by the
Investigation Division's Romeo
team, it entailed hundreds of hours of
painstaking surveillance, culminating
in a series of early morning raids in
London and the arrest of suspected
cocaine couriers in Sydney. *Above*:
Two ID officers study their briefing
documents before raiding a south
London flat. *Left*: An ID officer
carries one of the 'keys' – Customs
slang for a sledgehammer or other
tool, which may be used for breaking
down doors. Officers also carry 'writs
of assistance' – all-purpose warrants
enabling them to conduct searches
without applying to a magistrate, as
the police must do.

OPERATION RENAISSANCE

For a year the Customs tracked the movements of Michael Mescal in the belief that he was one of the organisers of the smuggling operation. Mescal, a Londoner in his thirties, was arrested by uniformed officer Brian Waite (*above*) at Heathrow in March 1986 after arriving on a flight from Rio. While Mescal was being searched, plain-clothes officers took the opportunity to examine his baggage (*left*). Nothing incriminating was found. Mescal was charged with conspiring to smuggle drugs into England and Australia. He protested his innocence throughout and in May 1987 was acquitted on both charges.

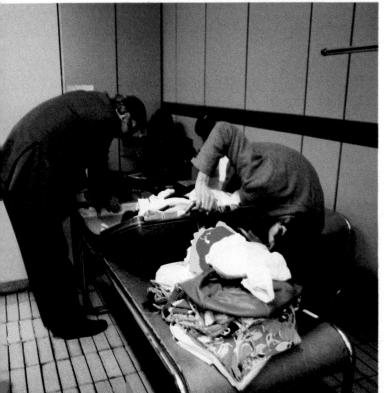

Three months before Mescal's arrest, 3 kg of cocaine were found inside a concealed compartment in a red Samsonite suitcase he had owned. The suitcase was brought into Heathrow from Rio by a man who was stopped in the Green Channel, and who was sent to prison for twelve years. *Left*: An official of the Government Chemist analyses the cocaine. Mescal, who was first questioned in a Customs interview room at Terminal Three (*below*), explained that he had bought the suitcase to carry currency and gems, and that he had lent it to a friend in South America. He denied knowing what happened to it after that, and no further evidence linking him to the suitcase was produced.

OPERATION RENAISSANCE

Shortly before the Customs' raid in London, three suspects were arrested 13,000 miles away in Sydney, Australia (*left*). Three Samsonite-type suitcases were seized and found to contain 4.5 kg of cocaine, neatly packed in transparent packages and concealed in a false compartment. *Below*: Hugh Donagher, the leader of the Romeos, examines one of the concealments with his Australian colleagues – a gratifying climax to a long and arduous investigation. In June 1987, the Romeos seized 57 kg of cocaine in a raid in London's Harley Street – the largest cocaine haul ever made in Britain.

THE RED AND THE GREEN

With 16 million people passing through Heathrow each year, the airport presents the Customs with a daunting challenge. In the 'rush-hour' between 6 and 10 a.m., a dozen jumbo jets disgorge thousands of passengers who head for the Green Channel after collecting their baggage (*above*). Which ones should the Customs stop? And are their decisions based on luck, instinct, or the 'revenue nose' – the mysterious sixth sense that officers are supposed to acquire? Whatever the answer, seizures of hard drugs such as heroin and cocaine are mounting, suggesting that the Customs are becoming more and more skilled in catching the smugglers out. *Left*: A passenger contemplates the choice – anything to declare?

THE RED AND THE GREEN

Passengers who go into the Green Channel (*left*), signifying 'nothing to declare', run the risk of being stopped by uniformed officers, whose questioning usually follows a well-tried routine. 'Is this all your baggage? Did you pack it all yourself? Are you are aware of your duty-free allowances?' Officers look for signs of nervousness or unease. Do passengers seem over-friendly? Do they look the officer in the eye? And can they account for where they have been? Officers believe that if they persist, a dubious story will eventually collapse. 'The more you go into it,' one says, 'the more they say, then suddenly the whole house of cards comes tumbling down.' Most passengers, however, are law-abiding, like the woman being questioned *above*, and before long are on their way home.

SURVEILLANCE

VAT investigations are among the most demanding and complex that the Customs undertake. And even though Operation Breaker, carried out in Birmingham in 1986, was relatively straightforward, it still required countless hours of watching and waiting for the target to show himself. *Above*: During a bitterly cold winter, two officers wait in hope of seeing their suspect. *Centre*: Officers spend up to twelve hours at a time in cramped surveillance posts, peering through a tiny aperture, camera at the ready, waiting for their target to appear. *Below*: After weeks of surveillance, Kirit Fatania, VAT fraudster, finally showed himself to a Customs investigation team – and a BBC camera-crew – outside a bank in Leicester. He was later arrested and sentenced to three years.

THE CUTTERS

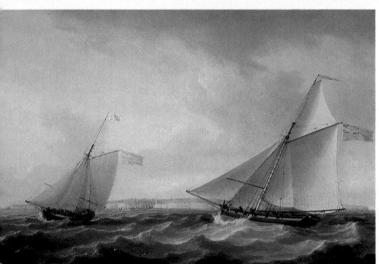

The Customs have been in the front line of Britain's sea defences against smugglers since Charles II introduced the first revenue cutters in the 1660s. In the 1820s (*left*) the cutters were the fastest vessels afloat. There were around ninety in all, heavily armed to deal with the threat of the smuggling gangs. There are seven Customs patrol boats – five 20-metre cutters and two 33-metre cruisers – in service today. They are no longer armed, and their crews do four-month spells between their normal Customs duties. In November 1986, the cruiser *Seeker* spent fifty-six hours in the Irish Sea in pursuit of cannabis smugglers. The photograph *above*, showing skipper Jim Nicholson at the helm, with first officer Chris Pratt and crewman Tom Hawthorne (with binoculars), was taken at dawn after a force eight gale.

THE CUTTERS

The *Seeker*, like her nineteenth-century predecessors, offers smugglers a formidable foe. At top speed (*above*) she cuts through the water at more than 20 knots. Launched in 1979, she is designed like a naval patrol boat, and has scored some notable successes. In 1981 she took part in a joint operation with the French Customs to track down an ocean tug, the *Sea Rover*, which was attempting to smuggle cannabis up the English Channel. In 1984, off the coast of Essex, she helped intercept a schooner, the *Robert Gordon*, carrying $4\frac{1}{2}$ tons of cannabis – Europe's largest single drugs haul. In November 1986, in Operation Bach, she helped seize $1\frac{1}{2}$ tons of cannabis at a beach in South Wales.

AUNTIE'S BAG

Some international flights arriving at Heathrow (*above*) are known as 'target flights' and receive the Customs' close attention. They are usually from the source countries of drugs – Colombia and Bolivia for cocaine, India, Pakistan and West Africa for heroin. They are often boarded by 'rummage crews' (*left*) – a term that applied to the officers who searched the holds of ships, and has now been extended to airports. The rummage officers look for drugs that may have been left on the plane for an accomplice to pick up. Sometimes they find drugs that frightened couriers have abandoned at the last minute.

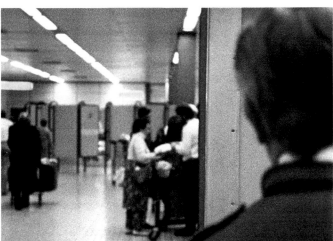

Baggage from the target flights is often examined on the airport tarmac before it is delivered to its owners. Officers may search through the cases themselves – or they may give the task to one of the Customs' dogs trained to sniff out drugs, like labrador Glen (*above*), waiting with his handler, officer Jessie Follington, before being led along the line of bags. In December 1985 the tarmac crew found a suitcase containing heroin off a flight from Pakistan. Its owner was questioned in the Green Channel – and filmed by the BBC at the same time (*left*). She was arrested and eventually sent to prison for six years.

POTEEN

Distilling illicit liquor, or poteen – pronounced pocheen – is a time-honoured activity in Ireland. Despite its romantic aura – poteen is also known as 'mountain dew' – it costs the Exchequer thousands of pounds in excise duty, and also carries severe health risks. In September 1986 the Belfast investigation unit raided an illicit still (*above*) housed in a farm near Ballymena (*left*). In a scene reminiscent of the US Prohibition era (*right*), officers tipped away hundreds of gallons of 'wash' – the liquid from which the alcohol is distilled.

POTEEN

The Belfast officers seized the distilling equipment, including the barrels that had contained the wash (*left*). The owner, John Wilson (*below*), had been observed selling his poteen in Ballymena market that morning. When he was arrested, he protested that he was a 'broken-down farmer' who had difficulty making ends meet. When the Customs officers left, Wilson went back to feeding his ducks.

With almost two million cars, four-teen million passengers, and one million commercial vehicles each year, Dover (*left*) presents the Customs with as much of a challenge as Heathrow. In the summer officers may have to examine one thousand cars an hour, and most are sent on their way with a mere nod of the head. Dover naturally tempts the smugglers, who reckon the odds against being detected are heavily in their favour. But the Dover Customs play the odds too, drawing on a mixture of instinct and experience to choose whom to search. They make several seizures of cannabis each week, together with some of heroin and cocaine. Ordinary tourists may risk taking through an extra bottle of whisky or pack of cigarettes – but one seizure filmed by the BBC far exceeded that. In July 1986, officer Pete Sokhi (shown in the BBC still *below*) searched a Volvo and found 160 bottles of spirits. He asked the driver what he was going to do with it. 'Drink it,' the driver replied. He received a suspended prison sentence.

THE CHANCERS

Dover harbour (*above*) has seen a soaring increase in traffic in the past ten years, and is now being modernised to attract even more. The Customs fear that drugs are increasingly being smuggled among consignments of freight, but they are handicapped by the sheer volume of traffic passing through. *Left*: Officer Debbie Walker questions a driver arriving in the freight lanes in the small hours; he is soon on his way. Despite all the difficulties, the Dover freight officers have made substantial finds, especially of cannabis and tobacco. But they still worry about the contraband they miss. 'It's horrifying to think at the end of the shift, what have I let through?' Debbie Walker says. 'But you just have to do your best.'

the bodily orifices counts as an intimate search, even if it is only a 'visual' search and there is no physical contact at all. The Customs define intimate searches more narrowly, as those which involve physical contact, like the search carried out by a doctor on the couple at Hull. The Customs do not consider searches where suspects merely have to remove all their clothes as 'intimate' and thus conduct them under the 1979 Customs and Excise Management Act, where fewer safeguards apply.

It is true that, like the police, the Customs have guidelines which officers are intended to follow, as when Hazel Shopland told Judy Carne she would be required to remove only one half of her clothing at a time, and Peter Brooke referred to these in his answers to MPs. But, on the evidence of some of the cases considered by *That's Life,* these guidelines are not always followed, as several passengers complained that they had indeed been required to remove all their clothes.

The confusion over just what constituted a strip-search presented the Customs with further difficulties. As the controversy grew, they were naturally asked how successful their searches proved to be. Since the Police and Criminal Evidence Act requires them to keep statistics, they were able to say that they had carried out – on their own definition – 816 intimate searches in 1986, and 224 had been positive. The Customs also said that 46,000 searches had been carried out under the 1979 Customs and Excise Management Act. They pointed out that this represented no more than one in a thousand passengers entering Britain. But they were unable to say how many of these were full strip-searches or what proportion achieved positive results.

The best guess comes from individual officers, who say their 'gut feeling' is that the success rate varies between one in five and one in eight. Inside the Customs, opinions vary on whether that rate is too high or too low in achieving a balance between attempting to control drugs and respecting individual rights. One senior official illustrated the dilemma by pointing out that the only way to be absolutely sure that no one was carrying drugs would be to subject every passenger to a full strip-search.

The issue is unlikely to go away. *That's Life* joined forces with the Consumers' Association and the National Council for Civil Liberties to press for legislation to bring Customs search procedures under tighter control. In reply to more than 5000 viewers who wrote asking what they should do if the Customs wanted to search them, *That's Life* forwarded a recommendation from the Consumers' Association that passengers unwilling to be searched should withhold their consent and say: 'I assert positively that you have no grounds.'

The National Council for Civil Liberties drafted an amendment to the Criminal Justice Bill which was before Parliament in June 1987. The amendment would have tightened up the grounds on which searches could be conducted, required officers to explain those grounds to passengers, insisted that all strip-searches were carried out by medical staff in proper surroundings, and given passengers the right of appeal. The amendment was lost, along with the entire Criminal Justice Bill, when the government called a general election. But the NCCL intends to persevere.

Inside the Customs, the immediate response was to consider ways of lessening the shock for innocent passengers who are searched. A recent management survey had shown that, despite the Customs' guidelines, training in this area was sadly deficient. Officers are now to be taught that instead of abandoning passengers after a search they should keep talking to them in an attempt to assuage the distress that many feel. Nonetheless the dilemma is unlikely to be fully resolved so long as drugs retain their present high ranking on the political agenda. Plenty of Customs staff remain embarrassed at what they are asked to do, particularly women officers who sometimes feel that their male colleagues ask them to conduct searches rather too readily.

Charlotte Lockwood is a 'one-ring', or assistant officer, who has worked at Heathrow since 1980. Although the number of women officers in the Customs is rising, there are still few in the higher ranks. It was not until 1971 that women could work as preventive officers at all, apart from a handful employed as 'search officers' when searches of women passengers were required. And it is precisely this matter, Lockwood feels, which marks a difference of approach, particularly towards women passengers from India or Asia, who may never have appeared unclothed even in front of their husbands, and who may be arriving in Britain for the first time.

'They often can't understand why they have been asked to be searched,' she says. 'My male colleagues will say, "Will you search this lady because she comes from India and she hasn't got a lot of money with her," or whatever reason they've got that she might be a drug smuggler. You take them in there and you don't want to actually say to them, "I think you could be carrying drugs," so you say, "This is nothing personal against you and we've been asked to bring you in here." Yet at the same time you've got to be thorough and do a good search. You know you can't be embarrassed because you want them to lift their top off or take their trousers off, and for them it's really humiliating.'

It appears that some male passengers may be almost as embarrassed that a woman officer should search their suitcases, particularly when she comes upon dirty underwear – 'They don't want us to pick it up in front of other passengers,' Lockwood says – or sexy magazines: 'They were probably going to ditch them in the toilet outside before they go home

Warning

Entering the GREEN channel
with goods to declare is an offence
and can lead to seizure of goods
fines or imprisonment

GOODS to declare

NOTHING to declare

?

DUTY FREE

If you are in any doubt
go into the RED channel

HM Customs and Excise

Welcome to Britain

If you notice anything unusual,
or if you know ANYTHING that you
think might help HM Customs and
Excise in their fight against drug
smuggling, you can now pass this
information DIRECTLY to
Customs investigation
officers...

DRUG
SMUGGLING

...just dial 100 and ask for:

FREEFONE CUSTOMS DRUGS

Your information will be treated
CONFIDENTIALLY and your identity
will be protected.

Your prompt action could help trap a drug smuggler.

HM CUSTOMS AND EXCISE – protecting society

The warning at Heathrow's Terminal
Three (*above left*) might seem inti-
midating – but then deterrence is an
important part of the Customs' role.
Other notices (*above*) are more wel-
coming – and seek the public's help
in the fight against drugs. *Below*:
Heathrow officer Charlotte Lockwood
shows a passenger the way. 'There are
times when I hate the job,' she says.
'But most of the time I like it. I like
it when I've done a good day's work
and I've been successful – when I've
found some revenue goods, a coat or
a video camera, or even some drugs
if I'm lucky.'

to their wives.' Lockwood can tell when men are carrying contraceptives. 'They look away as you're going through and you know you're going to find something.'

Lockwood also helps to explain the impassivity that some passengers interpret as coldness when they are being searched. It is, she says, an instinctive response to passengers who look as though they are becoming angry, particularly when they are asked to remove their clothes. 'They could turn round to you and say, "You're lesbians" and this sort of stuff. But you can't react in any way, otherwise you'd lose control of the situation, so you've just got to let the insults go straight over your head.'

Lockwood nonetheless believes she knows how they feel. 'If it happened to me,' she says, 'I'd be horrified.'

On 9 August 1985, the Customs staff at Heathrow received a visit from the Prime Minister, Margaret Thatcher. It was one of those occasions when Mrs Thatcher displayed her determination and her concern. The visit followed a spate of newspaper and television reports over the increasing use of heroin in Britain, and Mrs Thatcher inspected the Customs' haul from the previous week, which included 4kg of heroin, as well as 106kg of cannabis, 0.5kg of cocaine and 5300 Mandrax tablets, valued in all at over £500,000. She also examined a shaving-soap aerosol which had been used to smuggle heroin, a false-bottomed suitcase, a wooden table which had contained cannabis, and a hollowed-out ski.

Mrs Thatcher was typically uncompromising in her remarks. 'We have to beat the drug smugglers,' she declared. 'They can undermine a whole generation and corrupt everything.' She was then asked how the Customs could fight drugs effectively if they were hampered by a lack of staff and resources. 'If that is so we will put it right,' she replied. 'We have never scrimped in any way on resources for law and order and this is a very big part of it. Some of the sums involved make bank robberies look comparatively small. This is a very important matter and they must not be hampered by lack of equipment or by numbers of people. Anything more we can do will be done and must be done.'

It may seem surprising that such a forthright declaration should receive a mixed response among Customs officers, but that is precisely what occurred. One senior officer present was quoted as saying: 'It is absolutely wonderful – just what our staff wanted to hear. If Mrs Thatcher carries out her promises, morale here will soar.' But other officers were not so ready to endorse Mrs Thatcher's remarks, for they were feeling frustrations too deep to be assuaged by a single visit to Heathrow.

The sudden surge of drugs into Britain came at a bad time for the Customs, for the 1970s had already brought several major changes. In 1971 there was a wholesale reorganisation which abolished the Customs' distinctive career structure and brought them in line with the rest of the Civil Service. In 1972 the Customs were given the task of collecting VAT. That brought an influx of staff that further altered the service, as well as new work that many officers regarded as mundane and tedious. And the following year, 1973, Britain entered the Common Market, thus inheriting a vast range of new tariffs to be administered that seemed to multiply endlessly and attain levels of daunting complexity.

The Customs struggled to adjust to these changes as the flow of drugs increased. Then came the general election of 1979. The new government launched an attack on what it regarded as the non-productive elements of society. That included the Civil Service – and the Customs found themselves lumped in too. In keeping with the government's aim of cutting the Civil Service by 500,000 staff, the overall strength of the Customs and Excise fell from 28,870 to 25,309 over the next five years. Of the department's three main divisions – Customs, Excise, and VAT – the heaviest burden fell on the Customs themselves, which dropped from 7591 to 6552. And of these, the preventive staff – principally the uniformed officers at ports and airports – were the hardest hit, falling from 3400 to 2700.

By a painful irony, it was precisely now that the importation of drugs rose most dramatically. In 1979 the Customs seized 43kg of heroin; in 1984 the figure was 312kg. Cocaine seizures rose from 21kg to 78kg in the same period.

To this paradox was added the Customs' envious view that, while they were suffering from massive cuts, their colleagues in the police were rewarded with generous pay rises. The pay scales of the two services widened, so that police now earn about one-third more than Customs officers at equivalent levels. The higher up the scale, the greater the discrepancies become. As a Civil Service assistant secretary, the head of the Investigation Division, Dick Lawrence, earns £27,000 – roughly the same earnings, with overtime, as a detective-sergeant in the Metropolitan Police.

The police also appeared to benefit from the activities of the Association of Chief Police Officers, one of the most powerful pressure groups in Britain, nominally accountable to local police committees and the Home Office but in fact able to formulate its own policy on a wide range of subjects. Its members also speak their minds without inhibition on topics ranging from the miners' strike to AIDS. The dissatisfaction of Customs officers was increased by the fact that there was no equivalent body to speak out on their behalf.

In the Customs, the nearest counterpart to ACPO is the Board of Commissioners. It is the direct descendant of the seventeenth-century board which first met in the Board Room of the Custom House in Lower

Thames Street, overlooking the Pool of London. Today's Board meets in the Customs headquarters, King's Beam House – the 'King's beam' was the weighing post outside most Custom houses – in Mark Lane in the City.

The Board has nine members. From 1983 to 1987 its chairman was Sir Angus Fraser, a Scotsman who, after graduating from Glasgow University and spending two years on National Service, joined the Customs as an assistant principal at the age of twenty-four. In his spare time he became Britain's acknowledged expert on the nineteenth-century writer and traveller George Borrow, and in public he sometimes appeared a shy and thoughtful man.

Of Sir Angus's eight fellow board members, most were Civil Service administrators by background and only one had spent the major part of his career in the 'outfield', as an officer of Customs and Excise. To some Customs' staff, that provided sufficient explanation of the Board's reluctance to speak up in public – and its apparent inability to secure the resources the Customs needed.

In fact, unlike ACPO, the Customs Board, as an orthodox Civil Service body, has no right or power to criticise the government in public. In private, however, it is a different matter. Sir Angus Fraser's reputation among his colleagues was as a doughty fighter on the Customs' behalf, emotionally committed to their cause, and able to mix equally with Customs officers in the field as well as to argue their case among the Whitehall élite, particularly during the annual bids for expenditure, which occur behind closed doors.

A further explanation why the Customs have sometimes appeared to lack an effective political sponsor in the hurly-burly of Westminster and Whitehall lies in their historical role. Between 1983 and 1987 the most fluent politician on the subject of drugs was David Mellor, both as a Home Office minister and as head of the ministerial group on the misuse of drugs. Although Mellor sometimes appeared to speak on the Customs' behalf, the Customs – as traditional collectors of revenue – were in fact accountable to the Treasury.

Faced with the clamour from major spending ministries like Education, Health and Defence, Treasury ministers spend most of their energies resisting rather than encouraging their colleagues' demands. From 1981 to 1985 the Treasury minister responsible for the Customs was Barney Hayhoe, who is now chiefly remembered for telling the Customs that they had to accept their share of the Civil Service cuts. His successor, Ian Gow, was more expansive but was unable to fulfil his promises as he resigned after only a short time in office in protest at government policy on Northern Ireland.

When the government first imposed its cuts it thus largely escaped any

Many Custom houses, like Liverpool's (*above*), built in the 1830s, are structural masterpieces befitting the days when Britain was a great trading nation. The Long Room of the London Custom House (depicted in the 1800s by Rowlandson, *left*) was a bustle of activity as traders queued to pay their dues. The original London Custom House, close to Tower Bridge in the Pool of London, was destroyed in the Great Fire. It was replaced by Christopher Wren, but his Custom House was damaged by fire in 1715 and then burned down completely in 1814. Its successor, although hit by bombs in 1940, has survived to this day. Many smaller Custom Houses are architectural gems. That at Poole in Dorset (*below*) was built in 1814 and is still in use today. In the foreground stands the 'King's Beam' – the official scales for weighing goods and calculating duty, introduced by Edward I in the twelfth century.

controversy. It was only when the Customs' trade unions joined the battle that the debate entered the public domain. Two unions were involved: the Society of Civil and Public Servants and the Civil and Public Services Association. When the first cuts were imposed in 1979 they were slow to form any overall strategy. Instead they resisted in piecemeal fashion at individual posts and ports and admit now that they offered an easy target. The unions also felt inhibited over how much they should reveal about the effects of the cuts. They felt that the Customs' controls were being jeopardised, but they were also aware – like individual officers – that if they revealed the Customs' weaknesses, smugglers might be further encouraged. Some officers in fact feel they have already been reduced to a presentational role, where their most important goal is to *appear* effective rather than actually to be so. But to admit to that risks reducing their effectiveness still further.

In the end the unions decided that their greater loyalty was to their members. In 1983 they published a report declaring that Customs controls had reached 'crisis point' and that the problem of heroin was 'much more serious than officially acknowledged'. They pointed out that on average only one in a hundred passengers at Heathrow was questioned and that at peak periods the figure could fall to one in 400. 'We seek to demonstrate that large quantities of heroin are being brought into the UK with comparative ease and point out that the effects will be suffered for many years,' the report said.

When the report was published, the government promised that its findings would be considered by a House of Commons committee. The hearings were cancelled when the government called a general election. The unions tried again in 1984, this time arguing that 'the lowering of Customs controls has made a significant contribution to the rise in the smuggling of heroin. ... Despite the best efforts of the Customs Officers engaged on control and investigative activities, the Customs controls operated by HM Customs and Excise are no longer effective.'

For their pains, the unions received a sound rebuke. David Mellor, who had just been appointed head of the ministerial group on drugs, criticised the unions' 'extremely lurid press releases', and claimed that their sole aim was to secure more staff – or, as he elegantly phrased it, 'more bottoms on seats'. The unions persevered. They published two more reports, *United Kingdom – open house for smugglers* and *UK: drugs unlimited,* in which they concluded that 'the present level of Customs controls in the United Kingdom can no longer be regarded as effective' and that 'unless urgent action is taken, the dangers to the health and economy of the country from smuggling will increase'.

This time Mellor told the unions that their case was 'irresponsible', 'seriously misleading', and 'propaganda'. The unions' fears were not assuaged when Mellor made a well-publicised tour of South America, visiting four cocaine-producing countries and disbursing £1.5 million to help equip their anti-drugs forces, a move which he argued was vital if the fight against drugs was to be maintained on a 'broad front'. But even £1.5 million was a tiny amount compared to the US government's expenditure – in 1987 it allocated $300 million to a three-year programme in Bolivia – and Customs officers asked whether it could not have been used to boost their resources instead.

So when Mrs Thatcher visited Heathrow in October 1985, to declare herself an unequivocal supporter of the Customs, it was understandable that some officers should consider her conversion long overdue. That feeling was accompanied by anxiety at the spectacle of politicians suddenly espousing a cause from which they had hitherto averted their eyes. Some officers feared that the government was making a high-profile commitment to keep drugs out of Britain, while still denying the Customs the resources they needed. Their scepticism was increased when the government launched a propaganda campaign against heroin whose aim appeared to be to demonstrate the government's concern rather than do anything concrete about it. They also feared that if the campaign failed they could become the most convenient scapegoats.

Nonetheless, the year of Mrs Thatcher's visit brought the turning of the tide. In October 1984 Mellor had announced that a hundred Customs jobs which were due to be cut would be reprieved, and a further fifty were restored in June 1985. From then on, the Customs' strength continued to rise. They acquired greater clout in Whitehall by being grouped with the forces of law and order, and their new minister, Peter Brooke, found it easier to persuade his Treasury colleagues to fund the increase in staff and resources that Sir Angus Fraser and the Customs Board argued for. By 1988 the Customs' strength will have risen to 26,647, from its low point of 25,309 in 1984.

The unions are not slow to point out that this will still leave the Customs well short of their 1979 level of 28,870. They also point out that in the same period the Customs have had to contend with a fifty per cent increase in passengers and freight, and have taken on other new burdens that range from the expansion of the Common Market to the requirements of the Police and Criminal Evidence Act.

The official Customs response is to describe the reconsideration of priorities and streamlining of resources that took place while the Customs strength fell and rose. Preventing drugs and collecting VAT are now the most important goals. The Investigation Division has been continually strengthened, with further emphasis on targeting suspected smugglers and organisers; intelligence and mobile task force teams have been appointed; dog-training and aerial surveillance have been boosted.

The view that the government was now doing its best for the Customs was endorsed – with a certain ambiguity – by the House of Commons Home Affairs Committee, which stated in 1986: 'We urge the Government to give, as we believe it is doing, the highest priority to the provision to HM Customs of all the necessary manpower and equipment that may be shown to be essential for the attack on the drug traffic, and to ensure that there is no reduction in staff employed on drug-related duties while drug smuggling presents such an acute problem.'

However, a number of Customs officers are yet to be convinced. As part of the Customs' increase in resources, they were allocated £10 million to be spent on the research and development of new equipment. The Customs' technical experts, together with the Government Chemist, have been considering proposals for equipment that will detect drugs automatically, while causing a minimum of inconvenience, but as yet this remains a boffin's dream. The Government Chemist has been evaluating a security gate, similar to the explosives 'sniffer' installed at the House of Commons, which would analyse particles in the air by means of gas chromatography. But it remains crude and expensive, and does not react to well-wrapped cannabis which gives off no particles at all.

Other hi-tech schemes have so far proved wanting. British Airways have demonstrated a 'Condor' drugs-detection machine based on mass spectrometry, but it costs a formidable £2.5 million and has a very slow reaction time. There are proposals for equipment to detect drugs via their nuclear magnetic resonance, or through ultrasonics which would measure their differing absorption patterns, but none of these have advanced far beyond the drawing board.

For many officers at Terminal Three, the neatest symbol of these endeavours was the machine which stood at the entrance to the Green Channel for much of 1986. Emblazoned with the words 'Drugs Screening Unit', it resembled a security screening gate. The Customs' press office hailed it as a piece of sophisticated technological equipment which would deter or detect smugglers by sensing drugs from their aroma.

The Drugs Screening Unit proved less sophisticated in practice. It was based on American equipment developed in the 1970s as a safety measure for detecting refrigeration fumes, and was donated by the US Customs. The Government Chemist tested it and promised the Terminal Three staff that it would work. It indeed proved efficient at detecting heavy smokers, women wearing perfume, and diabetics. 'But I don't think we caught anyone with drugs,' a Terminal Three officer says.

For a time passengers were asked to pass through the gate in the hope that it would act as a deterrent, but late in 1986 it was quietly removed. At Terminal Three there was one conclusion to be drawn: there is no substitute for a trained, experienced and well-motivated Customs officer.

CHAPTER FOUR
SURVEILLANCE

The VAT computer should really have noticed that someone was running a fraud. The computer, housed near the VAT headquarters at Southend, processes six million returns each year from the one and a half million traders who are registered for VAT, and collects almost £5 billion a year on the government's behalf. Since financial transactions on such a scale sadly provide no shortage of opportunities for fraud, the computer has also been programmed to issue a warning when something appears amiss – a microchip equivalent of the 'revenue nose'. But in this instance the computer stayed mute.

Instead it was the hard-pressed staff of the Customs' local VAT office in Leicester who first suspected that something was wrong. Clerical officer Patricia Fisher – a girl-guide leader in her spare time – noticed a growing number of forms from knitwear companies which had been filled out in suspiciously similar handwriting. The company names had a familiar ring too, and most of their addresses were in residential areas of Leicester. Mrs Fisher wondered whether there really could be so many small family businesses making women's and children's clothes in their back rooms, all claiming VAT repayments of between £500 and £1000 each quarter. But for her alertness, and that of her colleague Susan Norton, the Leicester fraud might have gone undetected.

The files on the case reached Alan Huish in December 1985. Huish, a Welshman in his mid-forties, with greying wavy hair, was a senior investigation officer at the Birmingham branch of the Investigation Division, based in a typically anonymous tower block overlooking the traffic on the Birmingham Bull Ring. After joining the Customs at the age of twenty, he graduated to what was still called the Investigation Branch in 1971. It consisted of fewer than a hundred officers, regarded as an élite by the rest of the Customs, and Huish was one of just a dozen officers accepted that year out of 600 who applied.

Huish first dealt with pornography, then a political minefield by virtue of several spectacular trials, including the prosecution of the radical magazine *Oz* and the exposure of corruption among Scotland Yard's pornography squad. Huish survived, to join a VAT investigation team led by Dick Lawrence, the present head of the Investigation Division. He next headed his own team pursuing VAT evasion in West End night clubs, a task with distractions which included interviewing show-girls wearing nothing more than feather head-dresses and shoes. He spent from 1980 to 1985 on drugs work – heroin followed by cocaine – before being posted to Birmingham to head its eight-strong VAT investigation team. It therefore fell to Huish, when he examined the files collected by Mrs Fisher, to decide what action to take.

No VAT investigations are begun lightly. They can be frighteningly complex, can drag on for years, and may even never be resolved at all. One officer in Birmingham's local investigation unit had already spent four years trying to pin down a VAT fraud that kept growing before his eyes; each time he thought he was near the end he found a new aspect to be investigated. In another case the Birmingham ID had amassed *four tons* of files which were piled up around the office walls for months.

Some investigative officers claim to like working through the mountains of paper that VAT cases entail, pursuing a fraud like a strand in a skein of wool. Others admit that they find VAT impossibly tedious, and count the days until their spell of duty on VAT ends. Some older officers even contend that the point when the Customs assumed responsibility for collecting the new tax in April 1973 marks one of the darker moments in the Customs' history.

When VAT was introduced, replacing the old purchase tax in order to harmonise Britain's tax system with the rest of the European Community, the Chancellor of the Exchequer said he was determined that Britain should have 'the simplest VAT in Europe'. Businesses or traders who charged VAT were to pass the revenue on to the government; at the same time they would be refunded any VAT they had paid themselves. At first the Customs believed that the tax would prove as simple to collect as the government had claimed. They also assumed, in the words of one senior officer, that traders would 'play fair'. There were shocks on both scores.

The key to VAT was that it handed money to people who were then required to pass it on to the government. As a result, some of the most prestigious companies in Britain devised every conceivable method to delay their VAT repayments. A company owing £1 million can earn £10,000 interest on that sum in a month, and a new vocabulary had to be devised – involving such techniques as 'differential tax staggers', 'fragmentation' and 'disaggregation' – to describe what a senior VAT officer calls 'whole new concepts of tax avoidance'.

Tax *avoidance* is, of course, perfectly legal; tax *evasion* is not. Here the Customs had been more realistic about the capacity of human imagination for wrong-doing, and a special team had already been preparing for the new methods of tax evasion the Customs would have to deal with. The most basic was VAT 'suppression' – collecting the VAT and then simply failing to pass it on to the government – which soon proved prevalent in businesses dealing mostly in cash, such as construction, pubs and restaurants, and the rag trade.

But within six months of the introduction of VAT, the Customs found themselves dealing with ingenious variations of frauds they had encountered elsewhere. In the classic long-firm fraud, for example, a company gradually builds up a reputation for reliability – and then suddenly incurs a massive debt and vanishes. The variation, especially designed for VAT, was the *short-firm* fraud. New companies set up in business, claimed VAT repayments for two or three quarters, and then disappeared. On investigation they were found to consist of an office which had been equipped with desks, typewriters and telephones solely for the VAT officer's benefit.

Just as in other areas of their activities, no sooner had the Customs caught up with the latest methods of evasion and avoidance than new ones would be devised. After the short-firm fraud came the 'Phoenix syndrome', whereby a company which owes VAT and other tax declares itself bankrupt. A new company arises in its place, often with the same directors, leaving the Customs to try to collect the tax due from its predecessor. Next came the 'multicell syndrome', where traders pass VAT on through a series of companies. A company in the middle of the chain suddenly disappears, defying the Customs to track it down.

The most breath-taking VAT frauds arose from gold. At first VAT was charged on gold bullion but not on items made of gold, like coins. It was a simple matter to import coins, melt them down and convert them to bullion, making a trouble-free fifteen per cent profit – the prevailing VAT rate. When the law was changed so that VAT was charged on coins, some traders simply smuggled them into Britain instead. The frauds became so widespread that VAT investigation teams throughout Britain were involved, and the Customs estimate that the government lost £200 million before the law was changed. Some of the cases were so complex and extensive that it took up to six years to bring them to court.

One of the most spectacular was not concluded until June 1987, when three businessmen were convicted after a five-month trial at the Old Bailey and were sent to prison for up to four years. They were part of a gang which had made £20 million from a VAT fraud involving gold transactions in just seven months – and although the Customs' enquiries extended from Hatton Garden to Canada, Israel, Germany and Switzerland, none of that money was ever recovered.

VAT also provided an opportunity for professional criminals to increase their profits from other crimes. The gang who carried out the £26 million Brinks Mat bullion raid at Heathrow in 1983 made a further £1½ million in VAT as they worked the gold back into the legitimate gold market (although some VAT officers view the word 'legitimate' when applied to gold markets as a contradiction in terms). It was the Customs' analysis of the gold transactions which was largely responsible for securing convictions when gang-members appeared in court.

Some VAT investigative officers tend to acquire a jaundiced view of humanity: the fact that there are now 1.5 million registered traders, one commented, means that there are 1.5 million potential frauds. But to add insult to injury, when the Customs raided suspected VAT offenders they found themselves compared in newpaper headlines to the Gestapo.

Although politicians and media portrayed the raids as the persecution of small businessmen, most were directed at people suspected of major fraud. That was borne out by the findings of the Keith Committee into the Customs' enforcement powers in 1983, which concluded that Customs searches using VAT search warrants issued by magistrates were 'regularly turning up evidence of substantial frauds' and that they were conducting the searches in a 'responsible, not indiscriminate and generally well conducted' manner.

Yet the reputation remained. Even after the Keith Committee had reported, VAT continued to bring the Customs a bad press, with headlines in 1986 referring to 'The VAT Bully Boys'. Many Customs staff still felt that they were struggling against a tide of hostility, compounded by the suspicion that somehow the general public did not regard VAT offences as a real crime, even though offenders were claiming or withholding money which was not theirs. And although the VAT staff suffered less than others from the cuts of 1979–84, they did not see things that way. They felt that the new emphasis on drugs within the Customs gave VAT inquiries a lower priority, and that in the constant competition for resources the drugs teams usually won out.

Most of these considerations were present in Alan Huish's mind when he considered the Leicester fraud. As in all VAT cases, he had to weigh up how much money was involved, how many officers the case might occupy, and how high were the chances of success. But compared with most, the Leicester fraud was breathtakingly simple. *Step 1*: you fill in a form registering a company for VAT. *Step 2*: you fill in another form three months later showing that you have paid more VAT than you have taken in. *Step 3*: you wait for the computer at Southend to send you the balance between the two amounts.

That is, of course, the procedure followed by genuine traders claiming a refund of VAT. In this instance Huish suspected that the companies

THE EXCISEMAN.

The Customs and Excise have not always enjoyed a popular image. When Parliament introduced an Excise duty in 1643 to help pay for Cromwell's army, it was the first tax levied on goods used by the common people. The necessities of life – meat, salt, leather, beer, clothes – were all affected, and the Excise officers had wide powers of entry and search. The new tax was met with protests and riots, and in 1647 the Excise office at Smithfield was burnt down. But when the monarchy was restored in 1660, King Charles II retained the tax, which was gradually extended to more and more items, from tallow candles (taxed at 1d a pound) to commoners' funerals (4s each). Excisemen toured Britain collecting their dues eight times a year, and also ran the hated press gangs which kidnapped men in the streets and forced them into the navy. Small wonder that when Doctor Johnson published his famous dictionary in 1755, he defined Excisemen, like the one shown *left*, as 'Wretches hired by those to whom Excise is paid'.

The Excise have now assumed a more settled role, ranging from collecting taxes at breweries and distillers to issuing licences to pawnbrokers. Until this century the Customs were a separate department, working mainly at the ports where they levied duties and searched for contraband, like the group of officers (*below*) in the 1890s. Although the two departments were merged in 1909 to form HM Customs and Excise, to many people they remain 'the Customs'. While they still attract some opprobrium from tasks like collecting VAT, which began in 1973, they now stand in the front line of Britain's fight against drugs.

in question simply did not exist. The Birmingham investigation unit had already conducted a discreet tour of the suspect addresses. As Susan Norton had guessed, most were in flats and houses in residential areas, with no signs of knitwear businesses to be seen.

Further checking in the Leicester VAT files suggested that at least fifty bogus companies were involved. Whoever was behind them was claiming at least £500 for each company every three months, and had collected over £75,000 so far. Calculating that they would clear £1 million within four years if they were not stopped, Huish gave the task of finding the fraudsters to two of his most experienced officers, Barry Riley and Mel Starling. The investigation was called Operation Breaker, after the CB radio term for interrupting a smooth-flowing conversation.

Riley and Starling formed a neatly complementary pair. Riley, forty-five, from Derbyshire, had spent six years in the British army, including spells with the paratroops and special operations forces, before entering the Customs in 1964, eventually graduating to the Birmingham ID in 1976. He had a phlegmatic appearance which served to conceal the anxieties most investigative officers are prey to. Starling, thirty-one, from Southampton, had spent four years with an ID heroin team in London before being transferred to Birmingham in 1982. In contrast to Riley, he had a fast, nervous manner and openly admitted that he was a 'worrier'. The two men sought relaxation in the same manner, by escaping into the British hills. Riley went walking in the Peak District of Yorkshire, while Starling headed for the English Lake District. 'It's difficult to explain to people who don't do it,' Starling says. 'It's hard work walking uphill, but it's very tranquil – there's a calm that comes over you.'

The qualities the pair brought to the case were the customary ID attributes of dogged persistence, regardless of the vicissitudes of fate, coupled with a painstaking attention to detail which has so often served the ID well. They were guided throughout by Huish, who adopted a stabilising role when nerves began to fray, and negotiated when required with the upper echelons of the Customs' considerable bureaucracy.

The trio's first aim was simply stated: find your adversary. But when they considered how to approach that task, they made an embarrassing discovery. No one from the local VAT office had ever met any representative of the companies which had so far received over £75,000 of the government's money. That was certainly not how it was intended to be when VAT was introduced. Traders registering for VAT were supposed to receive an initial 'educational' visit from a Customs official who would present them with a 'VAT pack' of information about the new tax, to be followed by inspection visits once a year thereafter. Those days had long passed. Today traders receive a visit *on average* once every five years – and some are not visited for eight.

Even though Operation Breaker was less complex than most VAT frauds, it still occupied up to two dozen Investigation Division officers for weeks on end. The Customs are renowned for their painstaking preparations; briefings, like the one shown *left* in the ID's Birmingham offices, are given in meticulous detail. The operation was headed by senior investigation officer Alan Huish (*bottom*), a Welshman who joined the Customs at the age of twenty, and who has since become head of the ID's cocaine branch in London. The case-officer was Barry Riley (*centre*), who joined the Customs after six years in the army, including service as a paratrooper and on special operations. Huish and Riley are aware that VAT is not a popular tax, but insist that fraudsters must be brought to book. 'If someone went into a bank and robbed it of £75,000 there would be a hue and cry,' says Riley. 'Because this man's taken £75,000 Value Added Tax, most people think it's fair game. But that money belongs to the public, and he's stealing from members of the public. That is straight theft.'

As a result, none of the dubious returns in the Leicester case had ever been checked. No one had seen the VAT receipts on which they were supposedly based or even established whether the companies themselves existed. And no one had the remotest idea what anyone involved in the companies looked like.

The second discovery by Huish and his colleagues was almost as disconcerting: their adversary – singular or plural, male or female – appeared to know an unhealthy amount about the VAT system. With its microchip equivalent of the 'revenue nose', the computer had some twenty tripwires that were supposed to warn of dubious claims. They would be triggered, for example, if someone made a series of claims ending in round numbers, or several of over £1000. Somehow their opponents had bypassed these checks. And by closing down each company after only a few claims, they had further reduced the risk of an official visit. Huish and his colleagues concluded that they were dealing with an organised, knowledgeable and skilful team – probably with four members, Huish guessed.

Their immediate goal was obviously to learn more about their opponents. Here they faced the familiar problems, in Customs jargon, of 'showing out'. It would be tempting, for example, to pose as a salesman and call at the suspect addresses. But they had no way of knowing whether the owners or landlords were involved – and even the most innocent-seeming enquiries could betray the Customs' interest.

There was nonetheless one area where the fraudsters had broken cover. When someone registers a company for VAT they have to nominate a bank where their payments are to be sent. The Birmingham team looked up the banks' addresses and Mel Starling approached them for help. Several managers declined on the grounds that their dealings with their clients were confidential, but one official was more co-operative. He told Starling that his client was a tall, smartly-dressed Asian in his mid-twenties, with a moustache but, so far as he could recall, no beard.

The official particularly remembered his customer because he was surprised that he had opened an account in Coventry for a company based in Leicester. The official also showed Starling the business references the man had supplied but they proved only to lead back to other suspect companies. But the Birmingham team at least had a description to go on, and they concluded that the man was probably a 'gofer' – a minor member of the gang, running errands for the principals.

A crucial deadline was approaching. In early January the next set of VAT repayments would fall due, totalling £16,000 in all. That meant that the fraudsters would almost certainly have to reveal themselves, either at the company addresses where the advice notices would be sent, or at the banks where the payments themselves were transferred. This

presented the Birmingham team with the chance of mounting a surveillance operation on the addresses and banks in question to see who
called there. But first there was an important bureaucratic hurdle to
overcome.

Whenever the Southend VAT headquarters had learned in the past
that someone was making false claims it had immediately withheld all
further repayments. For the Investigation Division that proved
immensely frustrating, as their targets usually realised they were under
suspicion and disappeared. The delicate task of persuading Southend to
continue making the payments fell to Alan Huish.

When Huish broached the issue, Southend made it clear that it was
most unhappy at the idea of paying out good government money to
known criminals. In response, Huish deployed two arguments. He said
he was only too aware that Southend had already lost a substantial sum –
now calculated at £86,000 – but contended that the only chance of
recouping that sum was to pay out a little more. Uneasily aware that he
sounded like a gambler arguing that the only way to recover his losses
was to bet his shirt, Huish went on to point out that if Southend were
to halt the payments now, the suspects would almost certainly vanish.
Not without misgivings – which were to surface again later – Southend
agreed.

Birmingham laid its plans. The £16,000 due in January comprised
payments to twelve bogus companies. It would clearly be beyond the
Birmingham team's resources to watch all twelve addresses at once, and
so they decided to start by making just one repayment, trusting that the
fraudsters would assume that the others had been delayed in the Christmas post. The company they selected was named Sirawear, which had
lodged a repayment claim of £887. It had one particular advantage which
they were at first reluctant to admit. Its address was 17 Sandhurst Road,
a predominantly white area of Leicester. If the young Asian described
by the bank official was indeed one of their targets he would – to put it
as neutrally as possible – stand out.

The repayment notice for Sirawear was posted from Southend on 15
January. The next day a surveillance team composed of all eight members
of the Birmingham VAT team, known as the 'B' team, together with the
'A' team who usually handled drugs, took up their positions. Those
allocated to Sandhurst Road took it in turns to sit in a Ford Transit van
parked a short distance along the street, while those outside the bank
stood in the street as nonchalantly as they could, although they did warn
the manager in suitably vague terms that they were there, in case he
thought they were robbers planning a raid.

With one of Britain's worst winters of the century sweeping over the
Midlands, and snow lying a foot deep on the ground, it was bitterly cold.

The officers in the Transit obtained some comfort from Thermos flasks, while those outside the bank were relieved and thawed out at frequent intervals. Meanwhile the repayment advice, which had been dispatched in the normal manner by second-class post, took *six days* to arrive.

Even then the surveillance proved inconclusive. The team kept watch for a further four days after the letter had been delivered. They saw and photographed a number of visitors to Sandhurst Road, among them a young Asian man who arrived in a two-tone Ford Fiesta and *could* have fitted the bank's description. The team were in no position to follow him and when they checked the Fiesta's licence plate it appeared to be registered with its previous owner – and they could not risk approaching him in case he was involved in the fraud himself.

Already Huish, Riley and Starling were becoming worried at the effects on their team of spending so long on the operation to little effect. 'They're going to get absolutely brassed off,' Riley feared, 'and once you start the downward spiral. . . .'

They decided to try again, selecting a second company to watch, the Attwal Manufacturing Co. of 103 Bassett Street, Leicester, which had made a repayment claim for £951. This time, rather than wait on the Post Office, they asked Southend to send the repayment notice to Birmingham by rail. The plan was that two officers would collect the notice from Birmingham New Street station and take it in person to the Leicester sorting office. There it would be handed to the local postman for delivery on his morning round. The 'B' team would thus be ready and waiting in Bassett Street, confident that the letter would be delivered on time.

Everyone agreed that it sounded a fine plan in principle. But when the two officers arrived at New Street at 6 a.m. to collect the package containing the repayment notice, it was nowhere to be found.

Riley and Starling went ahead with the surveillance on Bassett Street in the hope that their targets would call there anyway. There was therefore considerable chagrin among the watching officers when they saw the postman make the delivery at number 103 that *should* have contained the advice from Southend, followed moments later by two young white men who called briefly at the house and then left again. An officer followed the two men into Leicester on foot but had to abandon them near the city centre for fear of showing out. However, as he reported later, their movements appeared in no way suspicious.

That night, Alan Huish reviewed events again with Barry Riley. By now Riley's anxieties were clear. 'The "B" team have got pains in their bottoms from sitting in the same spot for so long,' he said.

'We've just got to keep plodding on,' Huish reassured him. But later that evening Huish revealed his own worries. 'We're hanging on, just waiting,' he said. 'It will come, but it gets difficult because the lads get frustrated as the days go on and nothing is happening. It's a matter of trying to keep them together, keep their objectives clear and their morale ticking over.'

Huish also pointed out the havoc surveillance operations can cause to family and personal relationships. 'They're spending less and less time at home,' he said of his officers. 'The jobs and tasks are not getting done, and wives and children don't always completely understand the situation. It always happens in any lengthy surveillance and other things just go by the board.'

There was another problem Huish was aware of which he did *not* reveal at that time. As he later put it, someone at Southend 'lost his bottle'. By now Southend felt that all its previous misgivings were justified: here were repayments being made to a suspected criminal without any apparent result. It took all Huish's diplomatic skills to stiffen Southend's resolve.

In the morning Riley and Starling embarked on their third attempt to deliver a VAT repayment form, choosing a new company with an address at 16 Avon Street, Leicester, and a bank in Coventry. They decided to use British Rail again – a decision, Riley told the 'B' team in a briefing that evening, 'based on the principle that lightning won't strike twice, and British Rail will not lose the second letter'. Southend duly sent a package containing the new repayment advice to Birmingham that night. When two officers called at New Street at 6 a.m. they were told it had not arrived. British Rail, Riley remarked that morning, had scored a second 'own goal'. It was, he added with commendable restraint, 'unfortunate'.

Riley and Starling still sent the surveillance teams to Coventry in the frail hope – given 'luck and patience' – that they might see one of the fraudsters call at the company bank. Their patience was almost exhausted and they had no luck either. That night Riley's anxiety was starker than ever.

'It's getting increasingly difficult because this is the twelfth day for my team and maintaining the momentum and alertness is always very difficult when nothing appears to be happening and we have wrinkles like the problem with British Rail,' Riley said. 'I say things are going to happen and then they don't, and then the officers on the ground have got to live with the fact that things aren't going to form.'

Riley pointed out that the repayment advices should now be leaving Southend 'in a flood' and that their targets must surely be suspicious that so few payments had arrived. Then Riley turned his frustrations on their invisible opponent or opponents. 'We don't know what he looks like, we don't know how he thinks, we don't know anything about him,' Riley said. 'The feeling I've got is that perhaps he's a little hesitant. He's

One of the biggest problems on operations like the Birmingham VAT fraud is maintaining morale through the days and weeks of watching and waiting. 'The worst thing is boredom,' says case-officer Barry Riley (seen in the driver's seat, *centre*). 'It's repetition, day after day after day, watching the world go by – and hoping that the next vehicle is the one you're interested in.' Surveillance positions can be cramped (*top*), while Britain's winter weather hardly helps. *Below left*: An ID officer phones in to the operation control. Despite all the difficulties, Riley says, ID officers 'are like terriers – if they get their teeth into something, they won't let go'. In the end their reward will come, like the moment when their target came out of a bank in Coventry and walked past a Customs surveillance car – and was filmed by the BBC into the bargain (*below*).

not quite sure whether everything's going fine. But I've got to be in charge, not him. Once I know who he is and I know what he's going to do next, I'll also know what he's had for breakfast, what clothes he wears, whether he smokes, all that type of thing. We've got to keep it going and be ready so that when the time comes, we can strike.'

Riley and Starling now abandoned British Rail. Instead they typed out two repayment notices themselves. The first showed that a payment of £951 for the Attwal Manufacturing Company of 103 Bassett Street had been made to the Standard Chartered Bank, Town Hall Square, Leicester; the second, that a payment of £893 for Baltex Ltd of 47 Wharf Street South had gone to the Yorkshire Bank, also in Town Hall Square.

That evening, 29 January, they faced another crisis when the 'A' team officers who had promised to help the following morning were diverted to a drugs operation in Sheffield. Late that night they persuaded the Bristol ID to lend them four men. With so much time spent, and so many resources committed, the need for a successful outcome was becoming acute. 'The pressure is beginning to build on Alan and Mel and myself,' Riley admitted.

The first intimation that the long run of failures was about to end came the next morning. At 11.20 an officer in Bassett Street saw a two-tone Ford Fiesta pull up outside No. 103. He radioed a description of the driver to Riley, who was sitting in a car in Town Hall Square, Leicester. The officer said the driver of the Fiesta was an Asian in his mid-twenties, with 'a Crombie style overcoat, grey trousers, collar and tie, very smart, full bearded.' The officer was sure it was the same man, in the same car, who had been seen in Sandhurst Road a week earlier. The man left the house shortly afterwards, just missing the delivery of the repayment advice. This time it did not matter. Moments later an officer in Wharf Street South saw the man arrive at No. 47, where the post had already been delivered. After calling at the house the man returned to his Fiesta with an envelope in his hand.

'He's opening the envelope,' the officer radioed. 'He's looking inside. . . .'

In Leicester, Riley could not conceal his delight. 'It's great,' he said. 'Magic, absolute magic. This two minutes is worth the twelve days we've sat around waiting.' He then performed a most uncharacteristic act. Selecting the hit by Abba, he broke into song: ' "Money, money, money. . ." '

There was better to come. An hour later, as the 'B' team watched the two banks in Leicester's Town Hall Square, the same man drove round the square and parked nearby. He called in at the Standard Chartered Bank and then crossed the square to the Yorkshire Bank. Mel Starling was waiting inside. 'He's at the counter,' Starling radioed. 'He's carrying gloves and a briefcase.'

The man appeared to check that a payment had arrived and then withdrew a substantial amount of cash. 'He's done 'em both,' said Riley, referring to the two banks. Then, to Riley's further delight, the man left the bank and walked straight past him – and a waiting BBC camera – as he returned to his parking place. He climbed into the Fiesta and pulled away.

'It's a lift off, lift off, lift off,' radioed the officer who could see the Fiesta.

'Lift off, lift off, lift off,' echoed Riley to the other waiting cars.

The Customs' habit of repeating crucial instructions three times may seem strange to outsiders. In fact it is to guard against a break in radio transmission – even if two phrases are lost, the third will still get through. A 'lift off' signifies that a target suspect is on the move and that the surveillance team is to follow. There were five ID cars in all on hand, and it was difficult for them to follow their target in the heavy lunchtime traffic, and still guard against the danger of 'showing out'. But they still had the Fiesta in their sights when it finally reached a residential area of Leicester and pulled into a quiet cul-de-sac named Huggett Close.

While the cars held back, an officer strolled down Huggett Close. A few minutes later he radioed that the man had gone into No. 23, a tidy modern semi-detached house with a 'For Sale' sign in the garden and a new BMW in the drive. Riley, who had parked in the adjoining street, made a radio request to the Birmingham ID headquarters to check the address in the Leicester electoral register and to find out who owned the BMW from its licence plate. The answers came back within minutes. Their target's name was Kirit Fatania, and he appeared to be living with his parents at No. 23.

Riley was delighted – and now revised his earlier judgment that the man they had seen was merely a junior member of the supposed gang. 'The assumption you can make at this stage is that you've got the man who is actually doing the bizzo,' Riley said. And now that they had found him, he emphasised, they were not going to lose sight of him. 'We sit and wait, and if he moves we follow him, if he stays there we stay here, until we're satisfied that he's not likely to move again tonight.'

Fatania did not move again that day. That evening at the Birmingham office, Riley, Starling and Huish discussed the significance of what they had seen. In the first place, their suspect matched the bank manager's description in every respect except that he had a beard. Second, they had seen him collect a repayment notice from one of the bogus company addresses and then withdraw money from two banks. Finally they had followed him back to his home.

'With a brand new BMW outside, it can't be bad,' said Riley.

'Evidentially it couldn't be better,' Huish replied. He also agreed with Riley that Fatania was not merely a 'gofer', but 'very much further up the tree'.

Perhaps, Riley even suggested, 'he *is* the tree'.

'It's beautiful,' Huish told him. 'Absolute magic.'

Then Riley began to worry again. Supposing the 'For Sale' sign outside No. 23 meant that Fatania was about to move away? Was this his last fling?

Huish agreed that it was at least possible that Fatania might be setting his sights on a house more in keeping with his undoubtedly high income. 'If he's up to £200,000 a year,' Huish speculated, 'it's taking him out of this bracket.'

Riley agreed. 'You only get Civil Servants having to live in little houses like that.'

The fear that although they had tracked down their suspect he might yet slip away from them imposed an air of urgency over their next decisions. For there was plenty still to do. Before making an arrest, they had first to collect enough evidence to satisfy a jury of Fatania's guilt. Second, they had to find out whether he had any accomplices, or whether, as Riley now proposed, he was the whole 'tree'. Third, they hoped to find out what he had done with the money, in the hope of recovering as much of it as possible.

Reinforced by officers from the other Birmingham ID teams, and still acutely aware of the need not to show out, the 'B' team watched virtually every move Fatania made for the next week. It was not long before he led them to some of the money. The following morning, 31 January, he left Huggett Close and drove to a local branch of the Leicester Building Society. There he made a deposit, almost certainly, they supposed, the money he had withdrawn the previous day. After spending the weekend of 1–2 February at home he made a further tour of the false company addresses to collect the latest repayment advices which were now arriving by post from Southend 'like confetti', Riley said.

On 4 February the 'B' team had a fright. Until then they had taken up their positions around Huggett Close at seven each morning. Since Fatania had not once left before ten, they decided to start their sur-veillance at nine. By the time they arrived, Fatania had gone. At once they assumed the worst: he must have realised he was being watched and had gone into hiding. There were audible sighs of relief when he returned to Huggett Close that evening. But the shock they received prompted urgent discussions as to when they should make an arrest. Alan Huish felt that the time was near.

'In a situation like this you're always running the risk, you're walking a very fine dividing line between developing the job and keeping it under control, and suddenly losing it,' Huish said. 'The danger with this one now is that he will disappear before we get to him. We're at the stage where we're ready to go for him and one keeps one's fingers crossed that he doesn't disappear in the last twenty-four hours.'

Barry Riley was inclined to agree. And now that the moment was approaching, he admitted to a certain technical respect for what their opponent had done. 'I'm looking forward to the arrest of this man, because I want to see what makes him tick,' Riley said. 'This man to me is a challenge, he's got to have a very keen mind to be able to keep this job running – somebody with the mind of an accountant, who can understand books, who can lay it out correctly. He's a bit of a genius in a way. But now he's blown it, because the Investigation Division are on his tail.'

On 5 February Fatania visited more of his company addresses and an officer saw a pile of brown envelopes in the back of his Fiesta. Huish and his colleagues guessed that they contained documents concerning Fatania's false companies, which could provide the conclusive evidence they needed. They were now more than ever convinced that rather than dealing with a gang, as they had first supposed, Fatania was their sole target. That night they decided to arrest him on Friday 7 February.

February 6 brought the biggest scare of all. The 'B' team was following Fatania through Leicester that day – Alan Huish had proposed a 'light tail' – and Riley himself was behind Fatania when he stopped abruptly on a street corner, causing Riley to overshoot. 'He's never done that before,' Riley said in alarm.

Worse was to come. A stream of other cars passed the stationary Fatania, followed by another Customs' car driven by an ID officer from Bristol. The Bristol man unwittingly stopped behind Fatania and went to call Riley from a nearby phone box. Then, as he told Riley, he realised that Fatania was staring at him from his car.

'Is he deliberately clocking you or what?' Riley asked.

'Deliberately keeping an eye,' the officer felt. 'He's just sitting there looking at me.'

'Perhaps he's waiting to use the telephone kiosk,' a second officer, Bill Gale, suggested.

Riley was not convinced and told Gale to call off the surveillance.

'All vehicles abort,' Gale instructed.

'Tell 'em again,' said Riley.

'All vehicles abort, abort.'

Riley and Huish tried to evaluate what had happened. 'It could be that he was just looking for a telephone box,' Riley suggested.

'You're probably okay,' Huish assured him. But it was time to make the arrest.

That night, in the Birmingham office, Huish, Riley and Starling briefed a meeting of thirty officers, with the Birmingham VAT and drugs teams reinforced by officers from Bristol and Manchester. After explaining the fraud in some detail, Starling predicted that according to the pattern they had observed over the previous month, Fatania was likely to visit several banks in Leicester and Coventry to check that his repayments had arrived and to withdraw some money.

'Ideally,' said Starling, 'we would like to arrest him when he comes out of a bank after making a cash withdrawal from one of the accounts we know about. He'll be arrested on the pavement, and not in the bank premises. Alternatively he may have a sum of money with him which he may go to the building society tomorrow and pay in. Ideally we'd like to take him out before he goes into that building society with that money, but if both those events don't occur, then he will be arrested at his home in Huggett Close, if we can establish that he is there. At all events, Alan will call the knock.'

Alan Huish then spoke to the officers, and the public image of the Customs was clearly uppermost in the mind. 'The arrest,' he said. 'I want a quiet one. It's going to be out in the street and I don't want any fuss and I don't want any problems, I don't want any difficulties with the public, so please, if possible, a quiet one. If he becomes difficult then obviously you know what to do with him, and you can restrain him, and we'll take it away. But otherwise a very quiet and controlled arrest, please.'

At 7.30 a.m. on 7 February, a dozen officers, including Huish and Riley, met in a frozen car park behind a supermarket on the edge of Leicester. With Huish in control, they were to form the 'caravan' of five cars which would tail Fatania that morning. A second group, including Mel Starling, headed for the banks in Coventry and Leicester Fatania was most likely to visit. After a swift final briefing, the tailing cars parked in positions where they could pick up Fatania on any of his possible routes, with Coventry considered his most likely destination. Three chilly hours passed.

At 10.46 an officer concealed in a van at the end of Huggett Close radioed that Fatania had just come out of his house and was clearing the overnight snow from the windscreen of his Fiesta. He was wearing his usual Crombie overcoat, the officer reported, 'dressed for business'. At 10.52 Fatania and his mother got into the car and drove cautiously down the icy road. The watching officer radioed: 'Lift off.'

Fatania dropped his mother off at a nearby shopping precinct and continued into the centre of Leicester. The five Customs cars were behind him, leap-frogging into the lead at regular intervals. 'Come on, let's go to Coventry and collect your money, young man,' called Alan Huish from the control car. Then the lead car radioed that it had lost Fatania in heavy traffic.

'He can't be too far ahead,' said Huish.

'Come on, lads, don't lose him,' said Riley.

'Still temporary loss,' the lead car reported.

'Come on, come on,' urged Riley. Then the lead car radioed: 'Eyeball regained.'

After passing through Leicester, Fatania turned on to the M69 and headed for Coventry at a steady 60 m.p.h. The caravan remained a discreet distance behind, taking it in turns to occupy the lead position. It was now that the greatest moment of danger occurred and it was caused not by the Customs but by the BBC.

When the caravan had pulled out to follow Fatania in Leicester, one vehicle had been left behind. It was a BBC car, driven by production assistant Sally Benge accompanied by camera assistant Vicki Parnell. They had been waiting in the car park where the cars had first assembled and had attempted to follow the Customs' cars when they roared off. But they had skidded on the ice and ended up facing in the wrong direction. By the time they had turned round the caravan had gone. Guessing that Fatania and his pursuers were bound for Coventry, they headed for the M69. Driving at some speed, they soon overtook both the caravan and Fatania himself. They then compounded their mistake by braking hard and allowing the column of cars to pass them. When they slipped in at the end of the caravan the comments made over the radio by the Customs team were, in the words of Sally Benge, 'not polite to say the least'.

In fact Fatania continued smoothly on his way at between 60 and 70 m.p.h., seeming to remain blissfully unaware of what had occurred. After twenty minutes he turned off the motorway and drove into Coventry. A mile or so short of the city centre he turned down a side street named Walsgrave Road and parked. The five Customs cars stopped as close as they dared nearby.

Fatania got out of his car and walked briskly to the Natwest Bank on the corner of Walsgrave Road. He barely glanced at the 'B' team officers who were already standing outside. One of them followed Fatania in and a few moments later sent the whispered radio message: 'He's got the money.'

'When he comes out,' responded Alan Huish, 'take him on his way down to his car.'

'Don't blow it,' added Riley.

When Fatania came out five officers, headed by Mel Starling, were waiting. Unsuspecting even now, Fatania passed them and headed for his car. In a few paces they came alongside him and then blocked his path. Starling told him he was under arrest.

Fatania looked devastated. His face drained of blood and seemed to turn a greeny-grey. 'I was expecting it,' he said. 'But not this morning.'

Fatania made no attempt to deny his guilt. Both in the Customs car that took him back to Huggett Close, and in a long interview at Leicester police station that evening, he furnished Mel Starling with every detail of his fraud. Aged twenty-three, living with his parents and two younger sisters, he had attempted to start a knitwear company three years before. But the company failed – Fatania blamed his creditors for failing to pay their debts – and when he closed it down he made a claim for payment of VAT. He could not help noticing how easy that was, and so the idea of the fraud was born.

Fatania denied that he had any inside knowledge of the workings of the VAT system. It was true that he had once been a Civil Servant, working as a clerical officer with the Manpower Services Commission, and had even considered applying to join the Customs. But he had kept his repayments below £1000, thereby evading the computer's scrutiny, simply because that was the level of the payments he had received before. He had merely guessed that it was sensible to avoid visiting the Leicester office in person, and was relieved when no one from Leicester asked to call on him.

He had not been aware at any stage that the Customs had been investigating or following him. On 4 February he had driven to London to collect a payment advice which had been delivered there – one of just two addresses outside Coventry and Leicester – and to visit his fiancée. On 6 February, the day he stared at one of the officers inside a telephone box and Barry Riley was convinced they had 'shown out', he had merely been waiting to use the telephone himself. Fatania also claimed that he was on the point of closing down the fraud. 'You may not believe this,' he told Starling, 'but I do feel guilty. I wanted no more of it.'

Starling was not inclined to believe him. Among Fatania's meticulous files was a folder showing that he was expecting to make £107,815 from his frauds in 1986, on top of the £86,462.93 he had already collected. His aims – or perhaps his fantasies – may have exceeded even that, for when officers visited the flats and bedsitters he had rented they learned that he had spun some extravagant tales. He had told one landlady that he was a buyer for Marks and Spencer and travelled all round the world. He had assured another that he intended to be a millionaire by the age of twenty-five.

In other ways he cut a pathetic figure. He hardly ever drove the BMW he had bought, telling Starling that he thought BMWs were what successful businessmen were supposed to spend their money on. Starling asked why he had carried on if he had no real need of the money. 'There's no point in lecturing about it,' Fatania replied. 'The basic nitty-gritty was greed.'

After he had been identified at last, Kirit Fatania (circled *above*), was secretly filmed and photographed by both Customs and BBC outside his home in Huggett Close, Leicester. Finally (*left*) came the 'knock', when Fatania, who had been under surveillance throughout the previous week, was arrested after withdrawing some of the proceeds of his fraud from a bank. The ID team waited outside – and when Fatania emerged they pounced, surrounding him as he walked towards his car.

The BBC team followed Operation Breaker almost from the start. They too spent days of waiting in bitterly cold weather, and were present at the dramatic moment when Fatania was arrested. Cameraman Pat O'Shea closed in (*top*) with the Customs team, followed by producer Paul Hamann (with clapperboard). As Fatania was led away (*centre and bottom left and right*) he told the officers: 'I was expecting it.' He later made a clean breast of his crimes, admitting that he had set up at least fifty dummy companies to make fraudulent VAT claims. The judge at Leicester Crown Court told him that VAT frauds were just as dishonest 'as if you were to rob an old lady' and sent him to prison for three years.

Among the officers who had spent three weeks watching Fatania no sympathy for him was to be found. 'He's just bloody idle,' said one. 'Why couldn't he go out and do a decent day's work like the rest of us? He's been making £1000 a week over the past two years and he's even too idle to go out at a proper time in the morning. We've been getting up at six each morning and going out in the freezing cold while he sits in his bloody bed. That's what really rankles.'

Others were pleased that this VAT investigation had been brought to a speedy conclusion, and pointed out that, although it did not rank as a major case, the sums involved could have equipped an operating theatre in the National Health Service. But they still feared that the public might not view it in the same way. 'People look on tax fraud as something unimportant, whereas they react at once against robbery or heroin-dealing,' said Huish.

Fatania stood trial in Leicester Crown Court in May 1986. He pleaded guilty and the judge, Mr T. G. Field-Fisher, told him: 'I do not take the view like a lot of people do that the income tax authorities and the Customs and Excise generally are fair game. They are not. It is just as much dishonesty as if you were to rob an old lady.' He sentenced Fatania to three years in prison.

Among the 'B' team officers, the sentiment was expressed that Fatania could count himself lucky not to have received six years; Alan Huish thought that four might have been nearer the mark. Even so, they conceded, it could be chalked up as a good result.

CHAPTER FIVE

AUNTIE'S BAG

On Sunday 15 December 1985, as Pakistan Airlines flight PK787 touched down at Heathrow at the end of its nine-hour flight from Karachi, passengers glancing at their watches were pleased to see that they were arriving on time. The queues at the passport desks in Terminal Three were relatively light that evening and most of the passengers came through without undue delay. A small disappointment awaited some of them. As they gathered around carousel number four in the baggage hall, not all the suitcases appeared.

Not all the delays to baggage at Heathrow can be attributed to the sheer volume of traffic at the world's busiest airport. Sometimes the Customs are to blame. When flights arrive from countries known as sources of drugs – Colombia, Jamaica, Pakistan – officers often take a discreet look at the baggage before it reaches its owners. After being unloaded from the aircraft, the baggage is set out in an area behind the passenger terminal that is the territory of the Customs' rummage and tarmac crews.

The Customs rummage crews have a long and venerable history. The term 'rummage' is a nautical one, dating from Elizabethan times, and originally referred to searches of ships' holds. After a dedicated preventive officer insisted on interviewing Louis Blériot when he made his first landing by aeroplane from overseas in 1909, the term was inevitably extended to cover searches of aircraft, which are carried out after the passengers have departed. The rummage officers look for hiding places under seat cushions, in lockers and lavatories, in case a package has been left there for an airline or airport employee to retrieve – or perhaps abandoned after its owner suffered a last-minute loss of nerve.

The most fruitful searches these days are of the baggage lined up behind the arrival terminals. They may be undertaken by the rummage officers, the tarmac crew, or by individual uniformed officers who come on their own initiative. The Customs also use sniffer dogs which are led up and down the lines of baggage by their handlers. They are mostly gun-dog types – spaniels, labradors, retrievers – and have been in use since 1976. They and their handlers are trained by the RAF, receiving a fifteen-week 'multi-scent' course, at the end of which the dogs can sniff out cannabis, heroin, amphetamines and cocaine.

That evening at Heathrow, however, it was a human and not a canine sniffer who homed in on a brown suitcase from the Karachi flight. He picked it up ruminatively and then felt its sides. He was as certain as he could be, without actually opening it, that he had found a 'DB' or dirty bag.

Sitting inside the baggage terminal at that moment, watching passengers collect their suitcases while pretending that he was hardly interested in them at all, was Jim Kirk, a member of the local investigation unit based at Heathrow. Kirk, dressed in plain clothes and a dark anorak, was looking out for the unusual or the untoward: passengers who seem nervous or who split up and pretend not to know each other – the same clues that would alert the uniformed desk officers in the Red and Green Channels.

Then Kirk received a radio call. It came from the Customs control post in Heathrow's building 820, and had been relayed from the officer who had found a dirty bag on flight PK787. Kirk immediately went to the rummage area at the back of the terminal. A few moments later, satisfied with what he had seen, he returned. Soon afterwards baggage carousel number four creaked on its way, and the passengers from PK787 clustered round. There was one item which was bound to be the focus of considerable attention: a brown 'Prince' suitcase with a combination lock and an airline tag, PIA 63-25-97.

Not only its owner was looking out for the case; a number of Customs officers were now doing so too. Then an officer saw a tall young Asian man, accompanied by a short middle-aged Asian woman, pick it off the carousel and load it and several other cases on to a trolley. He gestured briefly to a uniformed desk officer, Bob Stephenson, who had already been briefed by Jim Kirk.

When the pair approached the Green Channel Stephenson asked them to stop. He questioned them and asked them to open several of their bags – though not the brown 'Prince' suitcase. Meanwhile Jim Kirk, who was watching from behind a partition barely ten yards away, spoke discreetly into his radio. 'Charlie One, Charlie One, Charlie Four. Can you go into the concourse and link up with Charlie Three and Yankee One and organise to take out any meeters? I'll give you lift off from the channel in a few minutes. A male wearing a maroon anorak, light-grey trousers, accompanied by a female. She's wearing a yellow cardigan and she has a neck bandage on and underneath the yellow cardigan she's wearing a grey-flowered ethnic-type dress.'

Top: Labrador Glen, a Customs sniffer dog, and his handler, Jessie Follington, examine suitcases lined up on the tarmac at Heathrow. Human 'sniffers' (*left*) usually examine the suitcases too. The glue used to make false compartments often gives off a more powerful odour than drugs themselves, while officers also test suitcases for their weight and 'feel'. They call suspect cases 'DBs' or 'dirty bags' – and in December 1985, officers at Heathrow's Terminal Three found a 'DB' on a flight from Pakistan. When the suitcase lining was cut away (*above*), heroin was revealed.

Stephenson finished questioning the couple and told them they could go. The young man loaded their cases on to their trolley and steered his way through the Customs area to the arrivals concourse, the woman by his side. Kirk followed a dozen paces behind, radio in hand.

'Charlie Four to all mobiles – lift off, lift off, lift off.'

When the couple reached the concourse, several plain-clothes members of the investigation unit were waiting. They saw another young Asian man, accompanied by a white woman with a baby in her arms, step forward to greet them. The group walked to the Terminal Three car park with the officers following them. As they reached their car the officers moved forward and arrested them. All four, plus the baby, were escorted back to the Customs' offices in Terminal Three; the young Asian passenger held firmly by Jim Kirk at one arm and a second officer at the other. He and the other man were shown into interview rooms and searched, followed by the two women. The Customs' custody officer noted: '17.30 arrested car park Terminal Three.'

Then Jim Kirk took the Prince suitcase into the interview room containing the young Asian passenger. Bob Stephenson was there too. After Kirk had opened the case, Stephenson produce a knife and started to cut a hole in the lid.

'I've cut myself,' Stephenson announced.

Meanwhile Kirk was struggling to open a narrow glass phial, finally managing to break off its top. By now another officer had excavated a hole in the suitcase lid. He inserted his knife-blade and scraped out a small amount of a sugary brown substance. He handed it to Kirk who tipped it into the phial, which contained a clear liquid. Within seconds, as the three officers watched, the liquid turned purple.

'Happy, Jim?' Stephenson asked.

Kirk was indeed happy, as the test, known as the Marquis test, brought final confirmation of what he had suspected since first examining the suitcase behind Terminal Three. The clear liquid in the phial reacts to being mixed with various drugs by changing colour. Yellow would indicate that the drugs concerned were amphetamines. Orange meant mescalin. Purple meant heroin.

The surge of heroin entering Britain in the past ten years is another symbol of the dramatic changes the Customs have undergone. Officers who joined the service before 1970 talk of the halcyon days when life, at least from today's depressing perspective, was delightfully simple. 'Smuggling used to be a gentleman's game,' says one. 'Heroin was something you only saw in films.'

The film in question was usually *The French Connection,* in which Gene Hackman portrays a harassed member of the New York police drugs squad. It was based on a real-life incident in 1962, when a French gang smuggled 51kg of heroin into New York packed inside a car. In the same year the British Customs seized no heroin at all. At first British heroin seizures were measured in grams; by the 1980s they were counted in hundreds of kilos, reaching a peak of 334kg in 1985.

Films like *The French Connection* and the television series *Kojak* usually portray heroin as a white powder but in fact the heroin entering Britain almost invariably comes as a brown substance with the feel and consistency of sugar. Kojak is sometimes shown tasting heroin as an improvised field test but British Customs officers would never do this as heroin's effect is so powerful. Were they to do so, however, they would find that far from tasting sweet, like sugar, heroin is overwhelmingly bitter. That is perhaps appropriate for a substance which, in the words of the judge who sent the organiser of a heroin-smuggling ring to prison for twenty-eight years in 1986, brings in its wake 'misery, degradation, crime and death'.

Ironically, heroin was first produced in the search for a safe and non-addictive painkiller. It is derived from a poppy, the *papaver somniferum* or sleeping poppy, which was known to the ancient Egyptians. They were almost certainly the first people to discover that the milky fluid which oozes from the poppy's seedpod could be used for the relief of pain. They dried and filtered it and then burned it and inhaled the fumes. Called opium, it was used by the Greeks and Romans too, and in seventeenth-century Europe was mixed with alcohol to produce the elixir known as laudanum.

In 1805 a German chemist isolated the active ingredient in opium and named it morphine. It was widely administered to the casualties of the American Civil War, but while it was a far more effective painkiller than opium it also proved highly addictive. In the 1890s the German pharmaceutical company Bayer produced a refined version of morphine which it marketed as a general medicine and painkiller, ideal for treating ailments from coughs to bronchitis. For a name, Bayer adapted the German word *heroisch,* which means heroic, and called it heroin. They claimed that it was non-addictive.

In medical terms, heroin is a painkiller and sedative which operates on the central nervous system to cause drowsiness and sleep. It also affects the brain's respiratory centre. People who use it for non-medical reasons do so for the intensely powerful sensations of pleasure it provides, producing a 'high' which some compare with sexual ecstasy or even death. It is followed by a deceptive sense of relaxation or well-being which may otherwise be in short supply for many people today.

Heroin is far too potent to be consumed in its purest form. Instead it is diluted or 'cut' with additives such as sugar or food colouring (heroin that is 'twenty per cent pure' contains one-fifth heroin, four-fifths additives). It is then consumed in various ways. 'Snorting' means inhaling finely-chopped particles of heroin, one nostril at a time. 'Chasing the dragon' refers to heating the heroin and inhaling the fumes. 'Mainlining' means injecting a heroin solution directly into a vein, usually in the arm. The scars this leaves are known as 'tracks'.

The precise bodily mechanism by which users become dependent on heroin is not yet fully understood. Heroin somehow replaces the body's natural defences against pain so that when it is pumped full of an artificial painkiller it stops manufacturing its own. When the effects wear off, even minor irritations become overwhelmingly painful. This causes the terrifying experience known as 'cold turkey', which refers to the goose pimples that develop when users cannot obtain supplies, along with muscle tremors and stomach cramps, rapid pulse and breathing, physical cravings and sheer fear.

There is a powerful psychological component to addiction too, caused by both the search for pleasure and the avoidance of pain which rapidly dominate addicts' lives. They neglect their diet and become vulnerable to disease. They mix primarily with other addicts and are likely to contract AIDS from sharing their hypodermic needles. They die from blood-poisoning and liver infections or from overdoses, which cause them to stop breathing.

From one perspective, heroin is not the most destructive drug in use today. There are reckoned to be 70,000 heroin addicts in Britain of whom around a dozen die through overdoses each year. Tobacco, by comparison, kills 100,000 people a year. But there is something especially insidious about a drug which creates addicts so quickly, and something especially callous about the people who supply it. Their trade depends on creating as many addicts as possible and appears somehow more obscene because the profits it offers are so vast.

In 1986 a kilo of heroin purchased in Pakistan for £3000 was worth between £150,000 and £250,000 when sold in one-gram lots at thirty per cent purity in Britain, and the size and value of some seizures beggars belief. In 1986 the Dutch police found 220kg of heroin in a container ship in Rotterdam harbour, worth at least £33 million on the street. In 1982 the US Drug Enforcement Administration seized 640kg in Iran, worth almost £100 million.

Another of the dilemmas of the fight against drugs is that profits on such a scale arise precisely because the drugs are illegal. One of the consequences of the American prohibition era was that it presented organised crime with an unparalleled opportunity to grow fat on the proceeds of illicit alcohol. In the same way, the heroin trade has attracted some of the most determined and ruthless criminals of all. Heroin was banned for non-medical use by a series of international conventions early this century. For the next fifty years the Mafia dominated the world heroin trade. In the 1920s and 1930s notorious Mafia leaders like Al Capone and Louis 'Lepke' Buchalter, head of the 'Murder Inc.' organisation, helped smuggle heroin from the Far East into the US, where it was sold in one-ounce packets with brand names like Red Dragon and White Horse – the origin of the slang terms in use today.

After the Second World War the Mafia struck an alliance with the French underworld known as the French Connection. The French imported opium from the poppy-fields of Turkey and converted it into heroin in laboratories in villas around Marseille. At first the Mafia smuggled the heroin into the US on cargo ships, switching to airline routes after the French Connection seizure of 1962. The French Connection was finally broken when the French government acted against the Marseille underworld and the US and West German governments persuaded Turkey to control the opium at source.

Another painful lesson of the fight against heroin is that as soon as one source is cut off another springs up elsewhere. After Turkey, the new supplies came from an area of south-east Asia known as the Golden Triangle, covering the borders of Burma, Thailand and Laos. When the Golden Triangle was hit by drought it was replaced by the Golden Crescent, which comprises the frontier regions of Iran, Afghanistan and Pakistan.

This time the US-based Mafia went into partnership with the traditional Mafia of Sicily to transport the morphine to Italy and convert it into heroin there. Much of it was smuggled into the US on Alitalia flights from Rome, often hidden in freight to be retrieved at US airports by airline or airport staff. When the US and Italian authorities raided the heroin laboratories the Mafia struck back with a series of ruthless assassinations. Their victims included the head of Palermo's flying squad, its top judge, and a local police chief who had just arrested six Mafia suspects and was gunned down as he was walking through the streets with his four-year-old daughter in his arms. The sense of hopelessness drug investigators sometimes feel was best expressed by a senior Drug Enforcement Administration field agent who said: 'Even if I lined up every known mafioso in the main square of Palermo and shot them all, in a week's time you could fill the square again with mafiosi who had come to take their place.'

Throughout this period, Britain had remained relatively unscathed. Elsewhere in Europe, particularly Italy and West Germany, heroin seizures and deaths from overdoses had soared. There had been some major heroin seizures in Britain, the largest being 32kg found at the London docks inside the tyres of two cars imported from the Far East in 1979.

But the Customs believed that most of the heroin was bound for the US, with Britain being used at a transit point. In the summer of 1979 all that changed.

On the day in question, Alan Huish was on duty at ID headquarters at New Fetter Lane. Huish – who later oversaw the investigation of Kirit Fatania for VAT fraud in Birmingham in 1986 – headed one of the ID's four heroin teams which was called to Heathrow that afternoon to investigate a heroin seizure. When they arrived they found that preventive officers had arrested a young Pakistani who had attempted to smuggle through a kilo of heroin concealed in his suitcase. Huish sent the heroin to the Government Chemist for analysis. A day or so later the analyst called Huish and asked: 'Where the hell does this stuff come from? I haven't seen anything like it before.'

Since the smuggler had flown direct to London from Karachi, Huish assumed that the heroin had come from Pakistan. Anxious to learn more, he sent a telex to the Drug Enforcement Administration's officer in Rawalpindi. The DEA's reply was stark: 'There is no heroin problem in Pakistan.' A rude awakening awaited both the DEA and the British Customs. 'Pakistan', says Huish, 'just exploded.' Of the vast increase in heroin entering Britain over the next five years, Pakistan was the source of no less than eighty per cent.

Senior British Customs officials admit today that the flood caught them unawares. 'For some time we were running along behind it,' Alan Huish says. 'We had no real idea what was happening in Pakistan.' Since the DEA evidently had no idea what was happening in Pakistan either, the Customs can perhaps be forgiven. What made the situation harder to interpret was that the increase – as so often where the ebb and flow of drug supplies is concerned – had been triggered by world events utterly beyond the Customs' control.

The initial stimulus came from the fall of the Shah of Iran. For several years Iran had been the main source of heroin for the Mafia, who either bought opium from Iran's own poppy fields or used Iran as a transit point for supplies from Afghanistan and Pakistan. When the Shah was overthrown in 1979, many middle-class Iranians took refuge in Britain, among them numerous members of SAVAK, the Shah's secret police. Many removed their assets from Iran not in the traditional form of gold, but as heroin.

The Iranian heroin rapidly helped stoke demand in Britain. Then, just as rapidly, it dried up. In Iran the Ayatollahs and their judges were meting out summary justice to drug dealers, with mass executions of up to twenty at a time. The Ayatollahs' rule also threatened the overland route from Pakistan and Afghanistan. Supplies from Afghanistan were further hindered by the Soviet occupation in 1979, and in 1980 Iraq's invasion of Iran converted many of Iran's poppy-growing areas into battlefields. Of the three countries which comprised the Golden Crescent, that left Pakistan.

The Pathan tribesmen who inhabit Pakistan's north-west frontier region have long proved adaptable to the changing political fortunes around them. A race of farmers and warriors living in one of the most celebrated areas of British colonial history, where the Khyber Pass crosses the frontier between Pakistan and Afghanistan, they are accustomed to the passage of foreign armies and pay little heed to lines drawn on maps. If the troops of President Zia of Pakistan arrive they will decamp to Afghanistan. If Soviet troops forage too close, they will move back to Pakistan.

The Pathans had grown and sold opium for decades, both for the medical trade and for the legal market. Opium was far more profitable than the alternative crop, wheat, and as supplies from Iran and Afghanistan dwindled in the early 1980s, the Pathans found themselves in a buyers' market. Their profits doubled from £600–£700 a year to £1500 or more.

Local dealers and middle-men were attracted too. At first they were content to take commissions from introducing buyers and sellers but then they set up their own conversion laboratories near the poppy fields. They also looked for new markets where they could sell the heroin abroad. The most obvious was the country to which they were linked by 400 years of colonial history, the home of a sizeable Pakistani population, and connected by direct flights every day of the year: Britain.

When the heroin flood reached Britain, the preventive staff at Heathrow found themselves trying to outwit smugglers who became increasingly inventive and bold. It was concealed in the same variety of containers as cocaine, ranging from model elephants to hollowed-out tables. Like cocaine too, heroin is malleable and was sometimes found to have been impregnated in suitcases or clothes. Couriers were sent on roundabout routes, or passed their hand baggage to other couriers who joined flights in Europe, reckoning – correctly – that they were less likely to be stopped. Accomplices were recruited at Heathrow to retrieve loads of heroin that had been dumped in waste-bins or on cleaning trolleys in the transit areas, to be taken through the security gates by members of the airport or cleaning staff.

One of the most alarming seizures came in July 1983 when an Asian woman living in Britain who was stopped in the Green Channel was found to be carrying 16kg of heroin in a holdall. The stop had been pure chance – assisted, of course, by the 'revenue nose' – as no Asian women who were British residents had been arrested before. The Customs could not help wondering how many similar couriers had previously passed through the Green Channel, relying on the odds against being stopped.

The Customs' instinct that a high proportion of heroin was escaping them was confirmed by other indicators. Between 1981 and 1983 the street price of heroin fell from £140 to £40 per gram, and purity rose to an astonishing fifty per cent. What made all this worse for the Customs was that the influx of heroin coincided precisely with the decline in their own strength, in line with the Civil Service cuts. While the political battle was fought out elsewhere, the Customs were compelled to meet the heroin threat from their own resources.

In 1979 the Investigation Division had four heroin teams, two concentrating on the Golden Triangle, two on Iran and Turkey. A fifth ID team was devoted to cannabis and a sixth to cocaine. When heroin began arriving from Pakistan an internal review by the Customs recommended that the ID's strength should be increased. It was not until 1982, however, that two more heroin teams were formed to concentrate on Pakistan and Afghanistan. Since the Customs' overall staff was falling, this inevitably meant diverting hard-pressed resources from elsewhere.

The ID acquired another fifty officers in 1985 and formed four new teams, two each for cocaine and cannabis. It then created a seventh heroin team by reassigning the Juliet team, which until then had worked at the main London overseas postal sorting offices, investigating packages found to contain drugs. (The Juliets' work was taken over by a local investigation unit, which found it impossible to follow up all the drugs it found – sometimes it simply threw them into a disposal bin instead of visiting the people to whom the packages were addressed.)

By now the ID had carried out a further reform. Originally it had mostly undertaken 'referral' work, following up drug seizures made by the preventive staff. Now it allocated half its teams to 'target' work, concentrating on suspects in the hope of collecting the evidence needed to take them to court. Operation Renaissance showed the pitfalls that this strategy entails but in fact the referral teams enjoyed considerable success, securing a high majority of convictions.

The Customs nonetheless felt hampered by a lack of information from Pakistan. To begin with they relied on the DEA who – despite the embarrassment of its initial verdict on Pakistan – had been unfailingly co-operative. But the British now felt the need to have their own officer in place. In April 1984, following delicate negotiations between the Pakistan government and the Foreign Office, who stressed that his aim gather information and that he would not encroach on the territory of the Pakistan police, an ID officer named Mike Stephenson took up the post of British Drugs Liaison Officer in Karachi.

Stephenson, a confident South Londoner, was something of a loner and did not fit easily into a conventional ID team. These attributes were ideal for posing as a drug dealer, and he got on well with the DEA. Stephenson took part in weekly meetings to pool intelligence with the Americans and with countries such as Sweden and West Germany which also had officers in Pakistan. His information proved invaluable for the ID's target work and he was rewarded for his success with an MBE in 1987.

But the work of the overseas officers was complicated by the realities of world politics and of life under Pakistan's president, General Mohammad Zia-ul-Haq. When General Zia took power in 1977 the West had tended to view him as an unreconstructed militarist and an Islamic zealot to boot. Those perceptions abruptly changed when the USSR occupied Afghanistan in 1979 and Zia became a bulwark against world communism.

That made Zia a worthy recipient of US aid, which rose to $3 billion a year, much of it devoted to sustaining the guerrilla forces, the Mujahedin, who were fighting the Soviet army across the border in Afghanistan. Zia was also provided with funds to suppress the heroin trade. He responded by declaring a ban on all opium production in Pakistan. Pakistani troops and soldiers raided laboratories and warehouses and seized as much as 400kg at a time. Within a year Zia announced that opium production had been slashed from 650 to 100 tons.

But the DEA discovered that these figures omitted opium grown in northern Pakistan – and here wider political considerations came into play. Since that was the base of many of the Mujahedin, now regarded as freedom fighters, it did not make sense for either President Zia or the US to deprive them of their livelihood and turn them against the government of Pakistan. The DEA itself did its best by providing funds to equip the Pakistan Customs with radios and vehicles. It sent staff to train Customs and police officers and helped to set up drugs task forces. But British journalists who visited northern Pakistan confirmed that the heroin trade had gone virtually unscathed.

At the bazaar town of Bara, close to the Afghan border, a dealer offered the *Sunday Times* reporter Simon Freeman sixty-five per cent heroin for £4500 a kilo. The dealer boasted that with a week's notice he could provide a truck-load, and said that he and his fellow-dealers set aside £2000 of their monthly profits to induce the local police and customs to avert their eyes. Freeman found policemen, supposedly receiving salaries of £150 a month, who were living in luxurious mansions, running foreign cars and smoking imported cigars. He concluded that the Pakistani raids were tokens, that the seizure figures were cooked up to impress Western governments, and that the police resold most of the heroin they seized.

Some surprisingly outspoken US officials confirmed Freeman's verdict. A member of the US State Department's narcotics bureau complained that Pakistan appeared unwilling to act against the major traffickers and that the drugs task forces which the US had helped to set up 'had not distinguished themselves by making arrests'.

The Western countries devoted their efforts to preventing heroin from leaving Pakistan. They concentrated on Karachi airport and spent the next two years helping the Pakistan authorities to surround it with a virtual *cordon sanitaire*. Passengers are now supposed to pass through four separate checks, including the latest West German sensory equipment, and their baggage is X-rayed twice. The US also provided funds to increase the pay of airport customs and police to make them less vulnerable to bribes.

The campaign succeeded to the extent that drug smugglers came to regard Karachi airport as one of the more hazardous embarkation points. But in their constant tactical war the smugglers switched their point of attack, and the close scrutiny paid to Pakistanis brought an influx of Nigerians into the trade. Nigerian dealers moved into Karachi, trading openly in five-star hotels. They used Nigerian couriers to take the heroin out of Pakistan and, although the Karachi Customs stopped thirteen couriers in one month, hundreds more undoubtedly got through. They were despatched to Britain from new embarkation points in West Africa, assisted by the theft of passports from a government office in Lagos which enabled them to conceal their previous journeys or equipped them with new identities.

Back in London, the ID remained as hard-pressed as ever. By one yardstick 1986 was a successful year, as heroin seizures fell to 175kg, compared to 334kg in 1985, bringing the hope that heroin imports were down. But the increase of stuffing and swallowing meant that individual seizures rose from 178 to 295, further swelling the Customs' workload.

The pressure had its effect on the work of the Customs' investigation units. The units have considerable autonomy and are responsible not to the ID at New Fetter Lane but to the Collectors at the head of their own areas. At Heathrow, the investigation unit is the first to deal with drug seizures made by the uniformed staff. However, it also has to report all seizures to the ID.

Once the ID would come out to *any* heroin seizure, no matter how small. Now it makes a series of pragmatic decisions as to whether it is worth doing so. Does the consignment appear to be for dealing or personal use? (As a rule of thumb that limit, which was once around 100g, is now set at half a kilo.) Do the couriers have any identifying papers? Are they prepared to talk about their contacts? And have any 'meeters or greeters' been spotted – people who have come to meet the couriers at Heathrow?

At 5.30 p.m. on 15 December 1985 at Heathrow's Terminal Three, following the discovery of a dirty bag on flight PK 787 from Karachi, it was still too early to tell whether the owner of the suitcase in question could be identified or how much heroin it contained – and so it would be premature to call in the ID just yet. The immediate task for Jim Kirk and his colleagues of the Heathrow investigation unit, therefore, was to determine which of the passengers they had arrested owned the suitcase. Was it the young man? Or the middle-aged woman? While the officers were careful not to jump to conclusions – 'they have a nasty habit of kicking you in the teeth', one says – the consensus view was that the young man was the more likely candidate.

Kirk's first attempt to question him proved inconclusive. 'Where is the key for the suitcase?' Kirk asked.

'This is my aunt's suitcase,' he replied. But he took a key from his pocket and offered it to Kirk.

'Key provided by him out of his right-hand pocket,' Bob Stephenson intoned. Kirk sat at a table and wrote the words in a notebook.

'No, no, Auntie's suitcase,' the young man insisted.

Kirk pointed to the Prince case. 'Where is the key for this suitcase?'

'It is my auntie's suitcase,' the young man repeated.

'Who has the key? Your auntie?'

'I need translator,' the young man replied.

'At the moment I will speak slowly so that you can understand, okay?'

'Yes.'

'Who has the key for this suitcase? You have the key?'

'Yes.'

'For that,' said Kirk, pointing to the Prince suitcase.

'My auntie.'

At this point Kirk gave up trying to question the young man in English and decided to wait for an interpreter. Ten minutes later Sid Pirzada, a uniformed officer with the Terminal Three Customs staff, arrived. He spoke fluent Urdu, the principal language of Pakistan, and he now helped Bob Stephenson, the uniformed officer who had first questioned the Asian couple in the Green Channel, to interview the young man.

Most officers dislike using interpreters as it slows the interview unduly, denying them the nuances of replies and making it harder to seize on contradictions. But as the suspect's English was so limited, there was no alternative – and the lines of his story soon became clear.

Through Pirzada, the young man told Stephenson that his name was Muhammad Mujahid. He was aged nineteen and he lived with his parents in the city of Lahore in north-east Pakistan. His family was poor – both his sisters had arranged marriages in prospect – and he worked as a trainee car mechanic. So who, Stephenson asked, was the woman he was travelling with? And how could he afford to visit England?

Mujahid told Stephenson that the woman was his aunt. She came from Karachi, 650 miles from Lahore – and Mujahid claimed that he had only met her once before in his life. When Stephenson seemed sceptical, Mujahid went on to explain that his aunt had telephoned his parents earlier that year. She had invited him to accompany her on a journey to England, where he would be able to find work and send money home to Pakistan. His parents had agreed. The family did not hear from the aunt again for six months. Then, three days previously, a cousin of his aunt had telephoned and told him to take a flight from Lahore to Karachi the following day. A day later Mujahid had flown from Karachi to London with his aunt.

Suspending judgment for the moment on the plausibility of the story, Stephenson turned to the Prince suitcase. Mujahid told him that he had brought only a small case containing his clothes and some dried food that his mother had given him for the journey. Stephenson pressed him again: who owned the Prince suitcase?

'It is my auntie's suitcase,' Mujahid replied firmly.

In an attempt to impress on Mujahid the seriousness of his predicament, Stephenson reminded him that he was suspected of importing drugs into Britain.

Mujahid seemed nonplussed. 'What sort of drugs?' he asked.

Stephenson then told him that he had the right to contact somebody to tell them he was under arrest.

'I should like to contact my auntie,' Mujahid said.

Stephenson found the request somewhat embarrassing, as he did not want to tell Mujahid yet that his aunt was under arrest, on the grounds that the less he knew about the progress of the investigation the better. He merely told Mujahid that his aunt was in 'the Customs area' and that his request would be passed on.

At that moment, in fact, Mujahid's aunt was in the next room. She was being questioned by a uniformed officer, Mike Beglin, with the assistance of a second Urdu interpreter, officer Madan Jaggi. Her passport showed that her name was Mrs Almas Begum Sheikh, aged forty-nine, a housewife from Karachi. On the face of things she cut an unlikely figure as a potential heroin smuggler.

Mrs Sheikh told Beglin and Jaggi that her husband was the managing director of a cooking-oil company with 600 employees. She was wearing a foam neck support, and she explained that she suffered from a bad back. She had come to England for treatment from a specialist whom she had previously visited just two months before. She had asked her nephew Muhammad to come with her so that he could help her, and to give him a holiday in England at the same time.

The two passengers accompanying the bag were arrested and brought into the Customs' interview rooms in Terminal Three. But which one owned the bag? Was it Muhammad Mujahid, a nineteen-year-old trainee car mechanic from Lahore, Pakistan? Or was it his aunt, Mrs Almas Begum Sheikh, a businessman's wife, aged forty-nine, from Karachi? When Mujahid was questioned by officer Bob Stephenson (*above*), he denied that the bag was his. But so did Mrs Sheikh when she was interviewed by officer Mike Beglin (*left*), even when the suitcase was opened in front of her.

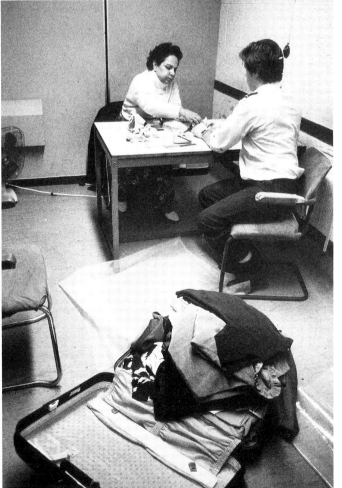

Although Beglin did not yet know it, Mrs Sheikh's account already differed from her nephew's in several respects. For the moment Beglin turned to the question of the Prince suitcase and asked if it was hers. At first Mrs Sheikh said she thought it was. Then Beglin told her he would bring the case into the room so that she could see it. 'We want to be sure,' he told her. When he brought in the suitcase, Mrs Sheikh seemed puzzled. She told Madan Jaggi that it *looked* like her suitcase. But, Jaggi reported, 'she says that there can be many suitcases of the same colour and she can't be sure unless she has seen the inside.'

Beglin put the suitcase on the desk in front of Mrs Sheikh and opened it. He asked Mrs Sheikh not to touch anything and then held up a child's dress. 'Do you recognise the clothing?'

Mrs Sheikh was emphatic. 'She says this is not her suitcase,' Jaggi reported.

Beglin spoke to Mrs Sheikh directly. 'Are you saying this is not your suitcase?'

Mrs Sheikh shook her head and opened her eyes wide. 'No.'

'Do you recognise any of the clothes at all?'

'No.'

Beglin decided to show Mrs Sheikh the heroin that was concealed in the suitcase. Confronting suspects with drugs can be a potent moment, sometimes producing a full confession, sometimes denials which none-theless have connotations of guilt. Beglin first showed Mrs Sheikh the lid, pointing to an incision which had since been sealed with sticky tape. Mrs Sheikh looked cross.

'She says she's not interested in looking inside that suitcase because that's not her suitcase,' Jaggi reported.

'Whether she's interested or not I propose to open it in her presence,' Beglin replied.

'It's up to you,' Mrs Sheikh told Jaggi.

Beglin carefully pulled away the sticky tape. Beneath it, he pointed out, was a plastic sachet containing a brown powder. 'Can you see that?' he asked.

Mrs Sheikh became animated, covering her eyes and then lowering her palms, before addressing Jaggi. 'She says in the name of God, I'm telling you that this is not my suitcase,' Jaggi said.

'Do you recognise that substance?' Beglin said.

Mrs Sheikh told Jaggi that she had performed Haj, by visiting the Muslims' sacred shrine at Mecca in Saudi Arabia. 'I do not believe in these things,' she said in Urdu. 'I pray five times every day and I do not do things like that.' Jaggi translated.

'But has she ever seen a substance like that, whether she's involved or not?' Beglin asked.

'She says she has never seen that powder.'

'What do you suppose that is?' Beglin asked Mrs Sheikh.

'She says she doesn't know anything about that,' said Jaggi. 'She says that for Muslims, Haj is a very important thing. A person who has been to Haj will not tell any lies. She says nobody even smokes cigarettes in her house.'

'I understand what you're saying,' Beglin said. 'But what I have to say to you, by the way you are answering my colleague, it appears to me that you know this is something prohibited, because you're speaking as if it is a prohibited thing to do.'

Mrs Sheikh closed her eyes and sighed in a show of exasperation before speaking to Jaggi again. 'She says she doesn't know what that substance is, she doesn't understand anything at all,' Jaggi said. 'She doesn't know anything about it.'

'So a fair summary of all that's gone on,' Beglin proposed, 'would be that she's denying the suitcase is the one that she brought, she's denying the clothing, we've opened up this incision. . . .'

Jaggi agreed. 'She says yes, this is not her suitcase, the things in the suitcase do not belong to her, she doesn't know anything about the powder.' For the moment, the interview ended there.

By this time a new officer had arrived at Terminal Three. It had become clear that the Prince suitcase contained a substantial amount of heroin, perhaps 2kg. In addition, the interviews with the two principal suspects were proving fruitful; there were also the two people who had met them to be investigated. At around 6.30 p.m. Jim Kirk had called the Customs control to report what had occurred. There was now no doubt that the ID should become involved.

Fifteen minutes later Dave Gourley, a higher executive officer with the Juliet heroin team, was telephoned at his home at Ashtead, Middlesex, where he had just come to the end of a two-week spell of leave. The head of the Juliet team, Bob Dearman, told Gourley that the local investigation unit had made a sizeable heroin find and asked him to go to Heathrow.

When Gourley arrived, Jim Kirk explained what had happened in more detail. He then pointed out the discrepancies between the stories that the two suspects had told, in particular over the reasons why Mujahid had come to England with his aunt. In addition, Mrs Sheikh seemed vulnerable through her answers when confronted with the heroin. As Mike Beglin had said, she appeared to have acknowledged that it was at least an illicit substance – if the suitcase really did not belong to her would she not simply have denied all knowledge of what it contained? Gourley was pleased with the results so far. In the first round of interviews, he said later, 'we like to hear as many lies as they want to tell us.'

Gourley now considered the couple who had met Mujahid and his aunt. They too had been questioned, and their answers had produced some suggestive details. The man came originally from Pakistan, his wife was born in England, and they ran a small restaurant in north London. Crucially the man was related to Mrs Sheikh: he was the brother of her cousin, the man who had telephoned Mujahid and asked him to come to Karachi. To the fertile minds of Gourley and Kirk it seemed that he had to be involved in some way: perhaps, they wondered, his restaurant provided an ideal distribution point for the heroin.

Although CEDRIC could offer no information on the couple, Gourley decided that their home should be searched. When he told them what he was intending to do, they obligingly lent him a front-door key to save the trouble of breaking down the door. The search was carried out by the rest of the Juliet team but the only items of interest they found were £2500 in banknotes, stuffed in a pillowcase. Back at Heathrow, the couple said that the money was the takings from their restaurant.

The investigation unit, meanwhile, had embarked on a second round of interviews with Mujahid and Mrs Sheikh. Mujahid continued to insist that he had nothing to do with the Prince suitcase or its contents. But he too was vulnerable on one detail which Stephenson now pursued. When Mujahid arrived at Heathrow he had told the immigration officers that he had come for a holiday and to help his aunt – the same account given by Mrs Sheikh. He had also shown the immigration officers £500 as proof that he would be able to support himself during his visit. But in his first interview with Stephenson he had said he had come to Britain to look for work. So which version, Stephenson asked, was true?

Mujahid admitted that he had lied to the immigration officers in order to gain entry to Britain. He also told Stephenson that his aunt had instructed him to hand over the £500 once they had arrived. Suspecting that further admissions were close, Stephenson pressed the point. Who had given Mujahid the £500 in the first place? Mujahid said it had been supplied by his aunt's cousin, the man who had summoned him to Karachi and the brother of the man who had come to Heathrow to meet him. The cousin had also provided his air ticket and had generally supervised the departure from Pakistan.

Stephenson reported his findings to his colleagues. For Mike Beglin, who was questioning Mrs Sheikh again, they offered an invaluable lever. But when Beglin told Mrs Sheikh what Mujahid had said she denied any knowledge of her supposed cousin. She also insisted that she had given Mujahid the £500 herself.

Sensing that she was weakening, Stephenson pressed her again over the inconsistencies. He also told her formally that the substance in the suitcase had been tested and found to be heroin. And he told her squarely that he did not believe her when she said that the suitcase was not hers.

At this point, Mrs Sheikh changed her story. She admitted that the suitcase was hers after all – but there must have been a terrible mistake. She told Beglin that four days before leaving Karachi she had gone to a local bazaar to buy a new suitcase for her journey, and a Pathan trader sold her the case for 500 rupees (£19).

Mrs Sheikh spread out her palms in a gesture of mystification. As everyone knew, the Pathans were notorious heroin dealers and she supposed they must have sold the suitcase to her in error as it was clearly intended for someone else. But Beglin looked sceptical and Mrs Sheikh began to cry.

Beglin stood up. Via Jaggi, he asked Mrs Sheikh if she would like a rest or a cup of tea.

'Chang?' Jaggi asked.

'Chang,' Mrs Sheikh replied.

Since chang – which means tea – was one of the few Urdu words that Beglin understood, he suggested that Mrs Sheikh should have a fifteen-minute break. But Mrs Sheikh suddenly leant down before him, her hands clasped in supplication. 'Please forgive me,' she said in Urdu. 'I bow down to your feet. I have performed Haj.' Then she turned to Jaggi. 'Please tell him the Pathans sold this bag to me. Perhaps they made it for someone else, they gave the bag to me in a hurry.' She started to cry again.

Beglin was visibly taken aback at this display of emotion. 'I want to speak to you again, but I want you to feel well,' he told her. 'Do you not feel well at the moment?'

'I am very ill,' Mrs Sheikh said in Urdu. 'I don't know whether I'll survive or not.' She mopped at her tears with the hem of her skirt.

'Take some rest,' Jaggi told her.

'No, I don't need any rest,' she said weakly. 'Ask what questions you want. All right, I won't cry.'

Beglin told Mrs Sheikh that he considered her story implausible, to say the least. 'People don't just throw away thousands of pounds worth of heroin for 500 rupees,' he said. Mrs Sheikh continued to maintain that she was telling the truth. But her story about the suitcase had yielded another contradiction. There were scratch marks around the lock and the remnants of a baggage tag attached to the handle, strongly suggesting that it had been used before. When Beglin put it to Mrs Sheikh that the case did not look new, as she claimed, she simply shrugged.

At ten o'clock that evening Gourley, Kirk, Stephenson and Beglin assessed what they had learned so far. They concluded that they had no grounds for holding the couple who had come to meet Mujahid and Mrs Sheikh – they had explained that the money the Juliets had found was the takings from their restaurant – and they were allowed to go. As for

Mujahid and Mrs Sheikh themselves, they had been compelled to revise their original view and now reckoned that Mrs Sheikh was the principal culprit. Both were charged that night with attempting to import heroin into Britain contrary to the Misuse of Drugs Act of 1971 and the Customs and Excise Management Act of 1979. Gourley produced a pair of hand-cuffs and asked Sid Pirzada to tell Mujahid what they were for.

'Could you explain to the gentleman that he is being detained overnight at Heathrow police station and he is going to be taken there in handcuffs?'

Mujahid was led away through the deserted terminal building, its strip lights garishly accentuating the desolate place it had become. Mrs Sheikh was led away too, after Madan Jaggi told her to pack her handbag. 'If you want to take any medicines with you,' he told her, 'take them now.'

Mujahid and Mrs Sheikh appeared at Uxbridge magistrates court the following morning and were remanded in custody. Gourley began to prepare the case for court, and as he did so, some more illuminating information emerged. The heroin was sent to the Government Chemist who reported that it weighed 1.955 kilos and was worth £97,750, based on its retail price in one-gram lots. It was also twenty per cent pure.

However, the heroin had not been mixed – 'cut' – with the usual innocuous substances like sugar, but with a cocktail of other drugs, which included methaqualone powder, phenobarbital, and phenacetin. All three drugs are depressants: methaqualone was once widely used in sleeping pills, phenobarbital is administered to quell epileptic fits, and phenacetin is a painkiller.

This combination of heroin and the drug cocktail had begun to arrive in Britain earlier that year. The drugs themselves, which are normally used by registered chemists, were being smuggled into Pakistan in increasing quantities and mixed with the heroin there. They brought the dealers two benefits: the first was to increase their profits, the second to make users even more dependent on them for supplies.

The first consequence of mixing the drugs with heroin was to increase the heroin's apparent strength. As the Government Chemist reported, although this consignment of heroin was only twenty per cent pure, the drugs gave it the effect of heroin that was thirty per cent pure. In that way, users were cheated of one-third of the heroin they thought they were buying. As one officer observed of the dealers concerned: 'They weren't even straight crooks'.

The second consequence was even more insidious. Like heroin, the drugs in the mix can cause both physical and psychological dependence. Thus users who consume them are likely to become doubly addicted, both to the heroin and to the added drugs. But if they remain unaware that the heroin has been cut in this way, they are likely to become

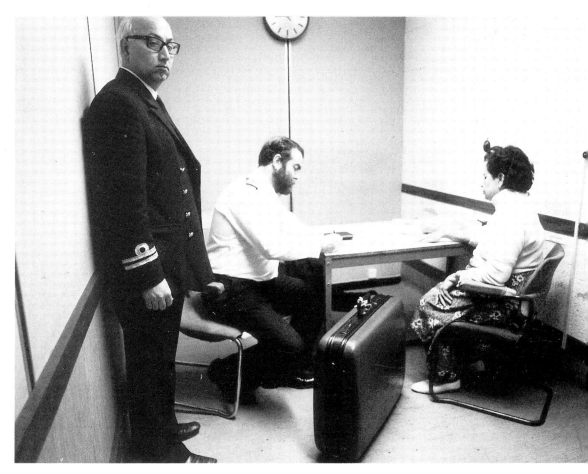

Both suspects were questioned in Urdu, with Customs interpreters translating questions and answers. *Above*: Mrs Sheikh, with interpreter Madan Jaggi standing by, continues to insist that the suitcase is not hers. Eventually she changed her story. Both she and her nephew, Muhammad Mujahid, were charged with importing heroin, and Mujahid was handcuffed and led away by Investigation Division officer Dave Gourley (*left*). Mujahid was eventually acquitted, although he was deported to Pakistan for having lied to immigration officers about his reasons for coming to Britain.

addicted to the drugs without knowing it, with all the disastrous effects that entails.

There were other dangers too. First, this combination of drugs is especially dangerous when consumed with alcohol. Second, they can cause withdrawal symptoms of their own, including physical convulsions. And third, most lethally of all, users who believe they are consuming thirty per cent heroin instead of twenty per cent may suffer from withdrawal symptoms because of the reduced dose. They may take more heroin to compensate and thus be at an even greater risk, either from addiction or an overdose.

For the Customs, the news of the chemist's analysis increased the contempt they felt for the organisers of the attempt. But after 11 February 1986 they only had one suspect left. The Uxbridge magistrates considered that there was insufficient evidence against Muhammad Mujahid and he was acquitted. However, for having lied to the immigration officers when he arrived at Heathrow, he was deported to Pakistan.

Mrs Sheikh stood trial at Isleworth Crown Court on 15 September 1986. She pleaded not guilty. She had changed her story once again, now claiming that the suitcase had been given to her by a relative at a wedding a few days before her flight. The jury did not believe her and she was found guilty. Judge Bathurst Norman told her: 'It is sad for a woman of good character to be in this position. But it must be made clear to anyone who is tempted by evil men that they will receive long sentences because they are trafficking in death.'

Mrs Sheikh was sentenced to six years and recommended for deportation. She began her sentence at Cookham Wood prison in Kent, where one of her fellow prisoners was Myra Hindley.

CHAPTER SIX

POTEEN

It is market day in Ballymena, a compact and friendly town in the lush, rolling countryside north of Belfast. The Saturday morning shoppers cluster round the fruit and vegetable stalls and there is a babble of shouts and conversations which merges with the laughs and clatter of glasses emanating from the adjoining pub, the Coronation Bar.

Then, booming out above the hubbub, the most recognisable voice in Northern Ireland is to be heard. 'Is it possible', asks the Reverend Ian Paisley, 'for a human soul to know this side of death, this side of eternity, that Jesus Christ has forgiven his sins, pardoned his sins, cast his sins out of sight, received him as a child of God and promised to bring him safely to heaven?'

Less than a hundred yards away a no less typical scene is being enacted. Close to the Coronation Bar a portly man in his fifties, wearing a chequered cloth cap and a tweed jacket, is sitting in his car listening to the radio. A second man, wearing a plain brown cap and a blue shirt buttoned to the neck, emerges from the Coronation Bar and approaches the car. The first man gets out and opens his car boot.

After looking around with conspicuous caution, he removes a vodka bottle from a cardboard box and passes it to the second man, who puts it into a rumpled brown paper bag. Five similar bottles follow. The second man removes a wad of ten-pound notes from his pocket, peels off three and hands them over. With a brief nod to seal the transaction the two men part, the first returning to the front seat of the car, the second heading for the market with the package held securely under his arm.

Through the grille covering the rear window of a shabby blue van parked some twenty feet away, officer John Hannon of the Belfast Customs Investigation Unit has been watching with a mixture of nervousness and satisfaction. 'There's a deal going down,' he whispers as the first bottle changes hands. He notes that it is a forty-ounce size and counts the bottles in turn: 'One, two, three, four, five, six.' He counts the ten-pound notes too, then reports that the man who has received the bottles is moving away. 'That's magic,' he says. 'Magic.'

Hannon has just observed the selling of poteen. Pronounced pocheen, the word comes from the Irish for 'little pot', and referred originally to whisky produced from a small still; today it is usually applied to alcohol that has been illegally distilled and sold without payment of excise duty. Sold for £5 at Ballymena market, and of far higher strength than legally-produced spirit, it offers buyers a saving of around £10 on a comparable bottle of whisky, gin or vodka, and gives the sellers a profit of around 200 per cent. To the government, the loss of excise duties is £8 per bottle.

The illicit distilling of alcohol is one of the most time-honoured activities the Customs have to deal with. It was part and parcel of rural life throughout both Scotland and Ireland in the eighteenth century. In 1798 an official enquiry reported that in Scotland it spread 'over the whole face of the country and in every island from Orkney to Jura', and the Excisemen who tried to collect the government's duties, often fighting ferocious battles with the distillers, were damned as 'blackguard loons that come down like locusts'.

The government finally assumed control in Scotland through land-owners who took over the stills and paid the duty of 2s 3d. per gallon, thereby laying the foundation of the modern whisky industry, with its small distilleries spread through Speyside and the Highlands and Islands. In Ireland the battles continued. The task of collecting the excise dues was undertaken by a revenue police force who proved no match for the illicit distillers, who produced probably two-thirds of Ireland's spirits until well into the twentieth century. Only after partition in 1922 did the Customs and Excise begin to exert control in the North. There are thought to be around 250 illicit stills in use today, although many produce only small quantities, usually for family and friends.

It is a topic that is the subject of a certain wry – or, dare one say, Irish – humour. The Customs in Northern Ireland recently took a Fermanagh farmer to court when his neighbours complained of the number of drunks lying in the road after drinking his poteen. The farmer claimed that he had only used the poteen for 'medical purposes' for his cattle. 'It might not have done them any good,' his lawyer said, 'but at least it made them happy.' (The farmer was fined £125.)

The Customs admit that in their effort to detect poteen, known other-wise as mountain dew, they face hostility from the community at large. 'There's a certain folklore surrounds this whole business,' admits Henry Snodden, joint head of the Belfast Investigation Unit, a Belfast man who joined the Customs in 1959 and now holds the rank of surveyor. Officer John Hannon, a member of the Unit, who comes from Newtownards, adds: 'Poteen in Ireland is looked upon as part of our culture and national heritage.'

The Customs had arrested Ballymena farmer John Wilson four times for making poteen but his activities continued unabated. On 21 September 1986 they tried again, setting up a surveillance post where they could watch Wilson in Ballymena market. From a van parked no more than a dozen paces away they watched and photographed Wilson in the act of selling poteen. *Frame 1:* Wilson, apparently looking around cautiously, walks towards his car. *Frame 2:* Wilson hands a 40-ounce bottle of poteen to a customer. *Frame 3:* Wilson is photographed in the middle of a second transaction. *Frame 4:* Wilson photographed as money changes hands – the crucial evidence of selling poteen.

Once stills were hidden away in remote rural areas so that they would not be given away by the smoke of the peat fire used for heating at various stages of the distilling process. Today, with gas or electricity, they may be housed in garden sheds or even, as on one notable occasion, in the bedroom of a council house. Even so, few people in Northern Ireland – where local dignitaries are as likely as members of paramilitary organisations to offer their guests poteen – would rush to give their neighbours away. But both Snodden and Hannon insist that poteen is a serious matter.

It is not just that the government is cheated out of substantial amounts of revenue. 'There's another side to it which the general public don't think of,' says Snodden. 'There's hygiene, for example. The poteen is made in unhygienic conditions, old bottles are used and they aren't washed out or sterilised. We have reports of children getting their hands on the stuff; from time to time we get reports of children running around drunk. We have a report of a café selling poteen injected into orange or Coke. It's fifty pence for Coke, but for eighty pence they will get Coke mixed with poteen.'

Nor were the Belfast Customs particularly amused by the activities of the poteen-maker they observed in Ballymena market. His name was John Wilson, sometimes known as Sidey, a reference to a physical handicap that had left him with a slight stoop. He lived with his wife and grown-up children ten miles from Ballymena on a farm with the intriguing name of 'Loonburn'. Wilson and the Belfast Customs had been engaged in skirmishing that had already lasted four years, during which time Wilson had been detected making or selling illicit alcohol on four occasions. He was prosecuted for the first three offences at Newtownabbey Magistrates' Court in 1984 and fined £1200. The Customs viewed the entire episode as an affront, partly because they considered that Wilson had escaped too lightly.

'The court listened to his story that he was a broken-down old farmer and the magistrate almost said, "How could this man have done this thing?" ' Henry Snodden says. Their anger was increased by the fact that Wilson's activities had continued unabated since. The Customs raided his farm again in 1985 and found 140 gallons of illicit liquor of awesome potency: 94 per cent proof, compared with the usual 70 per cent of whisky and gin. ('Enough to take Apollo up,' one officer said, suggesting that it would have sent a US space-rocket into orbit.)

The quantity, 140 gallons, also suggested that Wilson was distilling on a commercial scale, costing the government a theoretical loss of revenue of £5000. If, as the Customs guessed, Wilson was making 100 gallons of liquor a week, the unpaid duty could approach £200,000 in a year. 'He has treated the decision of the court with contempt,' Snodden said. contempt.'

The Customs were beginning to feel that they were being treated with contempt too. 'I am getting absolutely fed up with him,' said John Hannon. 'The officers who take part each time become known to him, he learns from each visit what not to do or say, and all these things don't help. He has got no respect for the law whatsoever.'

As a final straw for the Customs, the extent to which Wilson had benefited from his illegal activities was plain for all to see. His farm, nestling in the gentle fold of a glen, looked bright and prosperous, a cluster of freshly-painted white buildings crowned by a homely twirl of smoke. 'The house is totally transformed,' remarked Hannon as he pointed out Wilson's farm through the trees from a road passing along the side of the glen. 'He's built a huge extension and the main dwelling from the road looks totally different. The last time we went to do reconnaissance we simply couldn't find it because it had changed so much.'

It was in the summer of 1986 that the Belfast Investigation Unit learned that Wilson was still plying his trade in Ballymena market. The Unit had previously held its hand over Wilson's last arrest, in 1985, partly because he had denied actually selling the poteen. If it could now prove that Wilson was doing just that, then the two sets of offences could be linked and Wilson could be tried not by magistrates but in a higher court, where judges were known for imposing more severe penalties. 'The judges, I'm pleased to say, are taking a very strict line,' John Hannon says, 'and they are imposing some heavy fines.'

Compared with elsewhere in the United Kingdom, surveillance operations in Northern Ireland pose some very particular problems. As Hannon explains, this is partly because the rural farming communities are traditionally loyal and close-knit. 'They tend to know each other from miles around and it's like the old bush telegraph when strangers are in the area, especially if they're strangers that they have suspicions about,' Hannon says. It is also true that *any* unknown group in Northern Ireland is likely to arouse suspicion. A couple of men sitting in an unmarked car could easily be confused with an undercover unit of the security forces, exposing them to attack by paramilitary groups. Alternatively, they could be taken for paramilitaries, putting them equally at risk from the security forces.

It was for these reasons that the Investigation Unit decided to try to sneak a look at Wilson's farmhouse at night, reasoning that the bush telegraph would fall silent during the hours of darkness. Their aim was to establish that Wilson had constructed another still there, rather than elsewhere on his farm, which would also help them when it came to raiding the premises. John Hannon, as case-officer, was to make the attempt, together with officer Matt Bishop. Even they would admit that the operation was not a success.

In the first place, as they prepared to set off across the fields at 1.30 a.m. on a clear September night, there was a full moon, making it more likely that they would 'show out'. 'Matt,' said Hannon, 'we're going to have to be extremely careful here tonight, because I don't like that moon. It's the old rule – if you're going to show out, pull out.'

Even with the moon, it was not easy for the two Customs officers to find their way across the fields, particularly when they encountered a herd of cows. Then came a moment that appeared to confirm all their worst fears: a shot suddenly rang out from somewhere in the glen ahead. They headed back across the fields at high speed, the pounding of Hannon's heart competing with the noise of his breathing as he attempted to relate what had happened. 'There was a shot there and I didn't really know whether it was a shot from that farm – or even a bird scare.' A bird scare it proved to be: but as Hannon explained, 'better to be safe than sorry'.

Hannon nonetheless remained 'positive in my own mind that the still is in there'. And it was on that basis that he and Snodden laid their plans. At 7 a.m. on 20 September 1986, they were revealed to the rest of the Investigation Unit, reinforced by Belfast's mobile task force. The briefing took place at the unit's headquarters, housed above a bank in a building protected by closed-circuit television cameras, a mile or so from the centre of Belfast.

'Good morning,' said Henry Snodden breezily. 'The job today is a still at Ballyclare, a period of obs at Ballymena market, and a run to the still where hopefully the knock will take place. This man has been detected four times in the past and in respect of the first three occasions he was prosecuted at the magistrates' court. He pleaded guilty to those offences and the magistrate saw fit to fine the man £1200 because he was a broken-down old farmer on invalidity benefit. The fact that this penalty represented just a couple of weeks' income from this nefarious activity has now been exploited by the offender so we caught him again just before last Christmas.

'Since that time we've established that he's at it again. He's a bit of a thorn in our flesh and we feel it's important to catch him again, to positively involve him in dealing and hopefully at the next court he'll be dealt with in respect of his last two offences and that, we would hope, would put an end to it.'

The detailed instructions were presented by John Hannon. They were, in short, to watch Wilson selling poteen at Ballymena market; and then to follow him back to his farm, arrest him there, and raid his still. 'We have established from surveillance that normally on a Saturday morning Wilson arrives at the market between 9.30 and 10, accompanied by his wife and daughter,' said Hannon. 'They go off shopping, Wilson will hang around the car, then walk around the market, then goes to a local pub where he stays for approximately one hour, then returns to his vehicle around 11 o'clock and it's at this stage that he is visited by his various customers.'

To carry out the operation, the Customs would have no fewer than nine cars parked at various points in and around Ballymena, apart from the surveillance van from which Wilson's dealings would be observed. Other officers were to follow Wilson's customers and question them once they were safely away from the market. Wilson himself would be followed as he drove back home, although the quiet country roads made it far harder to mount a tail without 'showing out' than in busy urban areas.

Hannon was also wary of what would happen when they reached the farm, as Wilson had usually proved a truculent customer in the past. 'The whole family are a cheeky lot, they really are,' Hannon said. 'The old feller is one of the most obstinate people I have ever come across in my life. The daughters, they'll perhaps try to let down your tyres and the sons will come out as well and might give hassle.'

One officer was anxious on another score: 'Are there any farm animals that he could let loose on us or anything like that?'

The question was fielded by Henry Snodden. 'Well, there's a big billy-goat with a bell on it – and he could give you a donk up the rectum, so you need to watch that.'

In the event, the observation at Ballymena market could not have gone more smoothly. John Hannon and Matt Bishop together conducted the observation from the van, and relayed their observations to Henry Snodden who was controlling the operation from his car parked a quarter of a mile away. Hannon and Bishop were accompanied by the BBC cameraman Pat O'Shea, who filmed Wilson selling poteen exactly as Hannon described. The fact that Ian Paisley had chosen that very morning to deliver an entirely appropriate sermon at Ballymena market about the forgiveness of sins was pure coincidence.

Shortly after Wilson had completed his sale, Matt Bishop radioed that he seemed 'anxious to move'. Then came the word from Hannon that Wilson, accompanied by his wife and his daughter Sandra, was pulling out. The caravan of cars following Wilson leapfrogged past each other in the usual manner, but then, five miles outside Ballymena, one car found itself jammed immediately behind Wilson at a road-junction. Wilson and his daughter looked back.

'He's sussed the cars,' Henry Snodden announced. Wilson sped off and there was a disconcerting chase along narrow country roads before he was finally baulked by a Customs car. John Hannon got out and approached Wilson's car.

'Hello, Mr Wilson, you know who I am – Mr Hannon, senior officer,

Customs investigation. Where are you coming from?'

'You were following me,' said Wilson, 'so you should know.'

'Would you mind opening the boot, please?'

Wilson pulled a lever underneath his dashboard to release the boot lock, and got out of the car. As he did so, Henry Snodden took away his keys. Wilson snatched them back again and then saw Hannon rummaging through his boot. 'That's my car,' he protested.

'We're just having a look,' Hannon told him. 'Mr Wilson, I've reason to believe that there is illicit distillation taking place on your premises, and a search is going to be conducted.'

'Are they now,' said Wilson.

'Yes,' said Hannon.

Wilson got back into his car and a Customs officer tried to get into the back seat. Sandra Wilson objected: 'None of you boys are sitting on my knees.'

'Hold on,' said Hannon.

'That's my car there,' said Wilson. 'You'll not get in there.' He slammed the door and roared off down the lane. A Customs car reversed at high speed ahead of him and then turned, so that Wilson had an escort at front and rear as he reached his farm. In the yard beside the farmhouse further angry exchanges took place.

'John, calm yourself,' said Hannon. 'We're going to search the premises in the normal manner. Tell me this now, is there any illicit spirit—'

Wilson interrupted him 'Would you go to hell, out of my sight? Give me peace.'

Hannon tried again. 'Is there any illicit spirit on the premises, or a still?'

'I don't know,' Wilson said.

'Are you still the owner of the premises here, John?'

'No I'm not.'

'Who is the owner?'

'You find out – you know so much.'

By now, in fact, the rest of the Customs team had begun their search and within a minute or so a yell of triumph from an outhouse indicated that they had found the still. There were ten chest-high barrels containing the liquid 'wash' – which was in the final stages of fermentation. Nearby was the vat where the wash is heated to produce alcoholic vapour; and next to that, the condenser where the alcohol cools into liquid form. The Customs also found 105 litres of poteen, diluted from 92 per cent proof to around 80, already packed and ready to be sold. Hannon picked up one of the bottles and looked at it expertly. 'Fairly strong,' he guessed. Another officer, Wesley Dickson, agreed. 'It appears to be very, very good stuff.'

Meanwhile Hannon and Wilson had gone inside the farmhouse to

Above: After a high-speed chase along narrow country roads, Wilson was finally stopped close to his farm. Surveyor Henry Snodden, joint head of the Belfast Investigation Unit (back to camera in picture *above*), took away Wilson's keys; when Wilson saw officers searching the boot of his car, he snatched the keys back. *Centre:* Officer John Hannon of the Belfast Investigation Unit attempts to reason with Wilson. *Below:* After Wilson has been escorted back to his farmhouse, Hannon goes into his kitchen – followed by the ubiquitous BBC team, with cameraman Pat O'Shea in the lead.

continue their negotiations. As the following exchange illustrates, Wilson was proving as unco-operative as before.

Hannon: 'Okay, John, just for the record here, if you'd give me your full name.'

Wilson: 'You know it.'

Hannon: 'I know I do, John, I don't want any—'

Wilson: 'Then why ask me for it if you know it?'

Hannon: 'Because I have to, it's just for the record that I'm talking to you. Your full name?'

Wilson: 'I don't need to tell it to you any more. You can write that down there.'

Hannon: 'Okay. Is your full name John James Wilson?'

Wilson: 'Still the same.'

Hannon: 'And what is your full address?'

Wilson: 'You know it. You know where I live.'

Hannon: 'Okay. And your occupation.'

Wilson: 'Broken-down farmer.'

Henry Snodden came into the farmhouse to ask Wilson for a key to the main door of the outhouse containing the still. Wilson said he didn't have a key. By then, he had admitted that he was part-owner of the outhouse, but not of the still itself. Hannon pressed him again: 'Is that your poteen, John?'

'No it's not.'

'Who put it there?'

'Not telling.'

'I mean you have—'

'Don't even know it was there.'

Hannon turned to Wilson's poteen sales, telling him that the Customs knew they took place 'every Saturday at Ballymena market'.

'No way,' said Wilson.

'Occasional Saturdays you're selling it at Ballymena market.'

'No.'

'Eh?'

'Very seldom.'

'Ah-ha,' said Hannon, in triumph.

By now other officers had questioned several of Wilson's customers. One admitted that he had been buying poteen from him over the space of a year. Taken with Wilson's own qualified admission of selling – 'very seldom' – that added up to the evidence the Customs needed, along with the still itself. The Customs now prepared to tell Wilson that his equipment was formally seized.

Wilson declined to accompany the officers into the outhouse to witness this event, sending his daughter Sandra instead. In scenes reminiscent of

An innocent-looking outhouse (*top*) on Wilson's farm contained his illicit still. The photograph *left* shows the tank in which the 'wash' is heated, with officer John Hannon to the right and Wesley Dickson standing behind him. The alcohol evaporates and flows along the pipe to a still, where it cools into liquid form. *Below:* Officers tip away the wash, which is produced by mixing grain with water and allowing it to ferment.

the American Prohibition era, officers then tipped the barrels into a corner of the outhouse. The wash poured through a narrow drain pipe and ran out into the fields beyond, where it created some interest among Wilson's flock of geese.

A further task now fell to John Hannon. In accordance with Section 141 of the Customs and Excise Management Act, he was to tell Wilson that his car, which had been used for 'the carriage of goods liable for forfeiture under Section 25 of the Alcoholic Liquor Duties Act', was going to be seized too. Hannon approached this duty without relish. 'It'll be like putting the match to the blue touch paper,' he warned Snodden.

'He won't take that too well,' Snodden agreed.

Hannon went back into the farmhouse and spoke to Wilson. 'Now, er, the, your car – TIA 5272 – is being seized under the Customs laws. Under Section 141, it's being seized as forfeit, John, and you have the right – you have the right of appeal against for ... the forfeiture—'

'If anybody touches that car,' Wilson announced, 'I'll kill them.'

What ensued provides an illuminating example of the Customs' considerable powers of exacting penalties of their own choosing. The Act which permitted them to seize Wilson's car also enabled them to return it to him if he made what is termed a restoration payment. But first considerable manoeuvring took place. When Hannon told Wilson that his car had been seized, Wilson responded by saying that he needed the car in case he was taken ill and had to go to hospital. Then his daughter Sandra came out of the farmhouse and removed the car documents from beneath the dashboard. She was followed by Wilson himself who locked the car door. Hannon told Wilson to hand over the keys but he refused. Hannon threatened to arrest Wilson for obstruction unless he put the car keys on the farmhouse table.

Henry Snodden now joined in. 'I'll not touch the keys,' he promised. 'Just set them on the table.' When Wilson finally did so, Snodden told him: 'I'm in a position to offer you immediate restoration of that car, on payment of a sum of money.'

'I haven't got no money – first place,' said Wilson.

'Well, that is the condition that I'm talking about,' said Snodden.

'I'm almost eight hundred quid in the red, I had to go and pay me rates, the red notice came round for the rates.'

'Well, that is your own affair, Mr Wilson,' Hannon told him.

Sandra Wilson now intervened. 'If he does get the car,' she asked, 'how much is it going to be?'

'We'll let you know that,' said Hannon.

'We'd need to work that out,' added Snodden.

Hannon and Snodden withdrew to the farmyard, where they were joined by Wesley Dickson.

When the Belfast officers searched Wilson's outhouse, they found copious evidence of illegal distilling. *Left:* Wesley Dickson (right in picture) comes upon some of Wilson's bottles, while a colleague records the find. *Centre:* The Customs confiscate Wilson's equipment, including the barrels that contained the wash. Under Section 141 of the Customs and Excise Management Act, Wilson's car – which had been used for 'the carriage of goods liable for forfeiture under Section 25 of the Alcoholic Liquid Duties Act' – was also seized. The officers offered to return the car to Wilson if he paid a 'restoration' fee, and – after some haggling – this was agreed. *Below:* Wilson goes out to feed his ducks: he told the Customs he was just a 'broken-down farmer'.

'Two hundred and fifty quid,' Hannon proposed.

'We don't want to be unreasonable,' said Dickson.

'It's not a Roller, you know,' said Snodden.

'Two hundred to two-fifty,' said Hannon.

The officers returned to the farmhouse.

'We have discussed the matter,' Hannon announced. 'There is only one figure for the restoration, and that is two hundred pounds.'

'A hundred and fifty,' countered Wilson.

'There's no deal,' Hannon told him. 'We'll have to take the car.'

'Where am I going to get the money?'

It transpired that Wilson's son Ian, who was working at the other end of the farm, possessed a cheque book. Two officers, accompanied by Sandra Wilson, drove out to negotiate. Meanwhile John Hannon pointed out that if the cheque bounced there would be little they could do as they would have restored the car to Wilson long before. Snodden agreed that they were relying on Wilson's word, but added: 'I don't think there'll be any problem.' Then Sandra Wilson returned with a cheque for £200, and Hannon asked Wilson to sign a receipt for the car. 'Just put it on behalf of Ian,' Hannon suggested. 'Put "p.p. Ian Wilson".'

'Parish priest,' said Wilson.

Their business completed, the officers offered their farewells.

'It is my job, you know,' Henry Snodden told Wilson.

'Good luck to you,' said Matt Bishop.

'All the best,' said Wes Dickson.

'Bye bye,' said Mrs Wilson, who had remained silent until then.

'Right, Mrs Wilson,' said John Hannon.

For once, John Wilson said nothing. He waited until the officers had departed, and then went out to feed his ducks.

On 11 August 1987, John Wilson pleaded guilty at Ballymena Magistrates' Court to seven charges relating to illicit distilling and keeping and dealing in poteen. He received a four-month sentence and a £1500 fine, although on appeal the sentence was suspended and the fine reduced to £450 – less even than Wilson had received in 1984. 'It was a good professional job,' Belfast's Assistant Collector Dennis McNally none the less told the unit, 'and I'm very glad and gratified.'

Not all the Customs' work in Northern Ireland proves so gratifying. They have naturally experienced the same frustrations as their mainland colleagues in the period of turbulence the Customs have recently undergone. But there is also a uniquely Irish factor that adds to their difficulties. It consists of what is termed the 'land boundary' – the winding 365-mile border between Northern Ireland and the Irish Republic, created by the partition of Ireland in the 1920s, and the cause of controversy and violence ever since.

To begin with, the border was patrolled by the Royal Ulster Con-
stabulary but their task was taken over by the Customs in 1952. As there
were duties ranging between twenty and forty per cent on most farming
products imported from the south, the border offered a powerful temptation to smugglers. Goods carried by road were supposed to be brought
into the North at one of twenty official crossing-points where the
Customs maintained boundary posts. Anyone carrying contraband naturally chose one of the hundreds of 'unapproved' roads where there were
no Customs posts and they could enter the North unmolested.

Even so the life of a Customs officer had a certain idyllic charm,
which – as elsewhere in the service – has gained in lustre from today's
perspective. Older officers relate how they would catch smugglers by
waiting behind hedges and then leaping forward to thrust what was
termed a 'tuck stick' through the front wheel of their bicycles. It is also
told how the officer at the border post at the village of Pettigoe would
sit reading his newspaper, while traffic virtually jammed the unapproved
crossing-point half a mile away. One officer remarks: 'When I joined it
was sleepy valley time on the border.' He adds, however: 'That was
before the Troubles.'

It was the resurgence of 'the Troubles' in the late 1960s that changed
everything. The IRA viewed the border as an affront, a permanent
reminder of a divided Ireland, and in the North they set out to eradicate
every trace of it that they could. Where the Customs were concerned,
that meant destroying the boundary posts. The IRA began by planting
bombs big enough to break windows and loosen slates. At first the
Customs defiantly moved back into the posts. When the IRA used bigger
bombs the Customs set up caravans and Portakabins instead. The IRA
blew those up too so that by 1980 there was not a single boundary post left.

At that point, the Customs gave up trying to maintain a permanent
presence on the border. They now dispatch mobile patrols from bases in
the towns of Newry, Armagh, Enniskillen, Derry and Strabane. There
are seventeen patrols in all, consisting of an officer and two assistants to
each patrol-car. Although the Customs officially cover the entire border,
there are some parts which even the RUC regards as virtually no-go
areas and where the Customs are also rarely to be seen. In addition there
are ten 'freight-clearance stations' and there is a check-point on the
Belfast-Dublin railway.

The Customs say that these moves help them to make far more efficient
use of their resources. They also happen to coincide with another, less
explicit goal. In its war on what it calls the British occupation forces, the
IRA has nominated a list of military targets which include the British
army, the RUC, the part-time volunteers of the Ulster Defence Regiment,
judges and prison staff.

Against this background the Customs have taken a pragmatic view of their role in the conflict, namely that they do not wish to have a role in the conflict, and they appear to have preserved their independence and their lives through a series of delicate judgments about the limits of their operations. 'We play it right down the middle,' an officer says, 'and we keep as low a profile as possible. That's what's kept us safe.' Thus, while it is true that eight Customs men have died from acts of violence, none of the eight is believed to have been directly targeted because of his work. Four officers were killed at Killeen when an IRA man dropped the bomb he was about to plant, two were caught in the crossfire of a shoot-out with the British army at Killeen, and two were killed because they were members of the UDR.

The frustrations that the border now poses for the Customs were made clear to the BBC when two officers of the Belfast mobile task force, Martin Oliver and Michael Patterson, paid a brief visit to the notorious 'bandit country' between Warrenpoint and Crossmaglen. All that remained of the former boundary post of Upper Fathom was a lay-by and a line of foundation stones, long overgrown. The two officers then toured the maze of winding roads that criss-cross the border, taking care to pull back at the edge of the Irish Republic since it lies beyond their jurisdiction and to be seen there can cause a diplomatic stir. A number of unapproved roads were blocked by the British army but some of these have been restored by the local inhabitants so that the flow of traffic continues unabated.

'You see the immensity of the situation,' Patterson said. 'You see the contours of the land, and the number of crossings we have to cover – it's really unbelievable. It's really a hit-and-miss operation. You can strike lucky but once people are across the border there are so many areas and routes that they can head for.'

It was, Oliver added, 'a smuggler's paradise.... The likelihood of us catching anybody is pretty remote. We do our best but we know in our heart of hearts that we cannot patrol the whole thing.'

The results of the Customs' predicament are plain. Drivers who need their importation documents stamped by the Customs make it their business to call at one of the ten freight-clearance stations. Those who do not wish to be scrutinised by the Customs simply choose a different route. Some border villages have grown prosperous from offering a haven or conduit for goods smuggled either into or out of the North – the direction varying with the fluctuations of currencies and the vagaries of the EEC. Recently the South has seen an influx of consumer goods such as televisions, videos, and hi-fis. For a long time cigarettes and alcohol were smuggled into the North but recently they too have gone in the opposite direction.

One of the most spectacular and profitable ruses is known as a 'Carousel' fraud. It exploits the changing value of the 'Green Pound', the unit of currency used by the Common Agricultural Policy. If the Green Pound is higher in the North than in the South, then farmers exporting cattle from North to South must pay duty accordingly. Farmers moving cattle from the South to the North, however, are paid a subsidy of the same amount.

It takes only a small stretch of the imagination to realise the opportunities the system offers. By smuggling cattle from North to South, farmers evade the duty they should pay. If they import the same cattle back into the North they receive the official subsidy. If they repeat the process they receive the subsidy twice over. 'It's a merry-go-round,' says Henry Snodden – hence the name, the Carousel Fraud.

In theory cattle are supposed to wear ear-tags to prevent the fraud – and a lively trade sprang up for a time in counterfeit ear-tags. It is far easier to work the fraud with grain, where no distinguishing marks can be applied. The same load of grain may be taken round the carousel by different people, each collecting the subsidy due. 'It can be very complicated, and it's very difficult for us to prove,' Snodden says.

Similar frauds have been worked with calves, milk powder, potatoes and pigs – at one time, says Snodden, it appeared that 'there were more pigs being bought than were born.' In this situation the Belfast Investigation Unit does its best to perform a 'sweeper' role, attempting to piece together the frauds after they occur. Despite some notable successes, its officers are forced to assume that most cases elude them. 'There is a definite tendency on the part of Irish people to have a cavalier attitude towards legal matters,' Snodden concedes.

The Customs are also forced to assume that the border is vulnerable to the importation of drugs. This too can only be an assumption, because there has as yet been no significant drugs seizure on the border, leaving the Customs with the familiar problem of deciding whether this means that no drugs are coming in, or whether they are not detecting them. They are inclined to the second interpretation because of the obvious temptation the cross-border route presents.

For a drugs-smuggler, it seems straightforward enough. First land your drugs in the South – and the Republic's remote shattered western coastline offers countless havens. Then bring them across the border into the North – and you are already in the United Kingdom. In theory there are no further Customs checks on any route to the British mainland. The Customs guess that smugglers favour the short sea-crossing from Larne to Stranraer. The Belfast mobile task force visits it occasionally but otherwise the only permanent watch is kept by the Special Branch, who are in any case looking for suspected terrorists.

At the same time it appears that Northern Ireland does not have a 'drugs problem' itself – at least in comparison with the British mainland. Seizures of hard drugs anywhere in the North are minimal and when a cannabis case arises it is prosecuted more toughly than on the mainland. Whereas people caught by the British Customs with a small amount of cannabis may receive a 'compounded' penalty and avoid the courts, in Northern Ireland they are likely to be prosecuted – and may even be charged with dealing if they admit giving any to their friends.

It is a matter about which assistant collector Dennis McNally feels especially strongly. He regards the practice of compounding small amounts of cannabis as bordering on the immoral, and says that by prosecuting such cases the Northern Ireland Customs are 'laying down a marker'. He adds: 'The only way to combat drugs is to stamp it out in the market-place.'

The comparative scarcity of drugs cases offers some compensation for the problems presented by the border. But the Customs in Northern Ireland still share the difficulties faced by their mainland colleagues: staff cuts, shortage of resources, pressure of time and paperwork, and the frustration of feeling unable to carry out their task properly. Officers are supposed to check passengers on all trains from Dublin to Belfast. They are allowed precisely six minutes to do so, and thirty-two per cent of the trains receive no examination because staff are occupied on clerical duties.

It was probably significant that in the recent Civil Service pay dispute, around ninety per cent of the Northern Ireland Customs staff went on strike compared to fifty per cent in some parts of Britain. It is also noticeable that some Northern Ireland officers are more outspoken than their colleagues elsewhere, and as Martin Oliver and Michael Patterson returned from their tour they were clearly in a frustrated mood.

'I want to do the job and I don't like being told I can't,' Oliver said. 'The whole thing is a façade. It's like having a model officer with a cardboard arm which waves as you go past.'

Patterson was even more forthright. 'The smugglers have realised how thin we are stretched on the ground and they are reaping the benefit,' he said. 'But the public don't seem to realise they are being sold short. We were meant to provide a service and a deterrent and we don't provide either. It's ridiculous and it's a scandal.'

Even so, neither man was considering leaving the Customs or giving anything less than his best. 'It's personal pride,' says Martin Oliver. 'I like and want to do the job and in my unit we have a bunch of guys who are all of the same opinion. It's like climbing a mountain – there is no sense of achievement until you reach the summit.'

'You do your job to the best of your ability,' adds Michael Patterson. 'Nobody can fault you for doing that.'

CHAPTER SEVEN
THE CHANCERS

There is a point, high on the white chalk cliffs, from which Dover harbour resembles nothing so much as an ant-heap, with people, cars, lorries and boats scurrying hither and thither in pursuit of some aim known only to themselves. Seen from ground level, the bustle assumes greater purpose. Dover is the busiest passenger port in Europe, dedicated to speeding people, cars and freight on their cross-Channel journeys as efficiently as possible. In 1986, fourteen million people, 1.8 million cars, one million commercial vehicles and nine million tons of freight passed through. To the Dover Harbour Board, the figures justify its claim to be Europe's Premier Port. The Customs regard them with less enthusiasm.

With the white cliffs in the background, Dover provides one of the sturdiest images of Britain as an island nation. It has been Britain's principal Channel port since Roman times, being the nearest point to the French port of Calais, 21 miles away. A Roman lighthouse, Saxon church and Norman castle stand on the cliffs as emblems of the successive regimes who have used it as their gateway. Other celebrated travellers commemorated in the town are Captain Matthew Webb, who set off from near Dover when he became the first person to swim the Channel; and Louis Blériot, who crash-landed on the clifftop after making the first Channel crossing by air. In 1940, at one of the most anguished times in Britain's history, Dover received the fleet of small craft which rescued the British army from Dunkirk.

In the 1950s, as the British began to turn abroad for their holidays, Dover saw the first drive-on car ferries to replace the converted cargo boats that were loaded by crane. The Common Market accelerated the growth of road freight, and in the 1980s both holiday and freight traffic grew at phenomenal speed. In a familiar pattern, life for the Customs altered irrevocably too. What had once been an amiable sea-port posting became a job with pressures from all sides. Just as at Heathrow, the Dover staff found themselves in the front line of the fight against drugs. At the same time they had to contend with the vast increase in passengers

185

and freight – and did so in a period when the Customs staff suffered their worst cuts. Yet despite the frustrations they face, the Dover staff include some of the most dedicated officers in the Customs.

To most people in Britain, the uniformed staff at Dover *are* the Customs. Heathrow apart, there is no other point of entry where so many travellers come into contact with them, as they drive off the car ferries and head for home. Since they hope to do so as quickly as possible, they may regard the Customs as anything from an unavoidable inconvenience to an infernal nuisance. So what is in the officers' minds as they decide just which cars coming into the Green Channel they should search? Suzanne Reddecliffe, who has been in the Customs for five years, offers her personal guide.

'You look for the make of the car, the registration number, any stickers on the side of the car,' she says. 'I'm looking for signs of nervousness, how many people in the car, maps – things like that can tell me where they have been and whether what they're telling me is correct or not.'

By itself, Reddecliffe concedes, nervousness can be a poor guide. 'I don't know why people feel guilty when they go through Customs but they do. I feel guilty when I walk through Customs myself.' Yet there is always that mysterious sixth sense to guide an officer when something does not quite seem to fit. 'It's a feeling – other officers more experienced than myself get it more strongly.' Sometimes, she concedes, 'it's sheer luck'.

The most common offence among returning holiday-makers is to exceed the duty-free allowance, usually by the odd bottle or pack of cigarettes. Their response to being found out varies from truculence to remorse. 'Some people try and have a go,' says Reddecliffe. 'They'll give you a story – they didn't know you couldn't bring through 300 cigarettes. Others react very strongly – they're angry or upset, or they cry.' One passenger was so upset, in fact, that he started hurling his car tools around the car hall.

Some offenders protest that the Customs would spend their time better if they confined themselves to looking for drugs rather than duty-free goods. Reddecliffe says she was very puzzled the first time a passenger said that to her – 'because I'm trying to gain experience'. After all, she adds, 'it's not as if he had "drug-smuggler" written down the side of his car.'

The Customs term small-scale offenders 'the bottle and carton brigade'. They are sometimes also known as the 'chancers'. They are usually let off with a gentle reprimand and a request for the extra duty – although at that point a surprising number tell the Customs to keep the goods. For larger amounts, the Customs are likely to ask passengers to empty out all their baggage, dismantle roof-racks and so forth, costing them

Above: Dover, just 21 miles from France, has been Britain's busiest Channel port since Roman times. The Common Market has brought a new surge of goods, and the pressures on the Customs have multiplied. *Left:* Officer Donna Chaffey is almost dwarfed by a juggernaut arriving at the Customs post: after asking the driver if he has any alcohol or cigarettes, she waves him through. 'Everybody wants everything to be cleared as quickly as possible,' she says. 'At Dover where we're busy most of the time, it's ever so hard if you want to do the job properly.'

an inevitable delay before they are sent on their way.

For passengers tempted to run the gauntlet the best chance comes in the summer months, when cars may pour off the ferries in a torrent of up to 1000 vehicles an hour. Since the Dover Customs can examine barely one-twentieth of that number, an officer stands at the entrance to the Green Channel trying to make split-second decisions over which cars should be stopped. Officers in that position are hard pressed to say what criteria they apply. 'Let's just say it's needle-in-haystack time,' one says.

One of Dover's most spectacular finds in the summer of 1986 took place in front of the BBC's cameras. Since it was past midnight on an April night, there were comparatively few cars coming off the Calais ferry, and most were being stopped. At first, the elderly couple in the black Volvo 244GL seemed an unlikely prospect. They seemed even less likely when officer Pete Sokhi asked if they had any duty-free goods and the man replied that he had bought some cigarettes but no alcohol, as he didn't drink.

Something left Sohki uneasy: although he was addressing the couple together, the woman said nothing and looked fixedly ahead. So he asked the man to show him the cigarettes he had bought. When the man opened the boot he produced not just 400 cigarettes but four bottles of spirits as well. Since this meant that the man had lied about the alcohol, Sokhi decided to look in the boot for himself. He tried to lift out a suitcase and found it was remarkably heavy, so he opened it where it lay. Inside, to his astonishment, he found row upon row of neatly wrapped whisky bottles. He called a colleague and together they systematically searched both the boot and the interior of the car.

Out came dozens and dozens of bottles: whisky of half a dozen brands, from malt to bourbon, together with gin, vodka, brandy, liqueurs, wine and champagne, plus several thousand cigarettes and several hundred cigars. It took Sokhi and his colleague well over an hour to remove all the bottles and line them up on their examination desk and the next one to it, until in the end there were 160 bottles in all.

'What', Sokhi asked the man, 'were you going to do with it?'

'Drink it.'

It was in fact the biggest seizure of alcohol most of the officers at Dover had seen. Sokhi conjectured that it was a 'commercial' run and that the couple were intending to supply a pub. The couple, who were both in their sixties, admitted trying to evade excise duty but continued to claim that they wanted the drink for themselves, even when a further 100 bottles were found in their home in Sheffield.

The man said he was a labourer but still managed to produce £750 in cash to secure the release of his car after it had been impounded at Dover. Despite further inquiries, the Customs were unable to establish whether

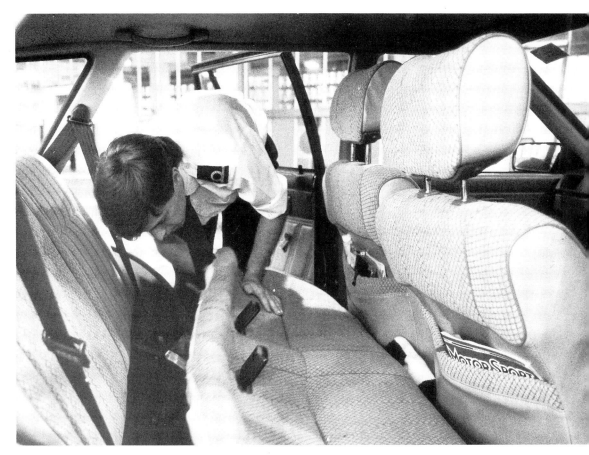

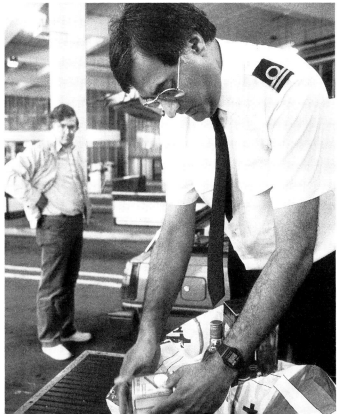

Officers working in the Dover car hall reckon they know most of the hiding places by now. *Above:* Darren Herbert looks underneath a back seat – a favoured place for hiding cannabis. Herbert has made several sizeable cannabis finds, including 40 kg concealed in a petrol tank. *Left:* Pete Sokhi checks a passenger's duty-free allowance, and finds it in order. But while the BBC were filming, Sokhi found a driver with 160 bottles of spirits. Sokhi's suspicions were first aroused because the driver's wife didn't look at him when he questioned her.

the couple did intend to sell the alcohol or merely proposed, as the man claimed, to drink it themselves. When the couple stood trial in April 1987 they pleaded guilty and received suspended prison sentences totalling four months each.

Sadly but predictably, the Customs' work at Dover is no longer limited to looking for excess drink and cigarettes, even on this gargantuan scale. The massive volume of traffic at Dover, coupled with the Customs' manifestly overstretched resources, mean that Europe's Premier Port offers an obvious attraction to drug smugglers. The pattern of seizures suggests that it offers a principal conduit for cannabis on the overland route from Morocco via Spain and France, and from Amsterdam, Europe's cannabis capital.

The increase in seizures has come later at Dover than at Heathrow. Whereas Dover is now making two or three major seizures a week, only three years ago a cannabis find of 20 kg would have been enough to bring most of the officers crowding round to look. Dover assumes that more drugs are coming their way because of the successes of its colleagues at Heathrow, providing yet another example of the phenomenon whereby smugglers who find one avenue blocked invariably seek out weaknesses elsewhere. However, the rising detection rate also reflects an improvement in its own methods.

In 1984 Dover formed a Drugs Intelligence Unit – the first British seaport to do so. Its members are to be seen standing at the entrance to the Green Channel, directing cars to the first of the dozen bays. As an evening in the car-hall illustrates, in deciding just whom to stop and question the Dover officers follow the same principles as their colleagues elsewhere. Do drivers match the pattern of past offenders? Can they give a satisfactory account of their journey? And is anything about them 'not right'?

A young couple with a child in a Rover 2800 aroused immediate suspicion: the car seemed too big for their probable income, the officer felt; besides, he pointed out, the car was dirty. His interest quickened when he learned from their passports that the man was not the father of the child, and was further aroused when the couple told him they had been on a day-trip to France.

Although drugs smugglers try to devise more and more ingenious methods, there are only so many places in a car where drugs can be concealed – and the Dover Customs reckon they know them all. The officer and a colleague unscrewed the door-sills, shone torches down the window frames, tapped the door panels (they give a dull sound if something is stuffed inside) and peered into the petrol tank with an instrument known as a spectroscope. But after half an hour it was clear that the couple were 'clean', and the officer told them they could go.

Much of the evening proved equally frustrating. A man was stopped and searched because he was alone in his car and he was wearing a sweater and jeans. He said he had been to France on 'business': he too was clean. A middle-aged Dutchman in an empty Mercedes Benz estate car was the next to be questioned. He said he was on his way to buy antiques at Bermondsey market; the officer believed him and let him go. The drugs unit stopped a Dutchman driving a car powered by LPG, or liquid petroleum gas. LPG fuel tanks have proved a popular hiding-place and the unit was encouraged when it saw that the fuel-gauge showed three-quarters full although the driver claimed the tank was empty. An officer examined the tank with a spectroscope – and found that the fuel-gauge was faulty.

Then an officer decided to search a couple who had been directed to his bay: 'they look scruffy,' he said. They were returning from a camping holiday in France and had two young children who were asleep on the back seat. As he turned out their baggage and began to search the car, the couple unfolded a pair of camp chairs and sat down to watch. When the officer asked the woman to wake up the children so he could look under the seat she protested, but her husband told her: 'They're only doing their job.'

There were no drugs under the seat or anywhere else. A second officer said that he would not have gone on searching when he saw how calm the couple were, but the first officer pointed out afterwards that, only a week or so earlier, the drugs unit had found a sizeable quantity of cannabis under a seat on which *four* children had been asleep – and had been congratulated for its perseverance in difficult circumstances.

Soon afterwards another officer stopped the driver of a Ford Sierra. The Sierra proved to have been hired. In addition, the driver's answers were suspiciously vague. He claimed that he had collected the car for a friend who had left it in France after setting off on a boating holiday. But he couldn't remember how long ago the friend had asked for his help, or the name of his friend's boat.

When the officer examined the car he found that the interior panels were loose, suggesting that they had recently been removed – and perhaps used to conceal either money or drugs. The officer became convinced that the car had been used for *something* illegal when the driver told him: 'You're wasting your time.' Like the Heathrow Customs, Dover has access to CEDRIC. It had no information to offer and there was nothing for it but to let the driver go.

Eventually the hunches pay off. Late that evening Officer Darren Herbert decided to question a couple in their mid-twenties who were driving a Granada Ghia estate car with X-registration licence plates. The man had curly hair and an ear-ring, and was wearing jeans and white shoes, while the woman seemed overdressed. It was enough for Herbert to feel that they didn't 'look right' for the car. He asked to see their passports: they came from Norfolk, and the man worked as a roofing contractor. Herbert asked where they had been: the man replied that he had taken his wife to Amsterdam 'for a break' as her grandmother had just died. Herbert considered his answers vague and hesitant; and there were long pauses which suggested that he was thinking carefully before he spoke.

Herbert decided to look underneath the car. He immediately saw that the petrol tank bore a fresh weld. In fact, that was to prove a red herring; but when Herbert looked more closely he noticed fresh scratches on the tank. He also saw that the threads of the bolts holding it in place were bright, showing that they had recently been undone. He called a member of the drugs unit, Hedley Beaumont, to look. When Beaumont tapped the tank it gave a dull sound and he told Herbert he was sure there was something inside.

Herbert asked the couple to wait in a room alongside the Green Channel and he drove the car to an examination pit at the far end of the car-hall. He and Beaumont climbed down into the pit, undid the fuel-tank bolts, and lowered the tank. When they removed the fuel leads they could see part of a brown package through the aperture.

Before long, the contents of the fuel tank had been emptied out. There were around sixty packages, each containing a number of chocolate-brown slabs. It was cannabis: 'It's Paki,' Beaumont said, meaning that it came from either Pakistan or Afghanistan. Each slab had been stamped with its manufacturer's trade mark, a pair of scissors, and there were 40 kg in all, worth around £100,000 at street prices – but now, as it lay scattered on the cement floor like fool's gold, worth nothing at all.

By now the couple had been told they were under arrest. The driver was brought across in handcuffs to look at the haul: he looked sullen, and said nothing. When two officers of the Dover investigation unit arrived the driver at first adamantly denied all knowledge of the cannabis. But finally he said: 'My wife doesn't know anything about this.' When the officer asked him: 'About what?' he gave no reply but it was enough to give himself away. The man eventually pleaded guilty and was sentenced to three years in prison. He incurred a further one year as he had previously received a suspended sentence for burglary, which was now activated. All charges against his wife were dropped.

For Herbert, it was the second major cannabis find he had made in five days, and he readily admitted that he relished the excitement it brought. 'I was supposed to go on leave tonight but I don't want to go now,' he said.

Left: Darren Herbert uses a spectroscope to scrutinise a petrol tank – often used for smuggling cannabis. The spectroscope, based on fibre optics, enables officers to peer round corners, and is an example of the 'hi-tech' equipment the Customs are introducing in their bid to beat the smugglers. *Below:* Officer Suzanne Reddecliffe examines the baggage of a 'walker' – one of Dover's foot passengers. The passenger was soon allowed to go. Reddecliffe looks for signs of nervousness, but agrees this can be misleading. 'I don't know why people feel guilty when they go through Customs, but they do,' she says. 'I feel guilty when I walk through Customs myself.'

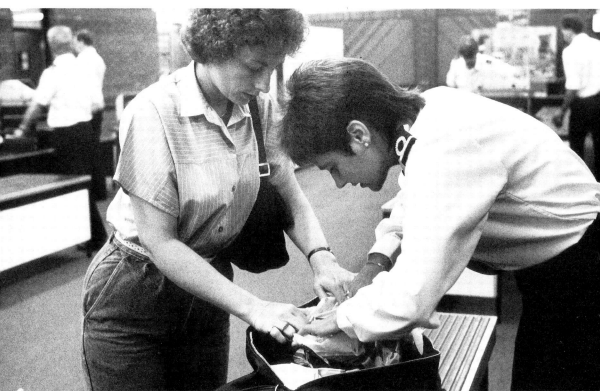

His colleague Beaumont added: 'The buzz can be better than sex – you get a tremendous high.'

The most obvious mistake made by the couple – or whoever packed the cannabis on their behalf – lay in not covering the scratches on the tank and the thread on the bolt, which should have been easy enough, with a dollop of dirt or grease. The second was more subtle, for it is apparent that the officers' revenue nose twitches if suspects do not conform to a set of social stereotypes. The couple appeared to be living beyond their means by driving a Granada Ghia Estate, and in fact it was later established that they had bought it only a month before – suggesting that they acquired it for the run. In the same way, another couple attempting to smuggle cannabis gave themselves away by driving a car that appeared *beneath* their scale: they were both wearing gold jewellery while driving an old, T-registered car.

Fortunately for Dover, some drugs smugglers give themselves away rather more easily, as was the case in an incident filmed by the BBC. A flaxen-haired young Dutchman who was arrested for trying to smuggle through 6 kg of cannabis concealed in the wing of his car had seemed, to officer David Webb, all too obvious a candidate for a thorough search.

'It was an old car, a young guy by himself, so it had to be worth a look, especially coming from Holland,' Webb explained. 'He didn't give a very good story and didn't have much stuff with him. The car's an old wreck and he was a little bit nervous. . . .'

There was a small drama when the Dutchman tried to make a break, but he was chased and grabbed by three officers and promptly hand-cuffed. However, he was to have the last laugh. He was sentenced to two years, but just before Christmas 1986 he escaped from Wayland prison in Norfolk, reaching home in time to send the prison staff a Christmas card.

From the pattern of the Dover finds it follows that the most successful smugglers are those who can blend most effectively with their fellow passengers. Officers feel that to pick passengers at random, simply because they look 'normal', is to stack the odds against themselves even more. 'You must have *something* to go on,' one said.

However, smugglers attempting to outwit the Customs in this manner are still prone to mistakes. One family acting as couriers who used their children as cover were trapped when an officer asked them where they had been on holiday. They replied that they had been to Paris. In that case, the officer asked, why was there a bucket and spade on the back shelf of their car? They had in fact been to Spain where they had collected a consignment of cannabis shipped from Morocco. If they had admitted they had been to Spain – common enough, after all – the officer's suspicions would probably not have been aroused.

Happily, some of the Customs simplest checks work too. In 1986 a

73-year-old pensioner returning from a day-trip to France was caught after an officer casually tapped the door of his car and noticed that it made a dull sound. There were 12 kg of cocaine inside the doors and, despite his age, the pensioner was sent to prison for nine years.

That seizure was crucial in confirming that Dover is now being used for 'hard' drugs as well as cannabis. Others indicate that major organisers are testing Dover with methods that Heathrow has come to know only too well.

Recently two couriers carrying heroin in their baggage flew from Bombay to Heathrow. There they took a flight to Brussels without passing through the British Customs, and they were joined by an accomplice who had started his journey from Heathrow. Once in Brussels the three men destroyed any evidence linking them with Bombay. They then hired a car and stuffed the heroin into the headrest. The two original couriers took the car to Dover on a ferry while the third man travelled as a foot passenger.

The hire-car proved the couriers' undoing. It was enough to prompt a thorough search, and on the floor of the car officers found a currency exchange form made out to the third man. When the couriers were asked why they had not travelled together, they had no satisfactory answer. The heroin was soon found in the headrest and the two couriers were arrested. So, too, was the third man, for the Customs found him waiting for his two accomplices nearby.

It was a notable success, the result of the curiosity and persistence that good Customs officers show. But Dover is only too aware that it remains vulnerable to the latest smuggling trends. In 1987 it detected several stuffers and swallowers, suggesting that smugglers using this method are also turning from Heathrow to the Channel ports – and Dover admits that as yet it lacks the expertise in this loathsome area that Heathrow has acquired.

In its attempt to stay abreast of the latest smuggling trends, Dover uses a number of methods similar to those adopted at Heathrow. It naturally has the assistance of CEDRIC, which is proving increasingly effective. Like Heathrow, it liaises with other government departments such as Home Office immigration officers and the Special Branch officers who work alongside them. Both telephone tips to the Customs on an internal line, pointing out passport stamps, for example, which show that travellers have visited source countries of drugs.

In the same way as Heathrow has access to airline passenger lists, the Dover intelligence officers scrutinise lists of ferry passengers at harbour booking offices. They also walk down the lines of departing cars, noting the registration numbers of likely prospects in the hope of intercepting them on their return.

One incident illustrates the factors the Dover intelligence team is looking out for. On 7 March 1987, an officer spotted a man in his thirties who aroused his curiosity. He seemed to fit every category the intelligence team is interested in: he was by himself, needed a shave, was wearing white shoes, was driving a dirty BMW, and was travelling to Ostend on a day-return ticket. The officer noted his licence number and when he returned to Dover that evening he was given a thorough search.

It was a false alarm. It was the weekend of the Zeebrugge disaster: the man was a graphic artist employed by a Sunday newspaper who had gone to Belgium to prepare a diagram of the *Herald of Free Enterprise*. 'What was that all about?' he asked the officer as he completed his search. 'Oh, just something that came up this morning,' the officer told him.

While the nature of its work makes such failures inevitable, Dover is relying on high technology to improve its chances. For years the task of watching out for the number plates of suspect cars was probably the least popular job at Dover. It was usually assigned to the junior Customs officers who sat on a stool at the entrance to the Green Channel, their heads bobbing up and down between the list and the oncoming cars for an hour before they were mercifully relieved.

Help is at hand. Like the police, the Customs have been experimenting with machines that will read number plates automatically. Early trials were disappointing – a machine tested at the entrance to the Dartford tunnel on the M25 proved highly fallible – but equipment has now been developed to meet the Customs' needs. Each car approaching the Customs area will be required to stop for a few seconds in a marked-off bay, and its number plate will be matched with a list of suspects held by a computer.

The machine is not entirely foolproof, as it remains uncertain whether it will be able to read dirty number plates, and the desk officers will still have to check cars against a computer print-out. Its introduction was also delayed by a familiar dispute over who would pay for the premises where the equipment was to be kept – was that the Customs' responsibility, or the Harbour Board's? But once installed it would almost certainly bring a major improvement to the Customs' chances of detecting smugglers.

The dispute over the installation of the number plate reader served to focus attention on another facet of life at Dover: the clash between the Customs' interests and those of the Harbour Board. Surprising as it may seem, it is the Harbour Board and not the Treasury which has to provide and fund the Customs' facilities.

In the view of the officers, the direct result of that apparent anomaly is that their working environment can be decidedly grim. During the bitter winters of 1986 and 1987 they shivered in temperatures that plunged towards zero, accentuated by the wind-chill factor caused by the car-hall opening at both ends. The officers came to work in thermal underwear, struggled to fill in forms with pens whose ink froze, and attempted to thaw themselves in the feeble supply of warm air wafting from grilles in their examination benches.

The officers' discomfort was increased by the Board's remarkable success in attracting new traffic to Dover. Between 1979 and 1984 the number of passengers rose from nine million to almost fourteen; cars increased in the same proportion, and coaches soared from 50,000 to 120,000. That caused a further clash, for while the Board has the entirely understandable aim of ensuring that cars and passengers clear the port as quickly as possible, that conflicts with the Customs' equally understandable aim of carrying out the checks they wish to make.

If queues of cars build up, the Customs are likely to hear before long from the harbour's Customs liaison officer, Bill Hargreaves, a former Customs man who was the Collector at Liverpool before joining the Harbour Board – and is thus regarded by some at Dover as a 'gamekeeper turned poacher'.

While officers view the Board without affection, they reserve part of their anger for the government, pointing out that the greatest rise in traffic at Dover, in the early 1980s, came precisely when the Customs were suffering their worst cuts. When the cuts were reversed, however, Dover's staffing did move in step with the increase in traffic. In 1987, too, their working conditions were improved. Plastic curtaining at the entrance to the car-hall helped cut down the wind, and the heating was boosted. A car-ramp was installed so that officers could look underneath cars without having to climb down into a greasy examination pit.

Yet a sense of grievance remained. In the summer of 1987 the Dover staff were among the most militant at the time of the Civil Service strikes in protest at the government's 4.25 per cent pay offer. They also resented being subjected to the conflicting pressures the dispute involved: since they universally shared the government's goal of wanting to keep drugs out of Britain, they could not understand why they were not paid properly for doing so, as one officer pointed out. 'You do have to wrestle with your conscience, going on strike when you know how important it is to stop drugs,' she said.

The officers in the car-hall also deal with the foot passengers – 'the walkers' – who flock off the cross-Channel ferries. The walkers' Customs area is certainly more warm and comfortable than the car-hall and is thus vastly to be preferred in the winter. The passengers can be a motley crew, ranging from the exuberant and flirtatious to the passive and bemused. They rank lower than car passengers as prospects on the simple grounds that they have fewer places for concealment.

Among likely contraband, the officers look out for pornographic magazines and video-cassettes, usually emanating from the sex-shops of Amsterdam. A passenger carrying *any* cassette is likely to have it scrutinised on a video-player in a small anteroom. A young man carrying five cassettes, for example, claimed they were recordings of the Wembley 'Live Aid' rock concert of 1985 – and so it proved. The incident was dutifully recorded in a ledger which showed that most viewings proved equally fruitless: among titles like 'Gardening' and 'Royal Wedding' only the occasional more suggestive 'Debbie does Dallas' and 'Group Sex (Teenagers)' were to be seen.

When pornography is detected the practice of 'compounding' once again comes into play. Each cassette is judged to be worth £25, each magazine £5. As a rule of thumb, pornography worth up to £30 is simply confiscated and the passenger is free to go. For amounts between £30 and £100, passengers receive a notice from the Customs asking them to pay a compounded fine – with the alternative of going to court. Amounts worth more than £100 are treated as an offence and passengers are likely to be prosecuted.

Even this approach has softened recently because of a legal anomaly in which the Customs were caught, whereby the laws controlling the *importation* of pornography are more strict than those governing its *possession* in Britain. In 1984, the Customs raided a gay bookshop in Bloomsbury, 'Gay's the Word', and seized hundreds of books – sixty-nine titles in all – which had been imported from the US. The bookshop's nine directors were charged under the Customs Consolidation Act of 1876, which forbids the importation of 'indecent or obscene articles', and were due to stand trial at the Old Bailey in the autumn of 1986. The anomaly arose because books actually published in Britain are subject not to the 1876 Customs Act, but to the Obscene Publications Act of 1959 – which defines obscenity far less stringently. It was heightened in the summer of 1986 by a judgment in the European Court over some inflatable sex dolls the Customs had also seized. The court ruled that under the Treaty of Rome countries could not ban the importation of articles unless their laws made manufacturing those articles illegal too.

In those circumstances, the Customs Board decided that it would be 'inequitable and impracticable' to proceed with the Old Bailey case, and instead negotiated a settlement. The books were returned to the bookshop on condition that, while fifty titles could be put on sale, the remaining nineteen were to be sent back to the US.

Since then, the Customs say, they have adopted a more relaxed attitude, recognising a 'changing climate' towards erotic material. Seizures have fallen – although the Customs emphasise that they still take a 'dim view' of pornography involving children and animals.

Where drugs are concerned, the Dover walkers are considered most likely to be carrying cannabis, particularly as many are returning from Amsterdam, where cannabis cigarettes can be bought over the counter in some cafés and bars. Inevitably, it seems, the passengers who are most likely to be stopped are those who most closely fit the image of the cannabis user: young people with scruffy clothes, unorthodox hairstyles, laden with rucksacks, especially when travelling on bargain-price overnight coaches.

Most stand by patiently when they are searched, some making conversation, others silent and impassive, as every item in their baggage is minutely examined, including packets of condiments, the lining of tents and the insides of tent-poles. Anyone found with an item connecting them with drugs – a packet that may have contained cannabis, even a reference in a diary to buying or smoking it while abroad – is likely to receive a full body search in an adjoining room. It was noticeable that even the passengers who had previously been chatty would emerge five minutes later somewhat mute.

It was noticeable, too, that the officers varied in their attitudes towards their suspects. One described the squalor of their coaches, with half-eaten sandwiches stuffed into the ashtrays and apple cores strewn on the floor. 'They're toe-rags,' he said. 'They expect to be searched anyway.' But a second officer, referring to the small amounts of cannabis that were likely to be found, responded: 'Let's face it, it's not really what we're looking for, is it?'

The search for cannabis in fact led Dover into the public arena in 1987, for one of the cases highlighted on the BBC's *That's Life* programme occurred there – the search of the seventeen-year-old schoolgirl who had a beer-mat from an Amsterdam café. The café in question was the *Bulldog*, and is one where cannabis cigarettes can be bought and smoked. Under the Customs' guidelines, that was certainly enough to warrant a body-search – and the Dover officers were taken aback by the controversy that broke around them. 'It's done us a lot of damage,' one said.

Darren Herbert, the officer who made two hauls of cannabis in one week in the car-hall, tends to agree. 'I don't like doing it,' he says, 'and I wish there was an easier way. But we don't have a sixth sense, as some people suggest, and when you're talking to someone you have to make a decision: do I let them go? Or do I carry out a search? It's a horrible thing – we've had pregnant women carrying drugs and people using children. But it's got to be done.'

The cars and walkers are one half of Dover: the other, on the far side of a security fence that divides Dover East 'A' from Dover East 'B', is freight. And if the pressures on the officers dealing with cars and walkers are heavy, those on the officers handling freight can seem overwhelming. Even more than cars, freight is the success story of the Dover Harbour Board. Where the ferries once carried the occasional lorry as well, Britain's entry into the Common Market and the growth of road traffic mean that juggernauts now surge off almost unceasingly. Around 1500 arrive every twenty-four hours and during the busiest period as many as 1000 can pass through Dover in one night.

These figures confirm the problem that freight poses. Small amounts of hard drugs are depressingly easy to conceal deep inside a consignment of goods, and the steady rise of imports into Britain in the 1980s has created even more work for the Customs. The proportion of freight examined has fallen steadily, from 8.5 per cent in 1980 to 5.4 per cent in 1986.

Two bleak official verdicts confirm the Customs' anxieties on this score. In 1986, Home Office minister David Mellor told a House of Commons committee that 'most heroin, in fact over 60 per cent, is now arriving in freight'. The two Customs unions agreed. 'Unless urgent action is taken,' they asserted, 'the dangers to the health and economy of the country will increase.'

The problem is most acute at Heathrow, as air-freight is unaccompanied, and any seizures of drugs are far harder to follow up. Officers posted to the Heathrow cargo terminal watch a torrent of goods flowing towards them on conveyor belts, requiring them to make decisions at a speed which one describes as 'worse than a joke – it's criminal'. When the BBC's Paul Hamann was shown the cargo sheds at Heathrow he decided not to film there for fear of offering an open invitation to smugglers.

The Dover officers do at least have a driver they can question. The lorries pouring off the ferries first pass through immigration control and then head for the Customs preventive post, an extended archway across the freight lanes that is, if anything, even more exposed to the elements than the car-hall. As the queues of lorries grow, it is hard for the officers involved not to be daunted by the immensity of their task.

'The biggest problem, as you can see,' says Officer Gordon Bines, 'is the sheer volume of stuff that we're dealing with. You have to be really selective in what you do. Trying to do the job thoroughly with vehicles of this size involves a lot of time and a lot of people as well. You couldn't do what you want to do to every single vehicle – it's impossible.'

His colleague Debbie Walker agrees. 'The turnover of traffic is so great, with the staff we've got and the time we've got, it's like looking for a needle in a haystack. It's a never-ending task. Unfortunately it doesn't matter how many staff we have, it's not going to alter the situation that greatly. You just have to try not to hold up the traffic too much, and do your job as best you can.'

Walker's remarks echo those made in the car-hall. But in trying to decide which lorries to stop, she and her colleagues have less to go on since lorry-drivers usually have a clear and provable purpose to their journey which is unlikely to fall apart under questioning. The officers still do their best to look for the obvious signs, as Walker explains.

'First of all, it's got to be the driver's reaction to the initial questioning,' she says. 'Is he at ease with you? Is he twitching all over the place? If you're looking up the lines of traffic, is he fiddling around with something? Then you've got the reactions to your questioning. Where's he come from, where's he going? You've got to think all the time, is it going to be worthwhile for him to smuggle?

'Obviously if you've got a driver that's coming over, dropping his load in Dover and going straight back out, he's got no need to smuggle. But on the other hand he could be going to London and you remember little bits of information and you think, well that factory was a bit suspect. It is really just what you remember, where they've come from, and how they react.'

Two incidents filmed by the BBC show how much time searches consume. Since fewer than one per cent of the lorries arriving at Dover receive a full 'turn-out', meaning that their goods are unloaded and searched, selecting just which lorries to examine becomes a major decision. Gordon Bines's suspicions were aroused when he spoke to the driver of a refrigerated lorry carrying Danish bacon – although paradoxically Bines was intrigued not because the driver was nervous, but because he appeared unnaturally calm.

'When I said, now what have you got, he was really laid back,' Bines explained. On the other hand, when the driver climbed down from his cab and went to open the back of the lorry, Bines said, 'he sort of shot round, and he seemed a little bit nervous'.

When Bines climbed inside he thought he had seen an important clue. Among the cartons of bacon at the back of the lorry he could see the corner of a black bin-liner sticking out – and bin-liners are sometimes used to wrap contraband, especially smuggled tobacco. For Bines, it was enough to decide that the lorry should receive a full 'turn-out', and he asked the driver to take it to a special chilled loading bay.

In theory, the Dover Harbour Board is supposed to provide the staff to remove goods from lorries, but that is another bone of contention as it seems to the Customs officers that there are never enough staff on duty, creating another obstacle to their work. In this case Bines simply carried out the search himself, removing carton after carton – there were 529 in all – so that he could examine the bin-liner.

By now the driver seemed neither laid-back nor nervous, helping Bines with a friendly smile on his face. When Bines finally reached the bin-liner he found it was a false alarm: it had simply been used as extra packing around one of the cartons, and both driver and load were 'clean'.

In a second incident, Bines helped to turn out a lorry carrying a bulging load of water-melons. That too seemed a reasonable choice, as water-melons are not worth much as a load and were in bad condition, suggesting that the true reason for the journey could lie elsewhere. 'It sounds quite good,' said Bines, who added that he might perhaps find 'a false bulkhead containing some drugs'.

The first signs were encouraging too: several screws appeared to be missing from the bulkheads. In addition, Bines noted, the driver climbed aboard the lorry with him. 'Another sign,' Bines said. 'It's just a reaction – I think they've something to hide when they come in with me, so I'm hopeful.'

Bines and his colleague Dave Jones escorted driver and lorry to the unloading bay, where Harbour Board staff started to lift out the melons, one by one. Two hours later all the melons had been removed, the floorboards lifted, the bulkheads unscrewed, the petrol tank inspected with a fibrescope, the wheels removed and the tyres X-rayed. Nothing.

'That's the way it goes, I'm afraid,' said Dave Jones. 'A bit disappointing.'

'A bit disappointing' is a minimal description of the frustrations the officers suffer as days or weeks can elapse without a seizure. The notion that untold amounts of drugs could be passing them by is one that preys on their minds. 'It's something you'll never know,' says Debbie Walker. 'But just to see the amount coming into the country – it's got to be coming through somewhere, and I suppose Dover is as good a place as anywhere, although we hate to admit it. It is horrifying to think at the end of the shift: what have I let through tonight?'

Gordon Bines is equally realistic about the lorries he is unable to search properly. 'Quite honestly, it takes only a small package in one of these big vehicles,' he says. 'A kilo of coke in a big vehicle – there's no chance that we could really find it in the middle of a load.' The hardest thing, he adds, 'is to try and shut your mind off to it. You try to do each lorry that comes into your bay and you have to try to look at it like that. Because if you start looking down the line and seeing what's behind, it will frighten you to death. You've got to look at each one on its own merits and think, shall I let him go or shall I have a look in the back? Because if you start looking down the line to the rest of them, you'll never succeed.'

Eventually the finds come. The most frequent drug hauls are of cannabis, and although the freight officers make fewer seizures than their colleagues in the car-hall, they are usually of larger amounts: up to 200 kg or more. In sheer size, rather than value, the largest quantities of

Choosing the lorries for a 'turn out' – a full search, which can take several hours – is a major decision for Dover officers, as they can search only a handful of lorries out of the thousand or more which arrive each day. Officer Gordon Bines thought the driver of a Danish bacon lorry (right, in *top* picture) seemed too 'laid back' – later, he appeared 'a little bit nervous'. But the driver helped with the search, and by the time Bines had emptied the lorry (*centre*) it was clear that both driver and lorry were 'clean'. The Customs work closely with other government departments, and an official of the Ministry of Agriculture, Fisheries and Food, seen in the picture *above*, took the opportunity to look at the driver's load – all was in order. Officer Debbie Walker (*below*) sometimes feels daunted at her task. 'The turnover of traffic is so great, with the staff we've got and the time we've got, it's like looking for a needle in a haystack.'.

contraband consist of tobacco, for here the differences in taxation policies within the Common Market offer yet another obvious temptation.

In Belgium 50-gram packets of loose tobacco – used for rolling cigarettes or in pipes – are sold for around £1. Since the normal retail price for the same packet in Britain is £4 or more, the opportunity is clear, and the statistics of the tobacco trade confirm what is happening. Some twenty tons of Old Holborn tobacco, for example, are exported to Belgium each month. As hardly anyone in Belgium actually smokes Old Holborn, it follows that most of it is being smuggled back into Britain.

The smugglers sell the tobacco to middle-men for between £1.80 and £2 a packet. Most is then sold under the counter for between £2.50 and £3 in clubs, pubs and work-places in east London, south-east Essex and north-east Kent, costing the Exchequer around £1.2 million each month in lost revenue. The Customs find it a particularly aggravating matter, as they feel it is one of those offences where they have to battle against a tide of public opinion, similar in some ways to VAT.

Officers also feel that in the past the courts have not treated the matter with proper seriousness. Some tobacco smugglers are known to have earned £1 million or more from their trade, but since it ranks as an excise offence, the maximum sentence is two years – although recently some terms have been increased by judges imposing consecutive rather than concurrent sentences for several offences. But some officers talk of their bitterness on the occasion an alleged smuggler was acquitted by a jury after being caught red-handed with a load of tobacco at Dover. He was already serving another sentence – and they heard him laughing uproariously as he was led back to the cells.

On 22 July 1986 the BBC crew was filming when a small open-back lorry pulled up at the freight-control post. The driver said to the freight officer, Fred Rutterford, that he was carrying machine parts from Germany for his employer's firm in Norfolk. But Rutterford felt that the lorry looked rather low on the ground and turned to CEDRIC for guidance.

CEDRIC confirmed that the lorry was worth closer scrutiny, and Rutterford and his partner Michele Best asked the driver to take it to one of the examination bays. The driver seemed co-operative and keen to please, and he helped Rutterford undo the tarpaulins so that he and Best could start their search. But before long Best came upon a large brown cardboard box. There were hundreds of packets of tobacco inside.

The driver stood back sheepishly, and Best asked him how much tobacco he had on board.

'Altogether?' he asked.

'Yes.'

'Seven thousand packets.'

'It's all yours?'

'Yeah.'

'You loaded it, did you?'

'Yeah.'

'Where have you got to take it to?'

'That's my business.'

The driver was led away to the Customs' custody suite, where Michele Best chatted to him before the custody officer arrived. The driver told her that he had paid £7600 for the tobacco, adding that it had taken him some time to raise the money, but he had hoped to double it in the end. At first he claimed that this was his first attempt. But later he admitted he had smuggled two thousand packets through Dover just a fortnight before.

'It's a lot to get rid of,' Best suggested.

'You could get rid of a hundred thousand if you'd got them,' the driver replied.

In November 1976 the driver pleaded guilty at Maidstone Crown and received two concurrent sentences of nine months – one for the attempt for which he was caught, one for the successful run he admitted to Michele Best. For her and Fred Rutterford, it brought a welcome sense of triumph after the long shifts spend without reward. It was, said Rutterford cautiously, 'a good morning's work'.

Best was more forthcoming. 'I feel over the moon,' she said.

As part of Dover Harbour's continual programme of modernisation, further rebuilding is taking place to streamline the freight lanes. This will undoubtedly enable lorries to pass through more quickly; whether it will assist the Customs to the same degree remains a moot point. By 1988 or 1989 the Harbour Board hopes to have built a single check-point for both immigration and Customs' controls. After presenting their passports, drivers will be questioned by the Customs about their loads. Since their lorries may only be visible on a television monitor, the officers fear they will not have the same 'feel' for when a lorry should have a closer look.

By then, however, the Customs hope they will be able to make full use of computers programmed either with specific information about target vehicles, or with 'profiles' of suspect types. If they decide that a lorry should be searched, it will be directed to an examination bay. Otherwise lorries will drive directly to the Customs' Entry Processing Unit, or EPU, where – as at present – the duties payable on the loads are assessed.

Here too modernisation is under way. The Dover Harbour Board boasts that lorries can pass this second Customs control in less than an hour, and since the freight they carry brings revenue of over £1 million a day, it is clearly in the interests of all that the procedures should work as smoothly as possible. The Customs nonetheless find they are once again involved in compromises between speed and effective controls.

Until recently, officers in the main EPU office worked in conditions bordering on the squalid. It was cluttered and noisy, with plaster peeling from the walls, panels dangling from the ceiling, and a notice by an electric plug in the wall saying: 'I bet this is unsafe.' Equipment always seemed in short supply – even ballpoint pens were locked in a cupboard – and although it was widely recognised that the room needed air-conditioning, that was the subject of the usual dispute between the Customs and the Harbour Board.

Recently life in the EPU has improved. The decorations have been refurbished, and the arrival of computers has cut down on the competition for space. But the computers have brought new problems, particularly in respect of what is termed 'the Tariff'. Its full name is the Tariff and Overseas Trade Classification, and it comes in two volumes.

The first contains 271 pages detailing the procedures to be followed; the second has 1312 pages listing the duties to be charged. These have almost infinite variations, stemming from trade agreements going back to the pre-Common Market days of EFTA, the Common Market itself, and numerous preferential and bilateral deals with other countries. They also take account of licensing agreements which control the numbers of goods that may enter Britain.

For example, Britain has an agreement concerning the number of tee-shirts that can be imported from Turkey. Clothing importers have to apply for a licence and are usually allocated around 15 per cent of the amount they request. Unscrupulous dealers can beat that control by buying tee-shirts in Turkey and claiming they were made in another country, such as Greece.

The Tariff also makes arcane distinctions between types of goods. In 1986, for example, the EPU staff were greatly preoccupied over the difference between a computer unit and a computer part. A unit, in fact, is a large item like a keyboard or a VDU; a part is something within that unit, like a key or a screen. The rate of duty differs: it is 4.9 per cent on a unit, only 4 per cent on a part. In 1986, the staff suspected that some importers were misdescribing their goods, saving themselves 0.9 per cent of the duty – a sizeable sum when multiplied many times over.

Or take chemical products: because of convoluted trade negotiations in the past, products containing more than 30 per cent sugar, starch or milk imported from Austria attract duty of 7.6 per cent; imported from Switzerland, the duty is less. There are even products in the Tariff which few outsiders would have ever have heard of: items such as Kainite, Stockroos, Lacs and Salep.

At one time, officers checking goods would be expected to know the Tariff inside out. Now that the EPU has been computerised they are spared that. When drivers arrive at the EPU they hand over a form describing their goods to a freight agent, who enters the details on a computer known as the Direct Trader Input, DTI. That is checked in turn with a larger computer, known as the Departmental Entry Processing System, DEPS.

Much like the VAT computer, the DEPS computer is programmed with various tripwires. But in general, if the details on the form appear to tally, the computer calculates the duty and allows the lorry through. This is called 'Route Three' and occurs in 60 per cent of cases. The catch, for the Customs, stems from the fact that in those cases no one from the EPU is likely to check that the load on a Route Three lorry actually matches the description on its form. 'You could get a load of Cognac described as chipboard, for all we would know,' one officer says. That is a fairly extravagant example – but a misdescription of Turkish tee-shirts as Greek, or computer units as computer parts, is far less unlikely.

Before 1987, the officers in the EPU at least had the sanction of not allowing a load to pass through until they had scrutinised its form and agreed that it could go. Now there is a different emphasis: if the computer decrees that a load shall follow Route Three, then it is cleared automatically unless the officers intervene – and they have just thirty minutes to do so. The Dover Customs are understandably coy over how many Route Three forms they do in fact scrutinise, but the proportion is no higher than five per cent.

If, on the other hand, the computer allocates a lorry to 'Route One', that could mean that the load has triggered a tripwire concerned, for example, with Turkish tee-shirts, or that something on the form was inconsistent or incomplete. In those cases an officer checks the form before the lorry is allowed through. It is only when a load is allocated to 'Route Two' that the lorry is likely to be fully examined – and, just as in the preventive lanes, the staff and facilities available for such tasks are limited.

That naturally concerns the officers – and there is a further loophole of which they are aware. In theory, a dishonest driver and agent could simply not submit a form at all, and the lorry would be on its way without being checked or paying duty of any kind – 'and we would never know,' an officer says.

It also falls to the Dover Customs to carry out a number of checks for other ministries and government departments. At the time of the Chernobyl disaster in 1986, for example, a notice was posted in the EPU warning that most foodstuffs from Eastern Europe were banned. The officers look out, inter alia, for explosives on behalf of the Health and Safety Executive, prohibited plants for the Ministry of Agriculture, Fisheries and Food, and rabies for the Department of the Environment.

The diversity of their tasks illuminates the position they occupy at the heart of a complex and changing modern society, with all the pressures and contradictions that can involve. It is undeniable that officers occasionally feel overwhelmed by their work. But fortunately for the Customs, their future rests with dedicated and enthusiastic officers like Suzanne Reddecliffe.

'It can be very interesting and rewarding,' she said when the BBC filmed at Dover. 'It has the other side, where it's a bit boring or mundane, but you accept that.' She conceded that with all its constraints, Dover was likely to be intercepting only 'a small percentage' of the drugs passing through. 'There are not enough men and women on the station and not enough hours in the day,' she said. 'But everybody does their best and that's all we can do really.' Her ambition was clear: 'I want to join the Investigation Division.'

By the time the BBC series was transmitted, Suzanne Reddecliffe had already achieved her goal. She joined the ID at its London headquarters in August 1987, where her first assignment was to the team that runs the intelligence computer, CEDRIC. Within a year she was likely to become a fully-fledged member of an investigation team dealing with serious offences. She was undaunted by the stories of unrelenting pressure and long hours. 'I can't imagine any more satisfying work,' she said. 'I have a very good feeling about it all.'